# The Non-Executive Directors' Handbook

THIRD EDITION

*Brian Coyle*

The University of Law
2 New York Street
Manchester
M1 4HJ

 icsa. Publishing

 NEDA NON-EXECUTIVE DIRECTORS ASSOCIATION DEVELOPING PROFESSIONALS

Third edition published 2013
Published by ICSA Information & Training Ltd for the
Non-Executive Directors Association (NEDA).
ICSA Information & Training Ltd
16 Park Crescent
London W1B 1AH

Typeset by Paul Barrett Book Production, Cambridge
Printed by Hobbs the Printers Ltd, Totton, Hampshire

British Cataloguing in Publication Data
A catalogue record for this book is available from the
British Library.

ISBN 9781860725784

# Contents

# Foreword

The absolute necessity for non-executive directors to know what they are supposed to be doing has never been greater. Although the risks and rewards are not usually evenly matched, people like myself still elect to perform these roles because we genuinely want to make things better, and care about guiding the next generation of business leaders, just as my generation was mentored. However, the opprobrium and publicity given to failure can wipe out in minutes successful careers painstakingly created over many years.

The executives within a business are nearly always nurtured and developed as a group, often from within that organisation or from similar companies in the same sector. They are designed to act as a team, with a common view on how to take the business forward.

The non-executive directors are usually brought together piecemeal over time with a much more varied set of experiences and backgrounds. Consequently, forming an agreed view with such a potentially disparate and opinionated group can be very difficult. Every business I have seen that falls into difficulties has had a board that was less than effective and, at times, even dysfunctional. This is a failure on the part of the non-executives because they are expected to act as the 'grown-ups'.

What is common to being a non-executive is an understanding and application of the fundamental rules, guidelines and policies that boards are expected to follow. So whether you are an experienced non-executive in need of a refresh, or just about to take up your first appointment, this excellent Handbook provides both a comprehensive and a succinct summary of the essentials, which makes it a must-read for NEDs.

*Peter Williams*
*Senior Independent Director, ASOS plc*
October 2013

# About the Non-Executive Directors Association (NEDA)

The Non-Executive Directors Association ('NEDA') is an organisation dedicated to Non-Executive Directors (NEDs). The Association promotes and supports the day to day needs of NEDs at all levels – aspiring, new and experienced.

The objective of NEDA is to provide member NEDs with a comprehensive range of practical support, education and advice, in association with a number of key partner organisations, including the Institute of Chartered Secretaries and Administrators (ICSA).

NEDA provides direction to NEDs in three essential areas:

**Knowledge...** in an increasingly complex environment, NEDs must have proper knowledge of their duties and responsibilities. NEDA helps NEDs share their knowledge and experiences while also supplying them with the information and tools to stay up to date.

**Performance...** NED performance is critical, not just for the organisation but also for their personal reputation. NEDA helps NEDs to appreciate best practice.

**Independence...** NEDs need to be, and need to be seen to be, independent in order to provide the appropriate level of challenge, advice and support. NEDA helps NEDs understand what is meant by true independence and acts as a sounding board for complex issues.

For more information, and to join NEDA, see www.nedaglobal.com.

# Acknowledgements

ICSA Information & Training Ltd would like to thank the following for permission to reproduce material in this book:

Appendix 1: The UK Corporate Governance Code
Appendix 2: Improving Board Effectiveness Guidance

© FRC. Adapted and reproduced with the kind permission of the Financial Reporting Council. All rights reserved. For further information see www.frc.org.uk or call +44 (0)20 7492 2300.

# CHAPTER ONE

# The role of the non-executive director

......................

## OVERVIEW

Non-executive directors are appointed to the boards of companies to fulfil a number of different roles. The presence of NEDs on unitary boards such as those in the UK is intended to improve board effectiveness and contribute to better corporate governance.

Concerns about weak corporate governance – and its potential consequences – have evolved over time, and now relate to matters such as the leadership and effectiveness of the board of directors, the reliability of financial reporting and auditing, corporate disclosures, risk management, executive remuneration, relations with shareholders and corporate citizenship.

Countries have their own laws, regulations and guidelines for corporate governance. Most countries with established stock markets have a voluntary code of corporate governance. In the UK this is the UK Corporate Governance Code, and companies with a premium listing must comply with its provisions, or describe, and explain the reasons for, any non-compliance.

NEDs are therefore closely associated with the need for best practice in corporate governance, and boards of directors should establish a framework for effective corporate governance within their company.

## 1 BOARD DYNAMICS AND THE ROLE OF NON-EXECUTIVE DIRECTORS

Non-executive directors are directors without executive responsibilities in their companies. Their role differs in some ways between countries, as well as between types of company. Some countries have two-tier board structures, with non-executive directors in a supervisory board and executives in a management board. In unitary board systems, there is a single board composed of executive and non-executive directors, but the relative numbers of the two types of director can vary. NEDs are appointed to the boards of companies to make them function more effectively, but the influence of NEDs on the board depends to a large extent on the relationships and dynamics between the executive and non-executive directors.

### The role of executive directors

It could be argued that a unitary board needs only two executive directors in its membership: the chief executive officer (CEO) and the finance director. The CEO provides a link between the board and the executive management team, as leader of the executive team and therefore accountable to the board for management performance. The finance director provides expertise in accounting and finance, an aspect of the company's affairs that can drive much of the board's decision-making.

Executive directors have a balancing act to perform between their responsibilities as directors and their responsibilities as executive managers, which are different. The FRC's *Guidance on Board Effectiveness* (see below) stresses that executive directors have the same duties as other members of a unitary board and that their duties extend to the business as a whole, not just that part which is covered by their executive roles. In the boardroom, they should take the wider view of their responsibilities.

### The role of non-executive directors

Non-executive directors can contribute to the effectiveness of the board in companies of different types and size, but their contribution can be particularly valuable in companies where there is separation of ownership of the company from control, and the members of the board own a relatively small proportion of the total number of shares in issue. NEDs must work together with their executive colleagues to promote the interests of the company, but at the same time they must also act as policemen or monitors, protecting the interests of the shareholders against the risk of excessive self-interest by the executive management.

The UK Corporate Governance Code identifies four broad roles for non-executive directors:

(1) They contribute to the formulation of company strategy. As members of the board, they should 'constructively challenge and help develop proposals on strategy'.

(2) They should review the performance of executive management in meeting their agreed goals and objectives, and should also monitor the reporting of performance.

(3) They should monitor the integrity of the financial information produced by the company, and satisfy themselves that the systems of internal control and risk management are 'robust and defensible'.

(4) They have responsibilities for deciding appropriate levels of remuneration for executive directors (and possibly other senior management), and also have an important role in the appointment and removal of executive directors, and in succession planning.

The relationship of NEDs with their executive colleagues is therefore complex: part colleague and part policeman. This need to combine different responsibilities makes the role of the NED a difficult one to perform well and successfully.

### The effectiveness of boards and the role of NEDs: reports and guidance

The effectiveness of a board of directors and the quality of leadership that it provides for the company depends largely on the effectiveness of the NEDs in performing their roles. Poor corporate governance is most likely to exist when NEDs do not perform effectively. In the UK, the government commissioned an independent review of the role and effectiveness of NEDs, published in 2003 as the Higgs Report. The Higgs Report included guidance for non-executive directors and the board chairman. This guidance was adopted by the Financial Reporting Council (which took on responsibility for the UK corporate governance code) and issued as 'Good Practice Suggestions from the Higgs Report' – more commonly known simply as the 'Higgs Guidance'. The Higgs Guidance, which was subsequently reviewed by the FRC in 2006, included guidance not only on the role of the board chairman and NEDs, but also on the duties of the remuneration and nomination committees of the board and pre-appointment due diligence checks for new directors.

The 'Tyson Report on the Recruitment and Development of Non-Executive Directors', published by the London Business School in 2003, followed up on aspects of the Higgs Report that dealt with board diversity. The Report suggested that companies, when looking for NEDs to appoint to their board, might draw on broader pools of talent with varied and complementary skills, experience and background (including gender diversity) to enhance board effectiveness.

In 2010 the FRC published the *UK Corporate Governance Code (Appendix 1)*, and also commissioned the Institute of Chartered Secretaries and Administrators (ICSA) to consult on whether additional guidance was needed on sections of the Code relating to leadership and board effectiveness. This review of the Higgs Guidance, now known as the *Guidance on Board Effectiveness*, was published in 2011 (see Appendix 2). It builds on Higgs by offering up-to-date guidance on board roles (including the role of non-executives), board support, decision-making, board composition, risk, remuneration and effectiveness.

A government-commissioned report by Lord Davies on 'Women on Boards' was published in 2011. It made a strong case for greater diversity on boards, and recommended in particular that there should be a greater proportion of women on the boards of FTSE 350 companies and that in FTSE 100 companies, at least 25% of board members by 2015 should be women.

A revised version of the UK Corporate Governance Code in 2012 includes a provision that new appointments to the board should be made with due regard for diversity of membership, including gender.

In response to another recommendation in the Davies Report, executive search firms published a Voluntary Code of Conduct in 2011. This addresses the issue of gender diversity in board level appointments.

### Independence of NEDs and board effectiveness

Most or all NEDs should be 'independent'. This refers to independence from the management of the company or from a major shareholder. An independent NED should be able to make judgements that he or she considers to be in the best interests of the company, without undue influence from management. Independence of NEDs is a requirement for an effective board, and is an important issue when deciding the composition of a board. Independence is considered in more detail in Chapter 4.

### A balanced board

In the UK, it has been argued that an effective board needs suitable balance between executive and independent NEDs, and between the board chairman and the chief executive officer. In a balanced board, there is a suitable range of skills and experience, and no individual or small group should be able to dominate the board's decision-making. The UK Corporate Governance Code contains principles and provisions relating to the composition and balance of the board, which are described in Chapter 5.

## 2  CORPORATE GOVERNANCE

The introduction to the UK Corporate Governance Code states that corporate governance is about what the board of the company does and how it sets values for the company, and as such it must be distinguished from company management by full-time executives. The Code quotes the definition of corporate governance provided in the report of the Cadbury Committee (1992): 'Corporate governance is the system by which companies are directed and controlled.'

The Cadbury Committee report went on to state the following:

- Boards of directors are responsible for the governance of their companies.
- The role of shareholders is to appoint the directors and the external auditors, and to satisfy themselves that an appropriate governance structure is in place.
- The responsibilities of the board include setting the strategic aims of the company, providing the leadership to put them into effect, supervising management and reporting to the shareholders on their stewardship of the company.
- The actions of a board are subject to laws, regulations and resolutions by shareholders at company general meetings.

Sir Adrian Cadbury has defined corporate governance in much broader terms, to include the responsibility of companies towards society:

> Corporate Governance is concerned with holding the balance between economic and social goals and between individual and communal goals. The corporate governance framework is there to encourage the efficient use of resources and equally to require accountability for the stewardship of those resources. The aim is to align as nearly as possible the interests of individuals, corporations and society.
>
> Sir Adrian Cadbury, Global Corporate Governance Forum, World Bank, 2000.

At the heart of corporate governance is the relationship between the directors of a company and the equity shareholders. This can be compared with the agency–principal relationship. The board of directors of a company is the agent of the company, and acts on behalf of its principal (the shareholders). The agent must act in the best interests of the principal, and should be accountable to the principal for its stewardship of the company's assets.

In practice, this 'ideal' relationship between the directors and the shareholders does not always function as effectively as it should. The aim of the guidelines, rules and regulations on corporate governance is to improve the quality of governance, so that the directors fulfil their obligations to shareholders. In doing so, they should improve the performance of the company and meet the needs of its shareholders more successfully.


## 3 THE MAIN AREAS OF CORPORATE GOVERNANCE

Corporate governance emerged as an issue in the 1980s, initially in the UK. During the 1980s there were several financial scandals affecting major UK companies, such as the collapse of Polly Peck International and the business empire of Robert Maxwell. In each case the collapse was unexpected, and was subsequently attributed to misleading financial reporting and dominant chief executives.

It was apparent that some company CEOs and chairmen were dominating companies, and running them as personal empires. Others were simply running companies in their own personal interests rather than in the interests of the shareholders.

There was also concern that some companies might be 'window dressing' their published financial statements. In spite of the fact that company accounts were audited and the auditors stated that they gave a 'true and fair view', the financial picture presented by the accounts could not necessarily be relied on. There were suspicions that external auditors might not be sufficiently independent of senior management in their client companies, and that they might be allowing companies to get away with questionable financial reporting practices.

During the 1990s, attention in the UK switched to directors' remuneration and concern that senior executives were being remunerated in ways that did not provide sufficient incentives for them to work in the best interests of companies' shareholders.

During the 2000s, risk management emerged as a governance issue, with concerns that company boards were insufficiently aware of the risks to which their companies were exposed and that systems of internal control and business risk management were not sufficiently robust. Worries about inadequate risk management seemed to be justified by the collapse or near-collapse of several banks during the banking crisis of 2007–08.

More recently, senior executive remuneration has re-emerged as a controversial governance issue, with criticisms of the way in which percentage increases in senior executive remuneration have been much greater than pay increases for other employees.

Ethical issues and social and environmental issues are also discussed in the context of corporate governance and company reputation.

Figure 1.1 sets out the areas of concern about corporate governance that have emerged over time.

In the UK, recognition of the role of NEDs has developed with the perception that successful companies need an effective system of corporate governance to which NEDs can contribute. Experience seems to show that when companies get into serious difficulty, there is usually some evidence that poor governance and ineffective leadership by the board have contributed to the problem.

| **Leadership provided by the board** | **The effectiveness of the board** |
|---|---|
| Role of the chairman | Composition of the board |
| The role of the board | Skills and experience of board members |
| Responsibilities of board members | NED focus and support |
| **Accountability** | **Risk management and internal control** |
| Financial reporting and narrative reporting | Risk appetite and tolerance |
| Strategic report | Opportunity risk |
| External audit | Risk reporting to the board |
| **Remuneration of directors and senior executives** | **Relations with shareholders and other stakeholders** |
| Levels of pay | Dialogue and communications |
| Incentive schemes and rewards | Corporate citizenship |
| Rewards for failure | |
| **Corporate ethics, reputation, social and environmental issues** | **Strategy and governance** |
| Lack of protection for whistle-blowers | Strategic objectives |
| Corporate bribery | Leadership and direction |

**Figure 1.1** Issues in corporate governance

## 4 THE REGULATION OF CORPORATE GOVERNANCE

In most countries, including the UK, corporate governance is regulated by a combination of laws and other regulations and self-regulation by companies. In the UK, various aspects of governance are regulated by statute law, such as the Companies Act 2006. Listed companies are also required to comply with rules of the United Kingdom Listing Authority (the Listing Rules, Disclosure and Transparency Rules and Prospectus Rules). Voluntary self-regulation is through the UK Corporate Governance Code, which applies to all companies with a premium listing for their shares.

Many other countries have similar arrangements of voluntary codes of corporate governance, although the details and content can vary substantially between countries. The corporate governance codes of each country are accessible via the website of the European Corporate Governance Institute (see Directory).

Confusingly, regulations and codes of practice may sometimes appear to overlap. For example, the Disclosure and Transparency Rules include requirements for an audit committee (or similar body) for all listed companies, and the UK Corporate Governance Code also includes provisions relating to audit committees.

## 5 THE UK CORPORATE GOVERNANCE CODE: COMPLY OR EXPLAIN

The UK Corporate Governance Code is now the responsibility of the Financial Reporting Council (FRC). It came together over a number of years, beginning with the Cadbury Code in 1992, followed by the Greenbury Committee recommendations in 1995 and recommendations of the Hampel Committee in 1996. The Hampel Committee recommended that the corporate governance guidelines for listed companies should be brought together into a single code, and the first version of the Combined Code on Corporate Governance was issued in 1998. The Code underwent a substantial revision in 2003, and subsequent minor revisions. Another review led to the publication of an amended governance code, re-named as the UK Corporate Governance Code (also referred to as the UK Code), in 2010. The intention of the FRC is that the Code should be reviewed and revised if necessary every two years, as it was in September 2012 (see Appendix 1).

The UK Code consists of principles of good corporate governance, supported by some detailed provisions. These can apply to all companies, to a greater or lesser extent. Their prime focus, however, is on listed companies with a premium listing in the UK.

The UK Code is voluntary, but the UK Listing Rules (rule LR 9.8.6) require companies to disclose, in their annual report and accounts, that the company has:

- applied the principles of the UK Corporate Governance Code;
- complied with all the relevant provisions of the Code, or if it has not complied with all the provisions, it has provided an explanation of which provisions were not complied with, and the reasons for the non-compliance.

This approach is known as 'comply or explain'.

## EU Company Reporting Directive

The EU Company Reporting Directive contains a similar requirement. All quoted companies in the EU are required to include a corporate governance statement in their annual report and accounts. This statement must refer to the corporate governance code applied by the company (which country's code has been used) and whether and to what extent the company has complied with this code. This requirement is now included within the Disclosure and Transparency Rules in the UK.

## Implications of 'comply or explain' rule

It is important to stress that the rules for stock market companies apply to disclosure of compliance or non-compliance with a corporate governance code. Actual **compliance** with the UK Code is voluntary and by no means compulsory. If the directors of a listed company believe that it is in the best interests of the company, they need not comply with every provision in the Code, although they must explain the reasons for non-compliance in the annual report and accounts.

In many cases, non-compliance is due to the circumstances of the company, such as its small size or its complexity. The Code is flexible and companies must simply provide a good and sensible reason for any non-compliance.

In the UK (more so than in the USA), there is a concern that if corporate governance rules are applied rigidly, companies will adopt a 'box-ticking' approach to compliance, and the intended benefits will be lost. In 2012 the Financial Reporting Council (FRC) published a report on discussions between investors and companies about what constitutes an explanation under the 'comply or explain rule'. This commented that the explanations provided by some companies for non-compliance with the UK Governance Code were 'rather perfunctory'. The report concluded: 'Used properly, the Code-based "comply or explain" approach can deliver greater transparency and confidence than formal regulation which is purely a matter of compliance.'

### Unlisted companies and smaller quoted companies

There is no regulatory requirement for companies other than listed companies to comply with the principles and provisions of the Combined Code. However, the Quoted Companies Alliance (QCA), a body representing smaller and mid-cap quoted companies, has issued guidance in the form of 'Corporate Governance Guidelines for Small and Mid-Size Quoted Companies 2013' (see Directory).

These Guidelines, which apply to smaller listed companies and companies on AIM and the ICAP Securities and Derivatives Exchange, are consistent with the UK Code for listed companies, but not as detailed or rigorous. Even so, companies with aspirations to become listed companies should be expected to develop their corporate governance systems towards the standards set out in the UK Code.

The Institute of Directors (IoD) also issued 'Corporate Governance Guidelines and Principles for Unlisted Companies' in 2010, building on guidelines issued earlier in the year by the European Confederation of Directors' Associations (ecoDA). The IoD Guidelines contain 14 principles:

- eight of these apply to all types of unlisted company, and are simplified re-statements of basic corporate governance principles that should apply to all companies, listed and unlisted;
- one principle deals with family governance and corporate governance in family-controlled unlisted businesses;
- five principles apply to large and/or complex unlisted companies: these are similar to principles that are applied to listed companies by the UK Corporate Governance Code.

The main thrust of this guidance is that unlisted companies should adopt principles of good corporate governance, and as they grow they should improve their governance further, towards the standards expected from listed companies.

Many unlisted companies are led by their entrepreneurial owner-founder or are family-owned businesses. Any minority shareholders have only limited opportunities to sell their shares, and so are medium- to long-term investors. The IoD Guidelines suggest reasons why these unlisted companies should try to establish a good standard of corporate governance.

- The entrepreneurial founder may want to reduce their involvement in the business as they get older, or may need more advice from experienced individuals as the company grows.
- The company may need new sources of finance, such as bank loans, as it grows. Lenders or other capital providers may expect good standards of corporate governance as a condition of providing finance.

- Minority shareholders will have reassurance that although they are unable to exit from the company, their interests will be respected and safeguarded by the company and its board.

The IoD Guidelines suggest that a key stage in the development of corporate government in unlisted companies is the appointment of external directors (NEDs) to the board. 'Its effect on boardroom behaviour and culture should not be underestimated.'

The Guidelines are accessible on the IoD website (see Directory).

## 6 NEDS AND EFFECTIVE CORPORATE GOVERNANCE

In the UK, the role of NEDs is closely associated with achieving best practice in corporate governance.

The role of non-executive directors in corporate governance has changed since their importance was recognised in the Cadbury Code, which included a recommendation that a minimum proportion of board members should be independent NEDs. Independent NEDs are now expected to fulfil roles that were not expected of them 20 years ago.

- They are expected to provide a counterweight, so that a balance of power in the board is achieved, in which executive directors are not dominant and all-powerful.
- They provide the committee membership for the audit and remuneration committees and for a majority of the nomination committee.

The burden of expectation on NEDs, if anything, continues to grow.

NEDs need to be aware of their responsibilities and what they are expected to do. To carry out their responsibilities effectively, they should be kept well-informed, and they have a duty to ask for the information they need, if they do not have it.

The existence of a code of corporate governance, setting out guidelines for recommended best practice, might suggest that the role of NEDs is concerned mainly with compliance. This is not the case. Although NEDs are involved with the application of best practice in corporate governance, they are also directors of the company, with a duty to govern the company in the best interests of the shareholders.

NEDs sit on the board with executive directors, share the same responsibilities as directors, and work with their executive colleagues to provide strategic leadership and participate in making major decisions for the company.

For the relationship between NEDs and executive directors to work, there has to be a mutual recognition of what each group brings to the board table. The *Guidance on Board Effectiveness* section on the role of NEDs highlights how important it is for NEDs to show an appropriate level of commitment to their companies and to develop and refresh their knowledge and skills to ensure they continue to make a positive contribution to the board. Being well-informed about the company and demonstrating a strong command of key business issues will 'generate the respect of the other directors'.

## 7  BOARDROOM BEHAVIOURS AND EFFECTIVE BOARDS

Measures in the UK to improve corporate governance standards have been intended to reduce the probability or frequency of major corporate failures due to poor governance. It might have been supposed that this risk was reduced by the requirement for UK listed companies to comply with a governance code or explain non-compliance, and by providing official guidance to companies on a range of governance issues (such as the role of the chairman and NEDs, audit committees and monitoring the effectives of internal control). However in 2008, the UK was badly affected by the global crisis in the financial services industry, and emergency measures were needed from the government to rescue a number of banks – Northern Rock, Bradford and Bingley, HBOS, Lloyds and the Royal Bank of Scotland. Sir David Walker headed a review into the reasons for the banking failures, and one of the issues to consider was whether the various banking failures were attributable to continuing weaknesses in corporate governance within the banking industry.

In 2009, ICSA submitted a report to Sir David Walker (which was copied to the FRC) entitled 'Boardroom Behaviours', in which it suggested that the system of corporate governance in the UK was not 'broken', but its effectiveness had been undermined by a failure to observe some basic principles of boardroom behaviour. Some of the comments in this ICSA report have relevance to the role of NEDs within the board.

The report suggested that best practice in boardroom behaviour is characterised by:
- a clear understanding of the role of the board;
- an 'appropriate deployment of knowledge, skills, experience and judgement';
- independent thinking;

---

CASE EXAMPLE
................

## THE WALKER REPORT AND BOARD BEHAVIOUR

In 2009 the UK government commissioned a review by Sir David Walker into the corporate governance of UK banks and other financial institutions, following the global financial crisis that began in mid-2007.

The Walker Report included the following comments about the contribution of poor corporate governance to the crisis:

'Serious deficiencies in prudential oversight and financial regulation in the period before the crisis were accompanied by major governance failures within banks. These contributed materially to excessive risk taking and to the breadth and depth of the crisis. ... Board conformity with laid down procedures such as those for enhanced risk oversight will not alone provide better corporate governance overall if the chairman is weak, if the composition and dynamic of the board is inadequate and if there is unsatisfactory or no engagement with major owners.'

The report identified failures by NEDs as a major contributory factor in the inadequacy of corporate governance in the banks.

---

- the questioning of assumptions and established views;
- a challenge that is 'constructive, confident, principled and proportionate';
- rigorous debate;
- a supportive decision-making environment;
- a common vision; and
- achieving successful closure on individual items of board business.

The extent to which these desirable boardroom behaviours can be delivered depends in turn on:

- the characters and personalities of the board directors and how they interact with each other;
- a balance in the relationship between key members of the board, notably the chairman and chief executive officer;
- the culture of the board and the company; and
- the environment in which board meetings are held.

The ICSA report argued that the absence of formal guidance on boardroom behaviour was a weakness in the UK corporate governance system. Effective corporate governance depends not only on sound governance structures but also on appropriate boardroom behaviour.

## 8 CHECKLIST: A FRAMEWORK FOR EFFECTIVE BOARDS AND CORPORATE GOVERNANCE

There are different aspects of corporate governance, and issues in corporate governance may be categorised and analysed in different ways. It is important to understand how the different elements of corporate governance are interlinked. Companies should establish their own framework and apply an integrated and consistent approach. This framework should start with the achievement of business objectives, and should conclude with disclosure in the annual report and accounts. An example of such a framework is set out in Figure 1.2.

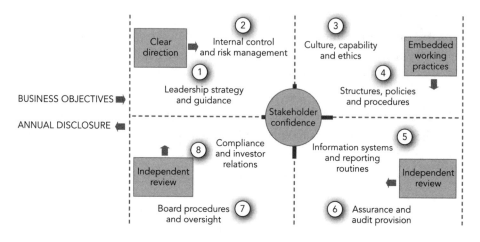

**Figure 1.2** A framework for effective corporate governance.

The following checklist sets out a framework of the requirements for an effective system of governance. It can be used by directors and their advisers to make a brief assessment of the effectiveness of governance within their company.

The items under each heading are guiding principles and key practice measures.

| | RATING | | |
|---|---|---|---|
| | Good | Average | Below average |
| **1. Strategy and management** | | | |
| 1.1 Business strategy and objectives are clearly defined and understood. | ☐ | ☐ | ☐ |
| 1.2 Implementation of strategy is monitored regularly. | ☐ | ☐ | ☐ |

|  | RATING | | |
|---|---|---|---|
|  | *Good* | *Average* | *Below average* |
| 1.3 Clear direction is provided by the board and senior management, towards meeting the strategic needs of the company and promoting its key behaviours. | ☐ | ☐ | ☐ |
| 1.4 The management team has the appropriate range and balance of experience. | ☐ | ☐ | ☐ |
| 1.5 The right people are in the right roles for implementing business strategy successfully. | ☐ | ☐ | ☐ |
| 1.6 Management demonstrate clear and transparent judgement, giving appropriate consideration to business risks in the decision-making process. | ☐ | ☐ | ☐ |

## 2. Internal control and risk management

|  | *Good* | *Average* | *Below average* |
|---|---|---|---|
| 2.1 Risk management policies and procedures are clearly defined, communicated and applied. | ☐ | ☐ | ☐ |
| 2.2 Risk management activities are integrated with business planning activities. | ☐ | ☐ | ☐ |
| 2.3 Risks are identified and assessed in all critical areas. | ☐ | ☐ | ☐ |
| 2.4 Ownership of risk is clearly defined by management. | ☐ | ☐ | ☐ |
| 2.5 Control procedures are well understood by management, and they are documented and consistently applied. | ☐ | ☐ | ☐ |
| 2.6 Risk treatment results in consideration of risk appetite and an appropriate response to risks (i.e. tolerate, treat, transfer, terminate as well as take in certain circumstances). | ☐ | ☐ | ☐ |
| 2.7 Risk monitoring and reporting routines are used to communicate progress. | ☐ | ☐ | ☐ |

## 3. Culture, capability and ethics

|  | *Good* | *Average* | *Below average* |
|---|---|---|---|
| 3.1 The company has an approved code of business behaviour and ethical conduct. This code of conduct has been communicated across the business. | ☐ | ☐ | ☐ |
| 3.2 Effective and comprehensive training programmes are in place. These include a company induction programme. | ☐ | ☐ | ☐ |

| | RATING | | |
|---|---|---|---|
| | Good | Average | Below average |
| 3.3 Governance, risk and control, business skills and competencies are assessed as part of the personal business development programme. | ☐ | ☐ | ☐ |

## 4. Structures, policies and procedures

| | | | |
|---|---|---|---|
| 4.1 The organisation structure is appropriate and is based on the key business activities of the organisation. | ☐ | ☐ | ☐ |
| 4.2 Policies, procedures and processes are clear, up to date and well-documented. The scale and scope of policies and procedures reflect the culture of the organisation. | ☐ | ☐ | ☐ |
| 4.3 Roles, responsibilities and levels of authorisation are defined and agreed. | ☐ | ☐ | ☐ |
| 4.4 Systems and procedures are flexible, capable of responding to changes within the business and within the business environment. | ☐ | ☐ | ☐ |

## 5. Information systems and reporting routines

| | | | |
|---|---|---|---|
| 5.1 Information systems (IS) are well-defined and support the strategic direction of the business. | ☐ | ☐ | ☐ |
| 5.2 IS investment, change programmes, security routines and system performance are well-managed, with appropriate reporting routines. | ☐ | ☐ | ☐ |
| 5.3 Business continuity plans (BCP) and disaster recovery plans (DRP) are defined, documented and tested. | ☐ | ☐ | ☐ |
| 5.4 Information provided to the business is timely, reliable and meets the needs of its users. | ☐ | ☐ | ☐ |

## 6. Assurance and audit provision

| | | | |
|---|---|---|---|
| 6.1 The role of all assurance providers, and the range of work that they do, is reviewed, approved and communicated. (This may cover external audit, internal audit, health and safety, security, environmental, insurance and compliance.) | ☐ | ☐ | ☐ |
| 6.2 Assurance activities are planned, integrated and co-ordinated. They are focused on the critical risks faced by the business. (For example, decisions about the need for internal audit are based on risks rather than the size of business operations.) | ☐ | ☐ | ☐ |

| | | RATING | | |
|---|---|:---:|:---:|:---:|
| | | Good | Average | Below average |
| 6.3 | Reporting to the board by assurance providers is 'fit for purpose', comprehensive and covers a full range of internal control areas. | ☐ | ☐ | ☐ |
| 6.4 | Any material weaknesses identified by independent reviews result in action plans that are followed through to completion. | ☐ | ☐ | ☐ |

### 7. Board leadership, procedures and oversight

| | | Good | Average | Below average |
|---|---|:---:|:---:|:---:|
| 7.1 | The board of directors has a clear definition of its mandate, and there is a clear definition and understanding of the role and responsibilities of individual board members. | ☐ | ☐ | ☐ |
| 7.2 | The chairman provides effective leadership for the board, so that all directors contribute to board decision-making and board meetings are constructive. Directors receive informative papers for board meetings in good time to study them before the meeting. The board is not dominated by one or two individuals. | ☐ | ☐ | ☐ |
| 7.3 | Members of the board have appropriate skills and expertise, and there is a formal and rigorous annual performance evaluation of the board, its committees and individual directors. | ☐ | ☐ | ☐ |
| 7.4 | There is an appropriate balance of executive and non-executive directors on the board. (The definition of 'appropriate' depends on the size of the business.) | ☐ | ☐ | ☐ |
| 7.5 | The NEDs make sufficient time available to fulfil their responsibilities and have a good understanding of the company and its business. Induction and professional development are provided for directors. | ☐ | ☐ | ☐ |
| 7.6 | There is an effective decision-making process at board level. Items of board business are resolved, without undue delay, disagreement, or uncertainty and lack of clarity. | ☐ | ☐ | ☐ |
| 7.7 | The board committees have clear mandates. These committees provide appropriate levels of both insight and oversight. | ☐ | ☐ | ☐ |

|  | RATING | | |
| --- | --- | --- | --- |
|  | Good | Average | Below average |

### 8. Compliance and investor relations

| | Good | Average | Below average |
| --- | --- | --- | --- |
| 8.1 All areas of external 'disclosure' required relating to financial, commercial, operational or other matters (such as disclosure requirements in the UK Corporate Governance Code) are well-documented and approved by the board. | ☐ | ☐ | ☐ |
| 8.2 All compliance matters for the business are defined and given appropriate attention. Compliance issues are dealt with on a timely basis. | ☐ | ☐ | ☐ |
| 8.3 The business has a robust and transparent investor relations programme. | ☐ | ☐ | ☐ |
| 8.4 The business satisfies the demands for information (and develops appropriate relationships) with investors, analysts and key stakeholders. | ☐ | ☐ | ☐ |

# Directors' duties and liabilities

....................

## OVERVIEW

In law, directors have certain general duties to their companies. Until replaced by statutory general duties in the Companies Act 2006, these legal duties were based on equity and common law, and directors had a fiduciary duty and a duty of skill and care to their companies. Although the general duties of directors have now been set out in the Companies Act 2006, as statute law, these are still based on the concepts of fiduciary duty and a duty of skill and care. There are also other statutory regulations for directors, such as rules relating to fraudulent or wrongful trading, but these are not duties.

Directors may become personally liable for a breach of duty. The greatest risk is probably the risk of civil liability for negligence or for a breach of the duty of skill and care. Civil action against a director may be taken by other directors, a liquidator, or (occasionally) by shareholders acting on behalf of the company.

NEDs should be aware of the personal risks that they may be exposed to, and should take measures to reduce these risks to an acceptable level. One measure for reducing the risks is directors' and officers' liability insurance.

Directors should also be aware of the legislation relating to market abuse and insider dealing, as well as the Model Code in the Listing Rules.

## Note

This chapter includes a general description of legal duties and obligations of directors, but for a more detailed study of the rules and regulations (for example, for details of all exceptions to the general rules) you should refer to the actual legislation or regulation.

## 1 DUTIES OF DIRECTORS: INTRODUCTION

### Fiduciary duty and duty of skill and care

In UK law, all directors owe certain duties to their company. Until the introduction of the Companies Act 2006, these duties took the form of a fiduciary duty and a duty of skill and care.

- A fiduciary duty is a duty of trust. 'Fiduciary' means 'given in trust'. The duty of directors is similar to the duty owed to a trust by a trustee. A director may be in breach of their fiduciary duties, for example, if they make a transaction that is for their personal benefit rather than for the benefit of the company.
- A duty of skill and care. Directors have a common law duty of skill and care to the company, and should not act negligently in carrying out those duties.

If a director is found by the court to be in breach of duty, they may be personally liable for the losses suffered by the company as a result. 'Breach of duty' may also be described as a 'wrongful act'.

Directors are agents of the company, and they owe their duties to the company itself, not the shareholders, nor the company's employees or anyone external to the company.

Civil legal action may be brought by a company against an individual director, or against several directors jointly, alleging negligence, breach of duty or breach of trust. In such cases, it is usual for the action to be initiated on behalf of the company by the rest of the board of directors, or by a liquidator of the company.

In certain circumstances, a legal action may be brought on behalf of their company by a number of shareholders (in a derivative action, on the company's behalf).

## What standard of skill and care is expected?

There have been several legal cases where the judicial decision has provided some guide to standard of skill and care expected of a company director under common law.

CASE EXAMPLES

# DUTY OF SKILL AND CARE

The case of *Re D'Jan of London* [1993] involved a company director who had signed an insurance proposal form, for a policy that included fire insurance cover. The form had been filled in by an insurance broker on behalf of the company, but contained an error, which the director did not see when he signed it. The company premises suffered fire damage, but the insurance company, finding the error in the proposal form, denied any liability under the policy. The company went into insolvent liquidation, and the liquidator brought an action against the director, on behalf of the company, claiming a breach of the director's duty of skill and care.

The court found that it would be unreasonable to expect a director to read every word of every document that he signed, but in this case the proposal form had consisted of a small number of simple questions that the director was in the best position to answer. It was therefore judged that he had been in breach of his duty of skill and care (although the court found him not liable on other grounds).

This case was notable because the judge ruled that the common law test of the director's duty of skill and care should be similar to the statutory test applied under section 214 of the Insolvency Act 1986. This statutory test is that the expected standard of skill and care is what would be expected of a 'reasonably diligent person' having both the general knowledge, skill and experience that may reasonably be expected of a person carrying out those functions on behalf of the company, and the general knowledge, skill and experience that the particular director has.

In the case of *Dorchester Finance Co. Ltd v Stebbing* (1989), two non-executive directors were held to be negligent for not attending board meetings of a subsidiary company, even though it was shown that it was not commercial practice to do so. The directors also signed blank cheques for a director who used the cheques to embezzle money from the company. It was held that the directors were accountants with long experience of acting in the financial affairs of various bodies, and consequently that they could not assert that non-executive directors had no duties to perform.

In a case involving the disqualification of three directors, *Re Barings plc (No. 5) (1999)*, it was held that the directors had failed to supervise their employees, and in particular a rogue trader in Singapore whose trading losses brought Barings Bank to insolvency. Directors must inform themselves of their company's affairs and collaborate with other directors to supervise those affairs, but in this case the directors had failed in this duty. Having no adequate system of monitoring was therefore a breach of this standard. Directors may delegate functions, but they nevertheless remain responsible for those functions being carried. The three individuals were disqualified from acting as directors.

Two of these three cases involved executive directors of the company, and it is more likely that executive directors rather than non-executives will be accused of breach of their duty of reasonable care and skill. However, the legal obligations of non-executives are the same as for executives.

## 2 DIRECTORS' DUTIES AND THE COMPANIES ACT 2006

The Companies Act 2006 (sections 170–177) introduced statutory general duties for all company directors (see Appendix 3). In summary these statutory general duties of directors are:

- to act within their powers;
- to promote the success of the company for the benefit of its members;
- to exercise independent judgement;
- to exercise reasonable care, skill and diligence;
- to avoid conflicts of interest;
- not to accept benefits from third parties; and
- to declare any interest in a proposed transaction with the company.

The Companies Act states (section 170) that the general duties 'are based on certain common law rules and equitable principles' and 'shall be interpreted and applied in the same way as the common law rules and equitable principles, and regard should be had to the corresponding common law rules and equitable principles in interpreting and applying the general duties'.

## Duty to act within powers

This duty is likely to have more relevance to executive directors than NEDs, although NEDs should make sure that their executive colleagues do not take decisions personally that ought to be reserved for the board. The *ICSA's Guidance on Directors' General Duties* (2007) suggests that when a group of directors meets, it must be clear whether they are attending a full board meeting, a committee meeting or an unofficial meeting. Unless they are meeting as a board, they would be in breach of their statutory duty if they reached decisions that should be reserved for the board as a whole.

## Duty to promote the success of the company

A director, in good faith, must act in the way he considers would be most likely to 'promote the success of the company for the benefit of its members as a whole'. The Act also states that in acting to promote the success of the company, a director must also have regard, among other matters, to:

- the likely long-term consequences of any decision;
- the interests of the company's employees;
- the need to foster the company's relationships with its customers, suppliers and others;
- the impact of the company's operations on the community and the environment;
- the desirability of the company maintaining its reputation for high standards of business conduct; and
- the need to act fairly as between members of the company.

The Act does not create a duty of directors to anyone other than the shareholders of the company, but directors are required to give some consideration to interests of other 'stakeholders' in the company, such as employees, customers, suppliers and the local community.

'Success' is not defined in the Act. Subject to any case law on the subject, success may be considered to be achieving an increase in the long-term value of the company. However, when there may be questions about whether the directors have given sufficient consideration to the interests of stakeholders (other than the shareholders), it would be advisable for minutes of the relevant board meeting to include details of discussions that led to the board decision – for example, with a decision to close a factory or office, it may be appropriate for the minutes of the board meeting to include how the board considered the impact of the decision on employees and the local community.

## Duty to exercise independent judgement

This duty could be of particular relevance to NEDs. NEDs must avoid falling into the habit of accepting the judgements of others – for example, the executive directors – without first thinking carefully about the matter. There is no problem with accepting the views of someone else, provided that the director has reached their opinion after careful consideration.

## Duty to exercise reasonable care, skill and diligence

This is similar to the 'old' common law duty of skill and care.

## Duty to avoid conflicts of interests

The Companies Act states that directors must avoid a situation in which they have, or could have, either a direct or an indirect conflict of interest with the interests of the company. An indirect interest might exist through the interest of a close family member, for example, or through ownership of another company. The duty to avoid a conflict of interests 'applies in particular to the exploitation of any property, information or opportunity', but it does not apply to a transaction or arrangement with the company. This aspect of the duty to avoid a conflict of interest continues even after the director has left the company.

The duty to avoid a conflict of interest does not apply in relation to any transaction or arrangement with the company, because such transactions are covered by the statutory duty for directors to declare their interest in any proposed transaction or arrangement with the company.

## What is a conflict of interest?

The Companies Act does not define a conflict of interest. However, it is generally considered that a conflict of interest is likely to arise if there is anything that might prevent a director from considering anything but the interests of the company (and promoting the success of the company) when reaching a judgement or point of view.

NEDs may have a conflict of interest, for example, if they hold more than one directorship, because the interests of the different companies may be in conflict.

## Authorisation of conflicts and potential conflicts of interest

The Companies Act allows conflicts of interest under certain circumstances. In broad terms, a director must not let a conflict of interest arise unless the board has given prior authorisation. Where authorisation has been properly given, conflicts of interest are permitted.

The Act therefore allows directors to authorise conflicts and potential conflicts of interest in advance, so that a director will not be in breach of duty even though a conflict does exist. The legal requirements for directors to authorise a conflict of interest differ for public and private companies.

- For a public company, the articles of association must contain a specific provision that permits the other directors to authorise actual or potential conflicts of interest.
- For private companies incorporated on or after 1 October 2008, the articles of association must not contain any provision that prevents the directors from authorising conflicts and potential conflicts.
- For private companies in existence before that date, the company's shareholders must pass a resolution that allows the directors to authorise conflicts and potential conflicts.

If the board is considering a matter in which a director has a material conflict of interest which has been authorised by the rest of the board, the director should not participate in the discussions, and should be asked to leave the boardroom while the matter is being discussed.

The company's articles of association may actually include specific provisions relating to how conflicts of interest should be dealt with. For example, the articles may be specific in requiring a director with a conflict of interest, as noted above, to excuse themselves from board discussions where a conflict or potential conflict exists.

### Consequences of breach

The consequences of a breach of this duty can include the director being liable for damages or compensation where the company has suffered a loss, or for the director to be required to hand over to the company profits made by the director from the conflicting interest.

### A conflict of interests questionnaire

In 2008, the Association of General Counsel and Company Secretaries of the FTSE 100 (the GC 100) published guidance for directors on how to deal with the duty to avoid a conflict of interests. The following checklist of situations where a conflict or potential conflict could arise is based on this guidance.

| Conflict of interests questionnaire | TICK |
|---|---|
| 1.  Are you a significant shareholder in the company? | ☐ |
| 2.  Are you a director or a significant shareholder of another company which is: | |
|     i.  A significant shareholder in the company? | ☐ |
|     ii.  In partnership with the company? | ☐ |
|     iii.  In a joint venture with the company? | ☐ |
| 3.  Does any external body you are associated with have any of the following relationships with the company? | ☐ |
|     i.  Supplier | ☐ |
|     ii.  Customer | ☐ |
|     iii.  Competitor | ☐ |
|     iv.  Bank (for example, a bank that provides or might provide finance) | ☐ |
|     v.  Distribution | ☐ |
|     vi.  Any other ongoing material relationship (for example, acting as an agent of the company) | ☐ |
| 4.  Are you associated with any adviser to the company? Examples of advisers are: | |
|     i.  Auditors | ☐ |
|     ii.  Tax advisers | ☐ |
|     iii.  Legal advisers | ☐ |
|     iv.  Pension or investment advisers | ☐ |
|     v.  Investment banking advisers | ☐ |
|     vi.  Management consultants | ☐ |
| 5.  Are you a member of a committee or a commission, or do you have a material position with a regulator, any department of government, a trade body, a professional body or a charitable organisation, which might: | |
|     i.  Influence government policy? | ☐ |
|     ii.  Prepare industry guidance? | ☐ |
| 6.  Are you a trustee of the company's pension fund? | ☐ |
| 7.  Do you hold a material position in any other pension fund that might hold shares in the company? | ☐ |

---

| Conflict of interests questionnaire | TICK |
|---|---|

8. Are you associated with an investment organisation of any nature, such as a hedge fund, venture capital organisation, private equity organisation or investment trust fund? ☐

9. Are you in a position where you (or another company in which you are a director or material shareholder) could make a profit as a result of your directorship of the company? ☐

10. Are you aware of any other circumstances where a conflict of interest with the company exists or might exist in the future? ☐

Notes:

There is no breach of duty when a director is in a situation that cannot reasonably be regarded as likely to give rise to a conflict of interest.

If you have any doubts or require any assistance, please consult the Company Secretary.

---

Conflicts of interest should be notified by a new director on appointment to the board, and changes should be notified throughout the director's term of office.

---

### CASE EXAMPLE
················
## CONFLICTS OF INTEREST

The meaning of conflict of interests has been partly tested by the case of *Thermascan v Norman* (2009).

Mr Norman was a director of Thermascan Ltd, but resigned from the company in 2008. He went to work for another company, but after a few months he was made redundant. Following his redundancy, he set up his own company, which operated in competition with Thermascan, and he approached some of Thermascan's customers. By this time, the restrictive covenants in Mr Norman's contract of employment with Thermascan (including a non-solicitation clause) had come to an end. Thermascan therefore applied for a court order under the Companies Act 2006 to prevent Mr Norman from canvassing or soliciting their clients, on the grounds that he was in breach of his duty to avoid a conflict of interests.

The court decided that in this case Mr Norman's approach to customers of the company did not amount to an appropriation of a maturing business opportunity for Thermascan, as there had not been any significant discussion

---

by Thermascan of a potential business opportunity with the customers concerned. Mr Norman was therefore not in breach of his duty to avoid a conflict of interests.

The court also decided that this case did not involve any continuing fiduciary duty after the former director's resignation, such as a situation where the resignation of a director is motivated by an intention to acquire business from the company for himself.

### Duty not to accept benefits from third parties

A director must not accept benefits from a third party that are given in connection with their position as director – for example, in return for doing something or not doing something. However, disclosure is not required where acceptance of the benefits could not reasonably be regarded as giving rise to a potential conflict of interest.

It would probably be considered a breach of duty for a director to accept an all-expenses-paid holiday from a third party (by virtue of being a director of the company) or to accept frequent invitations to hospitality events. On the other hand, it would probably not be a breach of duty to accept limited benefits, such as corporate hospitality for a day at a major sporting event.

Many listed companies have strict internal policies on the acceptance of gifts and corporate hospitality from clients, suppliers or firms of professional advisers. These might include a requirement for prior authorisation for the receipt of such benefits and for all benefits received to be recorded in an official register. (Company policy on giving and receiving hospitality must also comply with the requirements of the Bribery Act.)

### Duty to declare interests in proposed transactions with the company

This statutory duty is linked to the duty to avoid conflicts of interest. A director may have a personal interest in a proposed transaction with the company. (This is permitted by standard articles of association, provided the interest in a proposed transaction is declared to the rest of the board.) For example, a director may own a building that the company wants to buy or rent; or a director may be a major shareholder in another company that is hoping to become a supplier or customer.

If a director is in any way, directly or indirectly, interested in a proposed transaction or arrangement with the company, they must declare the nature and extent of this interest to the other directors. This declaration must be made before the company actually enters into the transaction. It may be given at a board meeting, or by notice in writing, or as a general notice of the director's interest in another body, such as another company (with which the company subsequently proposes to enter into a transaction). The other directors may then authorise the transaction in knowledge of the director's interest.

A declaration of interest is not required if it can reasonably be regarded as not giving rise to a conflict of interests, or if it can be reasonably supposed that the other directors are already aware of the interest. It is also not a breach of duty where the director is not aware of the interest that he has in a transaction, or where he is aware of an interest but unaware of the proposed transaction.

Failure by a director to disclose an interest in a proposed transaction makes the contract for the transaction voidable at the option of the company. The company can choose to declare the contract void, but need not do so. The company can also seek to require the director to account to the company for any profit or benefit that he has obtained from the transaction.

### Duty to declare an interest in existing transactions

A director is also under a statutory duty to declare an interest in an existing transaction with the company, where they have not previously made a declaration in a proposed transaction with company (under the provisions of section 177 of the Companies Act). Failure to make this declaration to the other directors is a criminal offence, for which the penalty is a fine.

### Related party transactions and the DTR Rules for listed companies

For listed companies, the statutory provisions about conflicts of interest and declaring an interest in proposed transactions are supplemented by the UK Disclosure and Transparency Rules (DTR). The definition of a related party includes any director of the company, any member of a director's close family, and any company in which a director or family member holds 30% or more of the shares. A related party transaction is a transaction between the company and a related party, other than in the normal course of business.

For most related party transactions above a minimum size, a listed company is required by the DTR to:

- make an announcement to the stock market giving details of the transaction; and
- issue a circular to shareholders with details of the transaction and then obtain the approval of the shareholders (prior to the transaction).

*Other restrictions on dealings by a director with the company*

The Companies Act 2006 includes other restrictions on transactions between a director (and persons connected with a director) and the company. This applies to all companies.

- Substantial transactions in non-cash assets. Formal shareholder approval is required before a director (or a connected person) can acquire substantial non-cash assets from the company or the company can acquire substantial non-cash assets from the director. 'Substantial' means assets exceeding £100,000 in value or exceeding 10% of the company's total assets if this is a lower amount. (Transactions below £5,000 in value are exempt from this rule.) If shareholder approval is not obtained, the director concerned and all the directors who authorised the transaction would be liable for any profit they have made, and must indemnify the company for any loss or damage it has suffered.

- Loans by the company to a director (or a connected person). There are complex rules restricting the ability of a company to make a loan to a director or a person connected with the director. The general rule is that a company is prohibited from making a loan to a director or from guaranteeing a loan by a third party to a director, unless the transaction has been approved formally in advance by the shareholders. Similarly a company cannot make a quasi-loan to a director without prior formal consent from the shareholders: a quasi-loan to a director is an arrangement whereby a company agrees with a third party to meet expenditure on the director's behalf. There are several exceptions from this general rule. These include:

  - loans to directors that are for less than £10,000, which do not need shareholder approval;

  - loans to directors to enable them to incur expenditure on the company's behalf, subject to a limit of £50,000 – for example, a company may assist a director with a bridging loan in a case where the director is required by his work to move home from one part of the country to another; and

  - loans by a bank to its directors.

## 3  OTHER RESPONSIBILITIES AND POTENTIAL LIABILITIES FOR DIRECTORS

Directors are expected to ensure compliance by their company with all relevant laws and regulations. These vary between types of company and different industries, but include laws and regulations relating to matters such as health and safety, environmental protection, employment rights, data protection, insolvency and wrongful trading. In some circumstances, directors, NEDs as well as executive directors, could become personally liable for failure to comply with current legislation. This chapter focuses mainly on the statutory duties of directors and obligations in relation to the Companies Act, but in practice responsibilities are much more wide-ranging, and directors need to be fully aware of what these are.

## Bribery Act 2010

The Bribery Act has implications both for ethical conduct and corporate governance within companies, as well as potential criminal liabilities for directors. The Act deals with bribery in the public and private sectors and makes it a criminal offence to:

- offer or pay a bribe, or ask for or receive a bribe;
- bribe a foreign public official; or
- in the case of a commercial organisation, to fail to prevent someone acting on behalf of the business to pay a bribe on behalf of the organisation (unless the organisation can claim as a defence that it has adequate procedures in place to prevent bribery).

The maximum penalty for an offence is ten years' imprisonment and an unlimited fine.

## 4   LIABILITY OF NEDS

Directors are not liable for the losses or debts of the company, unless they have given personal guarantees for a debt.

However, directors may be liable, in both criminal and civil law, for breach of their statutory duties. The risk of personal liability is probably higher for executive directors than for NEDs, but all directors have the same legal status and so in principle are equally liable for any breach of the law or other regulation.

A civil action may be brought against a director by the other directors, acting on behalf of the company, by a liquidator of the company or possibly by some of its shareholders. The Companies Act 2006 also makes it easier than it has been in the past for shareholders to bring a legal action against directors on behalf of the company. The Act provides for legal action by the shareholders against a director, subject to court permission and under certain circumstances. Legal action by shareholders will be possible in a statutory 'derivative action' where there is an alleged action or omission by one or more directors involving negligence, default, breach of duty or breach of trust. The procedures for bringing a derivative action are set out in sections 260–264 of the Act. They include safeguards designed to prevent individual shareholders from bringing actions that are not reasonable on the basis of the prima facie evidence.

Directors have statutory duties under a variety of laws and regulations, which vary according to the nature of the company and its business. For example, liabilities may arise under duties set out in the Financial Services and Markets Act 2000, the Health and Safety at Work Act 1974, the Environmental Protection Act 1999 or the Insolvency Act 1986.

For example, if a company is in insolvent liquidation, the liquidator may initiate legal proceedings against the directors. Insolvent liquidation occurs when a company does not have sufficient assets to pay its liabilities at the time of the liquidation. Under the provisions of the Insolvency Act 1986, if the liquidator of the company is able to show that directors were responsible for wrongful trading, the court may decide that the directors should be personally liable to make a contribution to the company's assets. Any such payment to the company by a director will be used towards paying the company's creditors in the winding-up process. Directors will only be liable if the court decides that before the liquidation of the company began, they knew (or ought to have known) that there was no reasonable likelihood of the company avoiding insolvent liquidation.

---

CASE EXAMPLE

### DIRECTOR LIABILITY ON WINDING-UP

In 1989, the liquidator of Produce Marketing Consortium Ltd applied to the court, asking that two directors of the insolvent company should personally contribute to the company's assets in the winding-up.

This followed a decision by the court that the directors were liable for wrongful trading, because they had allowed the company to continue in business in the belief – wrong and unrealistic – that the company could trade its way out of its financial difficulties. The court decided that the directors were liable for wrongful trading, but were not potentially guilty of fraudulent trading, because they had not acted dishonestly or with the intention to defraud the company's creditors. However, it should have been clear that the company would have to go into insolvent liquidation, and the directors had ignored a warning from the company's auditors about the company's situation.

The court therefore decided that the two named directors should be personally liable (jointly and severally) to contribute £75,000 plus interest to the company. This payment would be available to the liquidator of the company, as a contribution towards paying the company's creditors in the winding-up process.

The judge in the case said that although the directors had not acted fraudulently, this was no reason for making their liability only a small amount. The liability of any director in cases involving wrongful trading should be judged by the circumstances of the case.

### Directors' liability for directors' reports and safe harbour provisions

Any director of a company is liable to compensate the company for any loss caused by an untrue or misleading statement (or an omission) in the directors' report, the directors' remuneration report or a summary financial statement so far as the statement is derived from either of these reports (section 463, Companies Act 2006). The director may be liable only if they knew the statement to be untrue or misleading (or was reckless as to whether it was untrue or misleading) or they knew the omission to be a dishonest concealment of a material fact. (This protection for directors from liability for misleading statements, untrue statements or omissions when they did not know about them and were not reckless is known as 'safe harbour provisions'.)

Directors have no liability to anyone except the company in relation to these reports. They cannot be personally liable to shareholders or anyone else.

However, an amendment to the Financial Services and Markets Act 2000 was introduced by the Companies Act 2006 (section 90A, FSMA), giving investors the right to make a claim against a quoted company if they can show they have suffered a loss as a result of an untrue or misleading statement in, or dishonest concealment from, financial reporting disclosures by the company in its listing particulars or prospectus. The investor would also need to show that one or more of the directors of the company knew of the error or omission (or was reckless in not knowing about it). In this way, an investor may sue the company for misleading reports, and the company could then make a claim against any individual director(s).

### Comparing the potential liability of executive directors and NEDs

The liability of a non-executive director may be less in practice than for an executive director, for two main reasons:

(1) The time that a NED can devote to the company's affairs is considerably less than for an executive director.

(2)   The detailed knowledge and experience of a company's affairs will also be less for a NED than for an executive director.

The court will take these factors into consideration when it judges the liability of a NED for negligence or breach of duty. However, it still leaves a basic question unanswered. Allowing for the limited time that a NED has to spend on a company's affairs, and their relative lack of knowledge and experience of the company's affairs, what amount of skill and care would be expected of a NED in any particular situation?

The law is not specific on this point. Deciding whether a NED is in breach of duty will depend on the particular circumstances of each case.

## UK Corporate Governance Code

Before its replacement by the UK Corporate Governance Code, an appendix to the Combined Code on Corporate Governance gave some guidance on the liability of NEDs for a breach of their duty of care, skill and diligence.

It stated that it is up to each individual NED to reach a view on what they must do to comply with a director's duty of skill, care and diligence. The courts may take into account:

- the expected time commitment, to which the NED agreed on accepting their appointment (or any change in the expected time commitment that has subsequently been agreed);
- the requirement in the Code for the chairman to ensure that the board is provided with accurate, timely and clear information, to enable the board to discharge its duties properly;
- the requirement in the Code that NEDs should undertake induction after their appointment and should then continually refresh their skills and knowledge, and their familiarity with the company;
- the provision in the Code that directors, particularly NEDs, should obtain clarification of information or additional information from management, and should obtain professional advice where appropriate;
- whether the director has expressed concerns about a relevant issue to the board, and the concerns have been included in the minutes of a board meeting; and
- whether the director has resigned over a relevant matter, and has provided a written statement of their concerns to the chairman.

The UK Corporate Governance Code therefore recommended that a NED should take appropriate action to make sure that a court would consider that the NED has acted appropriately and has done as much as possible to fulfil their duties. In other words, will a court criticise the NED for failing in respect of any of the issues listed above, or criticise the company and its chairman (for example, for failing to provide relevant, timely and clear information)?

Although the same information does not appear in the UK Corporate Governance Code, it still remains relevant.

## 5   REVIEWING PERSONAL RISKS

All NEDs should make themselves aware of the personal risks to which they might be exposed. They should do this before accepting an appointment as a NED, and regularly throughout their term of office, by carrying out a risk review.

The risks faced by each individual NED will vary with circumstances, such as the nature of the company and the number of committee memberships that the NED has.

The purpose of a risk review should be to assess the potential risks that the NED faces personally, and to decide whether these are within tolerable and reasonable limits. A checklist of items to consider is given at the end of the chapter.

NEDs should also remain aware of the need to retain their non-executive role. There may be pressure on a NED to get more involved in the affairs of the company, to the point where they take on executive duties without necessarily realising that this is what has happened.

- If a NED takes on executive functions, they may become exposed to greater personal liability, in the event that something goes wrong and there are accusations of negligence, breach of duty or breach of regulations.
- When a NED takes on executive functions, they are no longer 'non-executive'. More significantly perhaps, they can no longer (under any circumstances) be considered 'independent'.

## 6   REDUCING POTENTIAL LIABILITY

In cases where individual directors disagree with a board decision, they may reduce their potential individual liability for negligence or breach of duty in the following ways:

- They should make sure that any concerns they have are expressed at a board meeting and are formally recorded in the minutes of the meeting.
- They should be prepared to resign if necessary. If they do not resign, they are still accountable.

- If the director resigns, possibly due to a disagreement with the rest of the board, they should provide a written statement to the chairman, for circulation to the rest of the board, setting out their concerns.

# 7 DIRECTORS' AND OFFICERS' LIABILITY INSURANCE

## Protection against personal liability

Directors may obtain some protection against personal liability from a combination of an indemnity from the company and directors' and officers' liability insurance. The law restricts the ability of companies to indemnify a director when a legal action is brought against one or more directors, and paying for their legal costs and any civil damages they have to pay.

However, companies are permitted to buy insurance for their directors and other officers (such as the company secretary), in the form of directors' and officers' (D&O) liability insurance.

## Indemnity from the company

A company is permitted to indemnify a director (under section 232 of the Companies Act) from any liability in connection with breach of duty or negligence, but with some exceptions. A company cannot indemnify a director against any liability to pay a criminal fine or regulatory penalty, in defending criminal proceedings where the director is convicted, in defending civil proceedings brought by the company (or an associate company) against him where judgment is given against him or in an unsuccessful application for relief from liability under the Companies Act.

This means that the company can indemnify its directors from liability for the cost of proceedings brought against them by a third party (including a regulator), including the cost of defending the case and even if judgment goes against them, but indemnity cannot be given for the payment of any criminal fines or regulatory penalties.

In addition, section 205 of the Companies Act allows a company that brings a claim against one of its directors to pay their costs of defending the case (on an 'as incurred' basis), provided that the director will be liable to repay this money if judgment in the case goes against them.

## D&O liability insurance

Since the ability of the company to indemnify its directors is restricted, a company will normally also obtain directors' and officers' liability insurance as further protection for its directors. However, the terms and conditions of these insurance policies can vary and it is important for a director to understand how much protection is provided (in terms of what is covered by the policy and what is the maximum amount of liability covered).

In general terms, the risks covered are personal losses or costs incurred by the insured individuals, as a consequence of their 'wrongful acts'. Wrongful acts include matters relating to breach of duty, breach of trust and negligence, and misstatements and misrepresentations – including statements made in the company's published financial documents about the company's financial affairs. Insured individuals are covered in the event of legal actions against them individually or actions against several directors (or the entire board) jointly.

The losses covered will normally include:

- civil damages awarded against the directors;
- the cost of out-of-court settlements; and
- costs incurred, such as legal fees.

D&O policies will have several exclusions, and it is important to check these carefully before accepting the position of director in a company. The exclusions will include:

- criminal fines or penalties imposed by a regulator or a criminal court;
- loss of earnings;
- liability for fraudulent acts; and
- liabilities incurred in certain jurisdictions.

For example, if the company has dealings in the USA, it is important to check whether D&O liability insurance provides cover for costs incurred in relation to US legal actions. For example, some D&O liability insurance policies cover the cost of a bail bond payable in the USA in relation to a legal action.

Examples of claims that are usually covered by D&O liability insurance include:

- following an acquisition of a company, a legal action brought by the shareholders of the acquired company against the former directors, alleging that they were misled about the terms of the acquisition;
- following the sale of a division of a company, a legal action brought by the purchaser against the company's directors, alleging that some aspect of the division's activities or performance was misrepresented to them; and
- action against the directors under health and safety legislation, or environmental legislation.

### Types of D&O liability insurance policy: limits to cover

There are several types of D&O liability insurance policy:

- Some provide cover up to a specified limit for all the named directors and officers, both for risks that the company is allowed to indemnify as well as for non-indemnifiable risks.
- Some provide cover up to a specified limit for all the named directors and officers, for non-indemnifiable risks.
- Some provide cover up to a specified limit for an individual director, for several different company directorships.

In addition, a policy may provide 'run-off cover' for liabilities arising after a director has retired, relating to any 'wrongful act' committed before retirement.

Policies normally provide a stated maximum amount of cover per claim, and/ or per year.

Each individual director should make sure that they have sufficient insurance cover for the entire period that they are a director.

Clearly, it is extremely important that directors are satisfied that the amount of cover is sufficient as any liabilities incurred in excess of the policy limits must be met by the director(s) personally.

### Corporate governance and D&O liability insurance

The UK Corporate Governance Code (provision A.1.3) states that the company should arrange 'appropriate' insurance cover in respect of legal action against its directors, but does not go into further detail. Providing D&O liability insurance is not, however, a legal requirement.

The Higgs Report (*Review of the Role and Effectiveness of Non-Executive Directors*, 2003) made the following comments:

- Although increasing the cover for D&O liability might reduce the personal exposure of individual directors, it does not remove reputational risk for the company. In addition, higher cover may paradoxically encourage more claims against directors, because there is more to gain financially when directors are covered by an insurance policy.
- There was no evidence that the risk of personal liability was deterring individuals from becoming company directors, at least in large companies. However, this situation might change in the future, and in particular deter individuals from accepting NED roles.

## ICSA Guidance Note: Directors' and Officers' Insurance

The Institute of Chartered Secretaries and Administrators has issued some guidance on directors' and officers' liability insurance (see Directory). This provides a fairly detailed summary of the issues that directors should consider, but stresses that directors should seek specific advice from a good broker or legal adviser.

The guidance note recommends that before their appointment as a director, an individual should:

- make sure that they will be covered by a D&O liability insurance policy;
- ask the company to confirm that it will notify the insurance company of the individual's appointment as director, so that the individual's name will be added to the list of individuals covered by the policy;
- check the liabilities that are covered by the policy (and what the exclusions are);
- check that the amount of cover provided appears to be sufficient; and
- check that the insurance cover will remain in place as long as needed, and that 'run-off cover' will be provided after the director has retired.

## 8  DEALING IN SHARES OF THE COMPANY

## Market abuse and insider dealing

In UK law, it is an offence to trade in the shares of a company while in possession of 'inside information'. In broad terms, inside information is information that:

- is not generally available;
- relates to the company or its shares; and
- if generally available, would be likely to have a significant effect on the share price (i.e. the information is 'price-sensitive').

Using inside information to benefit by dealing in the company's shares is, at the least, market abuse. It may also be insider dealing.

- Under section 118 of the Financial Services and Markets Act 2000, market abuse is a civil offence.
- Under Part V of the Criminal Justice Act 1993, insider dealing is a criminal offence.

The burden of proof is less for a civil offence than for a criminal offence.

Directors of quoted companies are 'insiders' and must be included in the 'insider list' that the company maintains. They must not deal in shares of the company when they have inside information, and they must not pass on inside information to anyone else.

In discussions with shareholders of the company, directors should be aware of the possibility that they may inadvertently say something that makes those shareholders 'insiders' themselves. Institutional investors will generally want to avoid becoming insiders, because it will block their right to buy or sell shares in the company without breaking the law, until the confidential information eventually becomes public or ceases to be relevant.

### The Model Code

The Model Code is a code of behaviour for the directors of listed companies and individuals with managerial responsibilities. The requirements of the Model Code are additional to the insider dealing and market abuse rules, and should not be confused with them.

UK listed companies – and their directors and senior officers – are required to comply with a Model Code, which is an annex to section 9 of the Listing Rules. The purpose of the Model Code is to ensure that directors (and other individuals discharging managerial responsibilities in listed companies) do not place themselves under suspicion of abusing inside information, especially during periods leading up to announcements of the company's results.

The Model Code does not affect the legislation on insider dealing or market abuse, but imposes procedural rules on listed companies. The Model Code includes the following requirements.

- A restricted person may not deal in the shares of a company during a restricted period. Restricted persons include directors of the company and connected persons.
- A restricted period is a 'close period' and any period when there is information in existence that may be considered as inside information. For example, when a company may be about to receive a takeover bid, inside information about the bid would exist during the period before any public announcement of the bid is made.
- A close period is a 60-day period before the announcement of a company's annual results and (for companies that publish interim results every six months) a 60-day period before the publication of the interim results.

In addition, the Model Code requires directors to obtain the permission of the chairman before dealing in any securities of the company at any time. Alternatively a shares and dealings committee of the board may deal with these matters. Having been given clearance to deal, individuals must then deal in the shares as soon as possible, and not later than two business days after receiving clearance.

Clearance to deal cannot be given during a prohibited period, except in very exceptional circumstances (such as when the prohibited person is not in possession of any insider information and is in extreme financial difficulties, in which case clearance may be given to sell shares.)

### Reporting dealings in shares of the company

Directors of quoted companies are included in the definition of 'persons discharging managerial responsibilities', for the purpose of the Disclosure and Transparency Rules and Listing Rules. A requirement of the DTR is that persons discharging managerial responsibilities in a quoted company must notify the company of any dealings they have in the shares of the company. The notification must be made within four business days of the transaction. The company must then notify the stock market.

## 9  CHECKLIST: REDUCING THE RISK OF PERSONAL LIABILITY

The following checklist is not exhaustive, but indicates what a NED should be aware of.

| REDUCING THE RISK OF PERSONAL LIABILITY | YES | NO |
| --- | --- | --- |
| **Time spent on duties** | | |
| Have you allocated the agreed amount of time to the company's business: | | |
| Over the past 3–6 months? | ☐ | ☐ |
| Over the past year? | ☐ | ☐ |
| **Financial reporting** | | |
| Does the company's financial reporting appear to be 'honest'? | ☐ | ☐ |
| Is there any possibility that financial information (and other information) issued by the company could be wrong or misleading? | ☐ | ☐ |
| If 'Yes', have you done anything about the matter? | ☐ | ☐ |
| Have the auditors voiced any concerns about any of the accounting policies used by the company to prepare its financial statements, or about any of the estimates in the financial statements? | ☐ | ☐ |

| REDUCING THE RISK OF PERSONAL LIABILITY | YES | NO |
|---|---|---|
| If 'Yes', have you done anything about the matter? | ☐ | ☐ |
| **Going concern status** | | |
| Is there any possibility that the company might not be a going concern and might be trading while insolvent? | ☐ | ☐ |
| If 'Yes', have you done anything about the matter? | ☐ | ☐ |
| **The company's risk exposures** | | |
| Does the company appear to have robust systems for monitoring and controlling risks? | ☐ | ☐ |
| Are its exposures to business risks and other risks within acceptable limits? | ☐ | ☐ |
| In your opinion, is the board reckless in allowing the company to operate with excessive risk exposures? | ☐ | ☐ |
| **Taxation** | | |
| Are you satisfied that the company is reporting its tax affairs correctly to the tax authorities? | ☐ | ☐ |
| Is there any risk of a dispute with the tax authorities about any aspect the company's tax liabilities? | ☐ | ☐ |
| **Regulatory and statutory issues** | | |
| Are there any regulatory issues that might expose the NED to personal risk? | ☐ | ☐ |
| If 'Yes', are you satisfied with the company's compliance with the regulations? | ☐ | ☐ |
| Have you declared all conflicts of interests or potential conflicts of interests to the company, and have these been authorised? | ☐ | ☐ |
| Have you declared your interests in any transaction with the company? | ☐ | ☐ |
| **Compliance with the UK Corporate Governance Code** | | |
| Are you aware of any non-compliance by the company with the requirements of the Code? | ☐ | ☐ |
| If 'Yes', has the company explained its non-compliance in the annual report and to your personal satisfaction? | ☐ | ☐ |
| **Directors' and officers' liability insurance** | | |
| Have you checked the terms of this insurance and the amount of cover provided? | ☐ | ☐ |
| Are you satisfied with the cover provided? | ☐ | ☐ |

| REDUCING THE RISK OF PERSONAL LIABILITY | YES | NO |
|---|---|---|
| **Dealing in shares of the company (quoted companies)** | | |
| Do you intend to buy or sell shares in the company? | ☐ | ☐ |
| If 'Yes', might you be at risk of insider dealing? | ☐ | ☐ |
| If 'Yes' are you aware of the times when you may not deal to avoid breaching the Model Code? | ☐ | ☐ |
| Notify the company of any dealings in its shares within four business days. | ☐ | ☐ |

# Becoming a NED

....................

## OVERVIEW

Individuals should not accept an appointment as a non-executive director without first doing their own due diligence review.

Key issues are finding out about the company, and whether the individual thinks that they can make a valuable contribution as a NED to this type of company. The individual should also establish what the responsibilities of the NED will be, whether they will have the time to do the work and what they will be paid. The remuneration of NEDs has risen as the demands of the job have increased, but the demands on NEDs' time have also increased.

The terms of the appointment should be set out in a formal letter from the company.

The UK Corporate Governance Code favours diversity of board members, and regular changing of the membership/composition of boards.

Having become a NED, the individual has to make sure of receiving formal and suitable induction, to become as effective as possible as soon as possible.

The term of a NED in office comes to an end sooner or later. It is important to be ready for leaving the company when the time comes.

## 1 APPOINTMENT AS A NEW NED

The formal procedures for appointing a new NED are the same as for any director. The procedures are set out in the company's constitution (articles of association).

The articles of association normally include the following provisions.

- The directors may appoint as a director anyone who is willing to act.
- The appointed person then holds office until the next annual general meeting (AGM).
- They then stand for election as a director at the AGM, and the shareholders vote on a resolution proposing the appointment.

The UK Listing Rules require listed companies to announce any new appointment of a director to the stock market, stating whether it is an appointment of an executive director, NED or chairman.

## 2 WILLINGNESS TO ACT: DUE DILIGENCE

Individuals must be willing to accept their appointment as NED. An appointment should not be accepted unless the individual is comfortable with the idea of acting as NED for that particular company.

The original Higgs Guidance (see Chapter 1) argued that prospective directors should carry out a thorough examination of the company before accepting their appointment, to satisfy themselves that it is a company in which they can have faith and in which they will be well-suited to working.

In its guidance note on due diligence, the Institute of Chartered Secretaries and Administrators made a similar point: 'By making the right enquiries, asking the right questions and taking care to understand the replies, a prospective director can reduce the risk of nasty surprises and dramatically increase the likelihood of success.'

Before accepting an appointment, it is therefore strongly recommended that an individual should do some 'due diligence' and find out what they can about the company.

### Pre-appointment due diligence checklist for new board members

The ICSA guidance note provides a non-exhaustive list of questions that the prospective director should ask. The questions are especially relevant for a non-executive director joining the company from 'outside', rather than for an executive director who is appointed from within the company.

## Questions to ask

The suggested questions in the pre-appointment due diligence checklist cover five broad areas:

(1)  Questions about the business

(2)  Governance and investor relations

(3)  The role of the non-executive director

(4)  Risk management

(5)  Ethical issues.

## What the prospective director needs to know

| | |
|---|---|
| **Questions about the business** | What is the nature and size of the business? What is the company's financial position and financial track record (for example, its track record of sales, profits and dividends)? What is its market share? Who is the competition? In some cases, the business may depend on a key licence or on regulatory approval or legislative approval. |
| **Governance and investor relations** | Who owns the company? Who are its shareholders? What is the relationship between the board and the shareholders? How does the board communicate with them? What is the structure of the board of directors? With some companies it may be important to identify the ultimate owners, to obtain assurance about the legitimate nature of the company's operations. It is also important to understand the company's record on corporate governance, and the extent to which it complies with the provisions of the UK Corporate Governance Code. Check whether there have been any reviews of the company's annual report and accounts by the Financial Reporting Review Panel (FRRP). |
| **Role of the individual as NED** An individual should not accept an appointment as NED unless they are satisfied that they can make a valuable contribution to the activities of the board. | Do I have the required knowledge, skills, experience and time to make a positive contribution? • Do I have knowledge of the industry? • Or do I have specialist skills or knowledge? • Or do I have relevant experience to make a positive contribution? Do the size, structure and composition of the board allow me to make a useful contribution? Why has the company offered the directorship to me? What particular skills or experience are they looking for? Can I meet the company's expectations? Are there any potential conflicts of interest? If I accept the appointment, will I be independent? |

| Risk management | A prospective director should:<br>• find out as much as they can about potential risks, both risks facing the company and potential liabilities that they might face personally<br>• obtain details and gain an understanding of the company's risk management systems. |
|---|---|
| Ethical issues | Is there anything about the nature and extent of the company's business activities that would cause concern both in terms of risk and any personal ethical considerations? |

## Sources of information

There are various sources of information from which answers to questions might be found. These include:

- the company's report and accounts;
- the company's articles of association;
- its latest annual returns;
- any social and environmental report that the company publishes;
- press reports;
- rating agency reports; and
- analysts' reports.

---

CASE EXAMPLE
................

# DUE DILIGENCE

An interesting example of willingness to act and due diligence would have been the decision of the NEDs joining PartyGaming, the online poker site, at about the time of its flotation in July 2006. In the prospectus for the flotation, the section on risk factors covered 27 pages. These included the comment that in the US, where the company had about 90% of its customers, its activities were 'considered to be illegal' and that the imprisonment of some key individuals such as directors could not be ruled out. In 2006, the US Congress passed the Unlawful Internet Gambling Enforcement Act, which made it illegal to provide internet gambling services to US citizens. The company's share price fell by over 50% in one day following the introduction of the new law. It was not until 2009 that the company was able to reach a settlement with the US government, removing the threat of prosecution against company directors and employees.

---

Many of these should be easily found on the internet, although a prospective NED should expect the company to provide them. The internet might also be a good source of published information that the company does not provide.

The original Higgs Guidance commented that published information about a company is unlikely to reveal any wrongdoing; however 'a lack of transparency' may be a warning to a prospective director to 'proceed with caution'.

### Induction

After their appointment, a NED should receive a programme of induction with the objective of learning more about the company and its affairs. Induction is considered in Chapter 10.

## 3  DIVERSITY

In 2003, the Higgs Report commented on the limited pool of non-executive directors, and suggested that this pool should be made much larger. The Report made the following suggestions.

- It is generally assumed that NEDs should be individuals with a business background. However, individuals from other backgrounds may have the qualities necessary for an effective NED.
- The potential supply of talent was therefore not being drawn on as much as it could be.
- There is a 'self-perpetuating tendency' for listed companies to assume that experience on the boards of other plcs was a necessary requirement for NEDs in their own company.
- Recruitment consultants have a tendency to identify potential candidates for NED positions from a small pool.
- Most NED appointments were therefore appointments of white males nearing retirement age with previous plc director experience. The small number of appointments of females was 'striking'.

A perceived lack of diversity has remained an issue since then, but has received significantly more attention in recent years as the composition and behaviour of boards has come under closer scrutiny.

### Diversity and the UK Corporate Governance Code

The UK Corporate Governance Code states that appointments to the board should be made on merit:

- against objective criteria, and
- with due regard to the benefits of diversity on the board, including gender.

The purpose of this requirement is to improve the diversity of talent that is available to the boards of listed companies, including the appointment of more women. Combined with the normal expected limit of six years to NED appointments, compliance with the UK Code may require listed companies to draw on different types of individual, with more varied backgrounds, for appointment as NEDs.

Using selected criteria, the nomination committee:

- should evaluate the skills, experience, independence and knowledge on the board, and
- in the light of this evaluation, prepare a description of the required role and capabilities for the new appointment.

The individual appointed should meet the requirements set out in this 'job description'.

The responsibilities of the nomination committee are described in Chapter 6.

## Women on Boards

Lord Davies of Abersoch's review into Women on Boards was published in 2011. It stated that 'boards make better decisions where a range of voices, drawing on different life experiences, can be heard. That mix of voices must include women.'

The Report fell short of proposing quotas, but it made a number of recommendations aimed at improving female representation on boards, including the following.

- All chairmen of FTSE 350 companies should set a target for the percentage of women they aim to have on their boards in 2013 and 2015.
- FTSE 100 boards should aim for a minimum of 25% female representation by 2015.
- Quoted companies should be required to disclose each year the proportion of women on the board.
- The UK Corporate Governance Code should require listed companies to establish a policy concerning boardroom diversity.
- Investors should be encouraged to pay close attention to diversity when considering company reporting and appointments to the board.
- Companies should periodically advertise non-executive board positions, to encourage greater diversity in applications.

In its annual Female FTSE Index and Report, the International Centre for Women Leaders at Cranfield University has consistently reported that women are under-represented on UK boards, although its 2012 report indicated some increase in women representation on the boards of FTSE 350 companies. As of 1 January 2012, 15% of directors on the boards of the FTSE 100 companies were women, 6.6% of executive directors were women and 22.4% of non-executive directors were women. The figures for the FTSE 250 companies were lower, with women making up 9.4% of all directors.

The same report found that 89% of FTSE 100 companies (and 54% of FTSE 250 companies) had at least one female director; and 50% of FTSE 100 companies (18.8% of FTSE 250 companies) had more than one female director.

The report argues that companies need to invest more in female talent at junior, middle and senior management levels in order to create a pipeline of women suitable to appointment to boards as executive directors.

In November 2012, the European Commission proposed EU legislation requiring all large listed companies in the EU to have boards consisting of at least 40% women by 2020. The initiative was associated most closely with Vice-President Reding, the EU Justice Commissioner. It is not yet clear whether the Commission's initiative will lead to legislation.

From October 2014, UK companies will be required to publish a strategic report, instead of a business review in their annual report. This report must disclose information about the numbers of men and women who were directors, senior managers and employees of the company. Mandatory disclosures may well speed up the pace of change.

## Board Effectiveness and Diversity

The FRC's *Guidance on Board Effectiveness* also looks explicitly at diversity, focusing not only on gender, but also on diversity of personal attributes, psychological type and background, to ensure that boards are not 'composed solely of like-minded individuals' and strike the right balance between challenge and teamwork.

The *Guidance* also highlights the role of the nominations committee in creating a balanced boardroom featuring a range of 'skills, experience, knowledge and independence'. In particular, NEDs should possess critical skills of value to the board and relevant to the challenges the company faces.

## 4  LETTER OF APPOINTMENT

A company should provide each new NED with a letter of appointment, setting out the terms of the appointment, including the expected time commitment.

This is sent to the individual after the board of directors has formally made the appointment. The individual is asked in the letter to confirm their acceptance of the appointment.

ICSA has developed a guidance note (see Directory) which provides a sample letter of appointment for new non-executive directors. This includes the following:

- **Contract status**. The letter should state that the arrangement is a **contract for services** and not a contract of employment.
- **Tenure**. The letter will state the initial period of the appointment (typically three years), subject to election or re-election by the shareholders. It may add that continuation of the appointment beyond three years will be contingent on satisfactory performance reviews. The appointment may be terminated earlier by either party giving written notice (with a minimum period of notice).
- **Time commitment**. The anticipated time commitment should be set out.
- **Role**. The letter should set out the role of NEDs in the company in general terms.
- **Fees**. The remuneration should be specified, together with a statement that the company will reimburse the NED's reasonable and properly documented expenses.
- **Outside interests/other commitments**. If the individual has any other business interests and has declared these to the company, these should be noted in the letter. The individual should also be asked to notify to the company any potential conflicts of interest, if these arise. The letter will also indicate whether the board will regard the individual as an independent NED in accordance with the provisions of the UK Code.
- **Confidentiality**. All the information received as a NED should be treated as confidential to the company.

The letter of appointment should also make reference to:

- arrangements for formal induction;
- the performance review process;
- directors' and officers' liability insurance;
- obtaining independent professional advice; and
- membership of board committees.

All newly appointed directors should receive a formal programme of induction, which may also be referred to in the letter of appointment. Induction is discussed in Chapter 10.

## 5 TERMS OF ENGAGEMENT

A prospective director must agree the terms of their appointment with the company, including matters relating to:

- tenure;
- time commitment;
- remuneration;
- resignation.

### Tenure

When an individual is first appointed as a NED, they are likely to be offered a three-year term of appointment, subject to re-election. There may be an indication in the letter of appointment that the term of office could then be extended for a further period at the end of the three years, subject to both satisfactory performance and re-election by the shareholders.

In deciding the most suitable length of period in office for a non-executive director, a balance has to be struck between:

- keeping the board refreshed with new members, and the need for an orderly change in membership over time, so that the board has the mix of skills and experience that it needs; and
- giving new directors time to learn about the company and grow into their role: the learning curve may be fairly long.

In addition, NEDs who are not performing to the standards expected of them should be asked to leave the company before the end of their term of appointment.

The UK Corporate Governance Code indirectly suggests that NEDs should not normally expect to serve more than six years with the company.

- There should be progressive refreshing of the board.
- Non-executive directors should be appointed for a fixed term, subject to re-election and to Companies Act provisions relating to the removal of directors.
- Any term beyond six years for a NED should be subject to particularly rigorous scrutiny, and should take into account the need for progressive refreshing of the board.
- All directors should be subject to election by the shareholders at the first AGM following their appointment.
- All directors of FTSE 350 companies should be subject to annual re-election by the shareholders.

- All directors of non-FTSE 350 companies should be subject to re-election at intervals of no more than three years. (Standard articles of association provides for one-third of directors to retire by rotation each year and stand for re-election. The directors who should retire and stand for re-election are those who have been in office longest since their previous election or re-election.)
- Non-executive directors may serve for terms in excess of nine years, subject to annual re-election. (However, when a NED has served for more than nine years, their continuing independence will be called into question.)
- When the board recommends to shareholders that a NED should be re-elected, the chairman should confirm that following a formal performance evaluation, the individual continues to be effective and to demonstrate commitment to their role.

## Time commitment

A NED must be able to commit the time that will be needed to perform their role to a high standard. This requirement is included in a main principle of the UK Corporate Governance Code: 'All directors should be able to allocate sufficient time to the company to discharge their responsibilities effectively' (Principle B.3).

In recent years the time commitment that companies require from their NEDs has increased. The time that a NED is expected to give to the company should be made clear before any appointment is made. The UK Code (Provision B.3.2) states that the letter of appointment should explain the expected time commitment, and that NEDs should give an undertaking that they will have sufficient time to carry out what is expected of them. This is reiterated in the *Guidance on Board Effectiveness*. The *Guidance* adds that the letter of appointment should also indicate the possibility that additional time commitment might be necessary when a company is undergoing a period of increased activity, such as an acquisition or takeover, or as a result of operational difficulties.

The Higgs Report, published in 2003, referred to a research finding that non-executive directors typically gave between 15 and 30 days to the company each year. However, many felt this was not enough for them to do their job effectively, particularly in view of the increasing demands of their role.

Since 2003, the required time commitment has probably increased.

The UK Code of Corporate Governance includes the following provisions:

- The letter of appointment of a new non-executive director should set out the expected time commitment.

- Non-executive directors should undertake formally that they could have sufficient time to carry out the role expected of them, taking into account their other commitments.
- If the NED has significant commitments to other roles, these should be disclosed to the board before the individual is formally appointed, with a broad indication of the time involved.
- If a NED takes on other commitments during their term of appointment, these should be notified to the board.
- The board should not allow any of its executive directors to accept more than one position as NED of a FTSE 100 company, and should not allow any executive director to be the chairman of a FTSE 100 company.

The 2006 UK Combined Code also recommended that no individual should be appointed to the chairmanship of a second FTSE company. However in 2007, following a review of the Code, the provision against any person being chairman of two FTSE 100 companies was scrapped. The arguments in favour of this view were that in some cases it should be possible for the same individual to have enough time to act as chairman of two FTSE 100 companies, and there was a scarcity of talented individuals capable of acting as chairman of a large public company.

The current UK Corporate Governance Code states that for the appointment of a chairman the nomination committee should make an assessment of the time commitment that will be required for the role, 'recognising the need for availability in the event of crises'. The chairman's other commitments should be disclosed to the board before appointment, and included in the annual report.

### Remuneration of NEDs

The provisions of the UK Corporate Governance Code on the remuneration of non-executive directors are fairly brief.

- The board of directors (or the shareholders, if required by the company's articles of association) should decide the remuneration of non-executive directors, within the limits set by the articles of association. Alternatively, if permitted by the articles of association, the responsibility for deciding the remuneration of NEDs may be delegated to a committee of the board, which may include the CEO. (In practice, this means that NED remuneration may be decided by the chairman and executive directors.)
- Remuneration for NEDs should reflect the time commitment and the responsibilities of the role.
- Remuneration for NEDs should not include share options or other performance-related elements. (But see the next point in this list.)

- If, exceptionally, share options are granted to NEDs, shareholder approval must be obtained in advance, and any shares acquired by exercising share options should be held by the individual for at least one year after ceasing to be a NED of the company.
- Holding share options in the company could affect the status of a NED as 'independent'.

In practice, the remuneration of NEDs depends on the size of the company and the industry in which it operates. Companies will often decide NED fees by making comparisons with other companies in their peer group.

Although NEDs should not normally be given share options, there is no reason why they should not receive their fee, or part of their fee, in fully-paid shares of the company.

When a company allows one of its executive directors to accept an appointment as NED of another company, it should be a matter of remuneration policy whether or not the individual should be permitted to retain any earnings from the appointment, or whether the earnings should be paid over to the company. If the individual is allowed to retain the earnings personally, the amount of the remuneration must be disclosed in the company's remuneration report.

### Higgs Report suggestions on the remuneration of NEDs

The 2003 Combined Code provisions on the remuneration of NEDs were based on recommendations in the Higgs Report, which went into more detail and made the following points.

- The appropriate level of remuneration for any NED should depend on the likely workload, the scale and complexity of the business, and the responsibilities involved in the role.
- It may be helpful, when setting remuneration for a NED, to use as a benchmark the daily remuneration of a senior representative of the company's professional advisers.
- However, there is a real risk that high levels of remuneration will affect the independence of thought of a NED, and this should be avoided.
- The annual fee for NEDs may be built up clearly from an annual fee, plus meeting attendance fees, plus an additional fee for the chairmanship of a board committee or for holding the position of senior independent director.
- The company should also pay reasonable expenses incurred by NEDs.
- There may be merit in paying NEDs wholly or partly in shares of the company instead of cash (but not share options).

In practice, variable fees for attendance at meetings are not a common feature of NED remuneration. The following examples are fairly typical, extracted from 2011 and 2012 remuneration reports of the companies concerned.

---

CASE EXAMPLE

## TESCO PLC

Here, the NEDs receive a basic fixed fee plus an additional fee for membership or chairmanship of board committees. 'The remuneration of the Non-Executive Directors is determined by the Chairman and the Executive Committee after considering external market research and individual roles and responsibilities.' Non-Executive Directors received a basic fee of £70,000 per annum. The Chairs of the Audit and Remuneration Committees received £30,000 (in addition to their basic non-executive fee) and Non-Executive Directors who were members of these Committees received an additional £12,000 for each Committee. The Senior Independent Director received an additional fee of £26,000. Excluding the chairman, there were eight Non-Executive Directors, all of whom were members of at least one committee.

'The Remuneration Committee determines the Chairman's remuneration, having regard to time commitment and packages awarded to Chairmen of other companies of a similar size and complexity.'

---

CASE EXAMPLE

## TAYLOR WIMPEY PLC

'The fees of Non-Executive Directors were determined by the Board in their absence taking into account the research carried out by independent remuneration consultants of fees paid to Non-Executive directors of similar sized companies and the sector-based peer group. Non-Executive Director fees are subject to the aggregate annual limit of £1,000,000 imposed by the Articles of Association and will be reviewed annually.

The basic fees of each Non-Executive Director were standardised at £50,000 per annum following the merger between Taylor Woodrow plc and George Wimpey Plc in 2007. The Senior Independent Director receives an additional payment of £10,000 in respect of the performance of this role. The standard fee for chairing a Board Committee (Audit, Remuneration and Corporate Responsibility) is £10,000. The Chairman does not receive any additional fee for chairing the Nomination Committee. The fees of the Non-Executive Directors have not been increased since the merger ....

Neither the Chairman nor the Non-Executive Directors participate in any of the Company's share plans or bonus plans and are not eligible to join the Company's pension scheme.'

CASE EXAMPLE
.................

## PUNCH TAVERNS PLC

'All Non-executive Directors have specific terms of engagement and their remuneration is determined by the Board based upon recommendations from the Chairman and Chief Executive (or, in the case of the Chairman, is determined by the Remuneration Committee based on recommendations from the Senior Independent Director and the Chief Executive) within the limits set by the Articles of Association and based on the median level of fees payable to peers in the same comparator group as that used for Executive Directors' remuneration. Non-executive Directors cannot participate in any of the Group's share incentive schemes or performance based plans and are not eligible to join any of the Group's pension schemes.

It is the Board's policy to take into account the following factors in determining the fees of the Non-executive Directors:

- the median level of fees for similar positions in the comparator group; and
- the time commitment each Non-executive Director makes to the Group (through membership of the Audit, Remuneration and Nominations Committees).

The following table sets out the Non-executive fees for 2011/2012 and the fees for 2012/2013:

|  | 2012/2013 | 2011/2012 |
|---|---|---|
| Basic fee | £42,000 | £42,000 |
| Senior Independent Director | £45,000 | £45,000 |
| Additional fees for chairing the Audit and Risk or Remuneration Committee | £10,000 | £10,000 |
| Additional fees for chairing the Nominations Committee or Governance Committee | £5,000 | £5,000.' |

## 6 LEAVING THE COMPANY

NEDs are not appointed on a permanent basis, and NEDs must accept that at some time the company will no longer require their continued services.

- A company may be reluctant to lose a NED who has contributed effectively to the work of the board. However, independence erodes over time, and when an NED is no longer considered 'independent', this may be a suitable time for the director to leave the company.

- Even sooner, a decision may be taken to replace a NED in order to renew and refresh the board membership, as expected by the UK Corporate Governance Code.

As a general rule, NEDs of listed companies should not expect their appointment to last for more than six years.

When a NED leaves the company, the parting should normally be amicable. The departure should be flagged in advance, and the chairman (taking advice from the nomination committee) will probably speak to the NED privately well in advance of the end of the NED's current term of appointment.

Occasionally, a departure may be the result of a disagreement with the company. The UK Corporate Governance Code (Provision A.4.3) states that on resignation, if the NED believes there is an unresolved matter about the running of the company or a proposed action, they should provide a written statement to the chairman, for circulation to the rest of the board. This should state their concern in writing, which will help to protect the NED against any possible future personal liability.

It is probably good practice for a NED, on leaving a company, to review what they have achieved during their term of office:

- What has been achieved by the company during the NED's term of office?
- What has the NED personally contributed to those achievements?
- Is there anything that should have been done better?

Answers to these questions may help the individual to be more effective as a NED with other companies in the future.

# CHAPTER FOUR

# NEDs and the board of directors

.....................

## OVERVIEW

Chapter 1 discussed the varied roles of NEDs, which make NEDs partly a colleague of executives on the board, and partly a policeman with responsibilities for monitoring what their executive colleagues are doing.

To comply with the UK Code, the majority of directors (excluding the chairman) should be independent NEDs and some of the board committees should consist either entirely of independent NEDs or a majority of independent NEDs. The independent or non-independent status of NEDs therefore has direct relevance to the composition of the board and its committees.

There are guidelines for assessing independence, one of which is the 'nine-year rule' that a NED who has served for nine years or more should not normally be considered independent. One of the aims of appointing independent NEDs is to achieve a balance of power on the board, reducing the risk that the board will be dominated by a powerful CEO or chairman.

NEDs should have the personal qualities and experience to carry out their responsibilities. They also need to be well-informed and well-advised. Once appointed, NEDs should make sure that they receive the information they need and that they maintain and develop their skills – through induction, development and timely access to relevant and reliable information. To act independently, it may be necessary at times to obtain independent professional advice, and not rely on the assurances of executives or even on the assurances of the company's own professional advisers.

There are still frequent criticisms that NEDs fail to carry out their responsibilities effectively.

## 1   WHAT IS EXPECTED OF NEDS?

NEDs have a role in strategic decision-making, monitoring the performance of management and the financial reporting process, the review of risk and controls, and (through committee work) the remuneration of top executives and the appointment of new directors.

It was explained in Chapter 1 that under UK law, executive and non-executive directors have the same duties and responsibilities, and may be equally liable for a failure to carry out their duties properly. In order to carry out their duties, NEDs should contribute actively to the work and decision-making processes of the board.

---

### CASE EXAMPLE

### EQUITABLE LIFE

The *Equitable Life* legal case has some relevance to the responsibilities (and liabilities) of NEDs. In 1999, Equitable Life initiated a court action for the right to force its policy holders to accept cuts in the bonus entitlements on their life policies. After winning its case in a lower court, it then lost on appeal in the Court of Appeal and then the House of Lords. It was unable to pay the huge cost of its wasted legal expenses, and having failed to find a buyer for its business, Equitable Life closed to new business in 2000. The legal proceedings continued, however. In one legal action in 2003, the new board of Equitable sued nine former NEDs for the recovery of millions of pounds of its losses. Although the action was dropped in 2005, the case brought attention to bear on the responsibilities and potential liabilities of NEDs.

In a judgment in 2003, Mr Justice Langley made the following findings.

- Directors cannot place reliance without question on their boardroom colleagues to do their work. NEDs cannot rely on their executive director colleagues to make decisions for them, and delegating a task to

---

the executive directors does not necessarily free them from potential liability for the consequences of what the executive directors do.

- The extent to which NEDs can rely on the executive directors and other professionals (such as the company's auditors) to do their work will depend to a large extent on the facts of the case.

The judge added that it was 'plainly arguable … that a company may reasonably at least look to non-executive directors for independence of judgement and supervision of the executive management'.

To fulfil their duties adequately, it may be argued that NEDs should:

- make sure that they receive a suitable formal induction on joining the board;
- keep themselves fully up to date with the company's business, and keep their skills 'refreshed';
- attend board meetings (and committee meetings) and demand sufficient information to prepare for the meetings, with sufficient time to study it beforehand;
- seek clarification of information that is not clear or complete;
- raise points of concern with management, either during board meetings or outside meetings;
- check the minutes of the previous board meeting to make sure that they are an accurate record of what was discussed and agreed, and include a record of any concerns that were expressed by the NED during the meeting;
- ask for independent professional advice on matters where a 'technical' judgement is required;
- ensure that problems that have been identified have been successfully or satisfactorily dealt with;
- as far as possible, monitor that the company has complied with legal and regulatory requirements, such as the requirements of the Companies Act, and in the case of listed companies, the Listing Rules and Disclosure and Transparency Rules, as well as the UK Corporate Governance Code;
- be satisfied that there is appropriate justification for any public disclosures by the company, including the annual report and accounts; and
- be satisfied that any issues raised by the annual performance review of the board, and communicated to the board by the chairman, are acted on.

## 2 INDEPENDENCE AND NEDS

Non-executive directors have been put forward as the 'custodians of the governance process', and all NEDs are expected to have a strong, independent-minded character. The Higgs Report (2003) made the following comment:

'Although they need to establish close relationships with executives and be well-informed, all non-executive directors need to be independent of mind and willing and able to challenge, question and speak up. All non-executive directors, and indeed executive directors, need to be independent in this sense.'

The Higgs Report identified other personal characteristics of non-executive directors, which are arguably linked to an independence of mind:

- Integrity and high ethical standards. (These characteristics are expected of all directors.)
- Sound judgement.
- An ability and willingness to challenge and probe. Within the 'collegiate' environment of a unitary board, non-executives must have the strength of character to obtain full and satisfactory answers to their questions.
- Strong interpersonal skills. The effectiveness of a non-executive director depends on exercising influence, not giving orders. To exercise influence, a NED must have the trust of their colleagues.

However, although independence of character is a desirable characteristic for NEDs, it is not sufficient on its own to make an independent NED. For the purpose of corporate governance, 'independence' of NEDs is defined much more strictly.

---

### CASE EXAMPLE

### NATIONAL ASSOCIATION OF PENSION FUNDS

Although published in 2002, the National Association of Pension Funds' guide for independent non-executive directors ('Independent directors – what investors expect') still has some useful insights into the distinction between independence and the more general role of NEDs.

The guide includes two brief lists: one about the qualities expected from independent NEDs and one about the requirements for NEDs in general.

It suggested that independent directors are expected to have the following qualities:

---

- willingness to contribute to strategy and to challenge executives on strategy and other matters;
- readiness to challenge the company's mergers and acquisitions policy;
- ability to contribute to board deliberations on financial and capitalisation issues;
- relevant experience for the needs of the company and its board;
- independence of mind;
- sufficient time to devote to the needs of the company and its affairs;
- 'integrity and a preparedness to resign over matters of principle, should that be';
- willingness to learn and continue to learn.

The more general requirements for NEDs are those relating to the roles of the NED, such as contributing to strategy, monitoring executive management and contributing to corporate governance functions, largely through membership of board committees. The NAPF guide also includes the following general requirements:

- 'To act as a sounding board – to contribute with the advantage of detachment.'
- 'To safeguard shareholders' funds by using the ability to challenge executive management and initiate change when necessary.'
- 'To be an effective part of the board team, but to "blow the whistle" if necessary.'

## Definition of independence for governance purposes

Independent NEDs must be independent in the sense that there is no possibility of a conflict of interest between:

- the best interests of the company; and
- either the personal interests of the director or other interests that the director might also represent.

Independent NEDs must therefore have no other significant connection with the company, other than their directorship.

This point can be illustrated by making a comparison with executive directors. Executive directors cannot be independent because they have potential conflicts of interest in areas such as remuneration and audit (since the remuneration of the directors may be affected by reported profits).

The independence of a non-executive director should be agreed by the rest of the board. The board is also required by the UK Corporate Governance Code to identify in each annual report the non-executives that it has identified as independent.

The board will decide that a director is independent if:

- they are independent in character and in judgement; and
- there are no relationships or circumstances that might possibly create a conflict of interest and affect the director's judgement.

Examples of relationships or circumstances that might possibly affect the director's judgement are listed in the UK Code. They include the following:

- When the director has been an employee of the company or the group within the last five years.
- When the director has a material business relationship with the company, or has had a material business relationship within the last three years. The business relationship may be direct, or the director may be a partner, shareholder, director or senior employee of another organisation that has such a business relationship with the company.
- When the director has received or receives additional remuneration from the company, in addition to their director's fee, or when the director participates in the company's share option scheme or a profit-related pay scheme, or when the director is a member of the company's pension scheme.
- When the director has close family ties with any of the company's advisers, directors or senior employees.
- When the director holds cross-directorships, or has significant links with other directors of the company through involvement in other companies or bodies. (Note: it should be unusual for NEDs of FTSE 350 companies to hold cross-directorships.)
- When the director represents the interests of a major shareholder.
- When the director has served on the board for more than nine years since the date of their first election.

The existence of any of these relationships is not 'proof positive' of a lack of independence. However, the UK Code states that the board of directors needs to explain (in the annual report and accounts) why it has decided that a non-executive director is independent despite the existence of such a relationship.

### The implications of independence

There are various implications of independence, and independent NEDs need to bear these in mind at all times.

- Independent NEDs should continue to show independence of character and judgement.
- Independent NEDs must continue to avoid all possible conflicts of interest, in order to remain independent.
- They should not (always) accept without question explanations that are given to them by colleagues and others.
- If in doubt on a matter of some importance, they should obtain independent expert advice.

The UK Corporate Governance Code states: 'The board should ensure that directors, especially non-executive directors, have access to independent professional advice at the company's expense where they judge it necessary to discharge their responsibilities as directors.'

## 3 THE NINE-YEAR 'RULE' ON INDEPENDENCE

The nine-year 'rule' comes from the general view that the independence of a director is likely to erode over time, as the director becomes more familiar with the company and less rigorous in their questioning. The Higgs Report commented that it would be reasonable to expect most non-executive directors to serve two terms of three years, and then give way to a fresh appointee:

'There will be occasions where value will be added by a non-executive director serving for longer, but I would expect this to be the exception and the reasons explained to shareholders' (Higgs Report 2003).

### Implications of the nine-year 'rule' and opposition to it

If the nine-year rule is applied, this means that:

- independent NEDs should be appointed for no more than three three-year terms; or
- NEDs who have served nine years but are contributing effectively to the board should be appointed for a further term, but may not be considered independent.

It would appear, however, that in about half of the FTSE 350 companies there is an independent non-executive director who has served for over nine years. In some companies there is more than one long-serving 'independent' NED.

In a submission to the FRC in 2005 (commenting on the 'old' Combined Code) the Quoted Companies Alliance wrote:

'It is important that the FRC and other bodies ... emphasise that a non-executive director ceasing to be independent is not a cause for the end of his directorship – if he is still contributing valuably he should be encouraged to remain a director although he is unlikely to be considered independent. This is particularly relevant for smaller companies where a director ceasing to be independent but remaining on the board does not change the number of independent non-executives required to be compliant.'

The problem of companies not wanting to lose non-executives after nine years because their independence may be subject to question is compounded by the fact that there is only a small pool of individuals who are perceived as having the qualities and experience to perform the role of NED in a large company. When it is difficult to find replacements, companies will be reluctant to let go of NEDs who are still doing a 'good job' with them.

The UK Corporate Governance Code is pragmatic in its approach and exceptions to the nine-year 'rule' are permitted. If the board of directors considers that a NED remains independent, they may be invited to stay on for more than nine years and still be considered 'independent' for the purposes of corporate governance. However, NEDs who have served longer than nine years should be subject to annual re-election (Code Provision B.7.1).

*The views of institutional investors and their advisers on the nine-year rule*
Institutional investor organisations and their advisers have expressed views about the nine-year rule.

In 2005, in its comments to the Financial Reporting Council about the 'old' Combined Code, the Association of British Insurers made the following comment about the nine-year rule:

'Some companies have described this as a rule and have urged that it be removed. However voting records show that the overwhelming majority of investors do not apply the provision as a rule and routinely re-elect directors who have served more than nine years .... While adopting a flexible approach, our members see value in retaining this provision as it provides a reference point beyond which there is a need to check whether independence is maintained.'

The National Association of Pension Funds (NAPF) takes a similar line in its *Corporate Governance Policy and Voting Guidelines* (revised 2011), and recognises that a pragmatic approach is required to the rule and a NED who has been on the board for more than nine years does not necessarily immediately lose their independence: 'The NAPF sees the nine-year 'rule' as a milestone rather than a fixed date. However, independence is likely to diminish with time and the onus is on the company to explain why a long-serving NED should still be considered independent. The Guidelines suggest that shareholders should look for statements by the company that the independence of a long-serving NED has been formally evaluated, and that the company has a policy for refreshing board membership and succession planning. 'This is perhaps the most important consideration' – retaining long-serving NEDs may act as a barrier to refreshing the board.

The NAPF Guidelines also stated that investors should have no problem with the existence of non-independent non-executive directors on the board, but the issue of independence may become an issue in terms of board balance (the UK Code requirement for a majority of independent NEDs on the board) and committee membership.

A board must not confuse 'independence' with 'skill and experience'. It may wish to retain a NED after nine years because of the depth of experience the individual brings to the board. However, this is not a test of independence.

---

CASE EXAMPLE
................
## DIRECTOR INDEPENDENCE

Research, Recommendations, Electronic Voting (RREV) is a joint venture between the National Association of Pension Funds and Institutional Shareholder Services, which provides a range of services for investment managers and pension funds. In a 2005 report, RREV described the pragmatic approach to assessing independence using the example of United Utilities. Its Senior Independent Director had been a non-executive director of the company since 1994.

The board and the Nomination Committee both carried out a review of his independence and both reached the conclusion that he remained strongly independent. The reasons they gave were his continuing financial independence from the company, his substantial other business commitments and his personal character and professional calibre.

RREV accepted these arguments, having obtained additional supporting evidence to support the board's view:

- Other individuals had retired as NEDs after nine years.

- The arrangements made by the company's remuneration committee were consistent with best practice.
- The company had a good 'track record' in corporate governance.

RREV reached a different conclusion in the case of Chloride Group. Its Senior Independent Director, who was also chairman of the remuneration committee, had been an NED of the company for 21 years. The board reported that it considered him to be independent after this time and valued the depth of his knowledge and expertise.

In this case, RREV decided that the board's review of his independence was not sufficiently rigorous, and it had confused 'independence' with 'skill and experience'. RREV therefore recommended that shareholders should vote against the director's re-election at the AGM.

## 4  PROCEDURES FOR OBTAINING INDEPENDENT PROFESSIONAL ADVICE

An important provision of the UK Corporate Governance Code, mentioned earlier, is that directors should have access to independent professional advice – at the company's expense – where they consider this necessary to fulfil their duties and responsibilities as directors properly (Provision B.5.1).

The Code does not specify in detail how or when directors might wish to obtain independent professional advice.

The right of directors to obtain advice, either collectively or individually, might be formalised by means of a board resolution. The ICSA Guidance Note on this issue (see Directory) suggests some wording for a board resolution that:

- gives recognition and approval of the right of directors to seek independent professional advice at the company's expense; and
- may establish procedures and limitations.

### Procedures

The company may require a director (or several directors jointly) to give prior notice of their intention to seek advice at the company's expense. The required procedure may be for notification to be made to the chairman, the senior independent director or the company secretary.

The professional advisers may be either:

- the company's own professional advisers, such as the company's auditors or solicitors; or
- other advisers where necessary, or when the director is not satisfied with the advice given by the company's own professional advisers.

The established procedures may require the company secretary to give an acknowledgement to the director(s) that the company will pay for the cost of the advice.

An alternative procedure may be for a member of the board, such as the senior independent director, to be given authority to commit the company to the costs of independent professional advice for directors. A director wishing to obtain advice should then obtain from this individual a formal acknowledgement that the company will pay the cost.

### Limitations

Independent professional advice should relate to accounting, legal or regulatory issues. It should not relate to advice concerning the personal interests of a director, such as the director's contract of service, the director's dealings in the company's shares or any dispute between the director and the company.

The company may also wish to control the amount of fees that any director or group of directors may incur to obtain professional advice. It may do this by requiring a director to obtain the formal agreement of the chairman or the senior independent director that the company will pay for the cost of the advice, whenever this cost will exceed a specific amount.

### Availability of advice

Advice obtained by a director at the company's expense should be made available on request to the rest of the board.

## 5 CRITICISMS OF NEDS AND CREATING AN EFFECTIVE BOARD

The provisions of the UK Corporate Governance Code, including provisions relating to induction, professional development and performance review, attempt to address the criticisms that have often been made about the ineffectiveness of NEDs. The most common criticisms may still be valid in some listed companies.

- NEDs have been accused of lacking knowledge of the company and its business operations. When this happens, they find it difficult to contribute to discussions about strategy, and often rely on explanations provided to them by executive director colleagues.

- NEDs are often ineffective because they cannot devote enough time to the company. If they are the executive director of another company, they will spend most of their time with that company, and its problems.
- Some NEDs may be reluctant to criticise fellow directors, and so might be tempted to go along with the opinions of colleagues, and be easily persuaded by their arguments.

The Myners Report in 2002, a government-sponsored report into pension fund investment, made the following criticisms:

- Some individuals held too many positions as NEDs of companies, more than they could serve effectively.
- When NEDs are also executive directors of other listed companies, there may be a 'You scratch my back and I'll scratch yours' mentality. By choosing not to ask difficult questions and putting executive director colleagues under pressure, they might hope to be treated in the same way by NEDs in the company where they hold their executive position.
- NEDs should help to make the board more accountable to the shareholders. However, shareholders rarely meet NEDs outside formal settings, such as general meetings of the company, where communication between NEDs and shareholders is limited.
- UK law makes no distinction between executive and non-executive directors. Both might be held equally liable for negligence or failure of duty. The threat of criminal or civil liability might make NEDs more inclined to support their executive director colleagues.

### Creating an effective board

The criticisms of NEDs can be overcome by applying principles of good corporate governance.

The Higgs Report suggested that the contribution of NEDs to the effectiveness of the board of directors will take time to develop.

- A culture of openness and constructive dialogue is needed, and an environment of mutual respect. The chairman has a responsibility for creating and maintaining these conditions.
- There is the potential for a virtuous circle. If NEDs interact constructively with executive colleagues, the perception held by executives of the value and contribution of NEDs will improve. This in turn will encourage executives to

be more open with the NEDs. This in turn will allow for even more constructive involvement by the NEDs.

However, Higgs also commented:

'Inappropriate or ill-informed non-executive contributions can quickly break this virtual dynamic, by leading to executive frustration or defensiveness and attempts to minimise the role of the non-executive directors. In turn this feeds the non-executive directors' suspicion of executive directors.'

It is also important to recognise that a major limitation on the effectiveness of NEDs is the 'asymmetry' of access to information between executive directors and the NEDs. The executive directors are much better informed than NEDs about many details of the company's business, and this can put the NEDs at a serious disadvantage in discussions at board meetings.

## Meetings of NEDs without executive directors present

Higgs recommended that the effectiveness of NEDs would be improved if the NEDs met occasionally on their own, without executive directors present, to allow for an organised discussion of matters such as:

- the provision of information to the directors;
- overall performance; and
- succession planning.

The UK Code includes a provision that the NEDs, led by the senior independent director (see Chapter 5), should meet:

- at least once a year to discuss the chairman's performance; and
- 'on such other occasions as are deemed appropriate'.

In addition, the Code states that if directors have concerns about the running of the company or a proposed action, they should ensure that their concerns are expressed in a board meeting and recorded in the minutes of the meeting.

# CHAPTER FIVE

# Effective boards and board meetings

.....................

## OVERVIEW

Various provisions of the UK Corporate Governance Code are intended to produce effective boards; these relate to the roles of the chairman of the board and the chief executive officer, and also the size and composition of the board. In listed companies, the majority of the directors, excluding the chairman, should be independent NEDs. The UK Code also identifies a special role for the senior independent director. The effectiveness of a board may also be improved by an efficient company secretary.

A requirement of the UK Code is that the board of directors should reserve certain decisions for themselves, to be taken collectively, and that these matters should not be delegated. In this way the board as a unit, and not senior executives, will make the key decisions for the company.

The board should delegate certain responsibilities to committees. One purpose of having audit, nomination and remuneration committees is to ensure that decisions are not taken by executive directors where they may have a conflict of interest.

The effectiveness of a board depends on how its meetings are conducted, how it reaches decisions and how it ensures that action points are implemented by the individuals responsible. The UK Code also requires that the annual report should include information on how the board operates.

## 1  THE ROLE OF THE BOARD OF DIRECTORS

The FRC *Guidance on Board Effectiveness* begins with the statement:

> 'The board's role is to provide entrepreneurial leadership of the company within a framework of prudent and effective controls which enables risk to be assessed and managed.'

An effective board is essential for sound corporate governance.

The UK Corporate Governance Code states as a main principle (Principle A.1) that every company should be headed by an effective board, which is collectively responsible for its long-term success.

The Code goes on to specify the role and responsibilities of the board in more detail.

- The board should provide entrepreneurial leadership for the company.
- Entrepreneurial leadership should be provided within a framework of prudent and effective controls that enable risk to be assessed and managed.
- The board should set the strategic aims for the company.
- The board should ensure that the necessary financial and human resources are in place to achieve the company's objectives.
- The board should review management performance.
- The board should set the company's values and standards.
- The board should ensure that its obligations to the company's shareholders (and others) are understood and met.

The effectiveness of a board can be judged by its success in fulfilling these roles. This depends to a large extent on the leadership that is provided, the composition of the board and the way in which the work of the board is organised and the way in which the various board members work together. The role of NEDs on the board should be seen within the context of the role of the board as a whole.

Note: The QCA's Corporate Governance Code for Small and Mid-Size Quoted Companies also gives emphasis to effective boards and includes a summary of factors for smaller quoted companies to consider.

## 2 THE CHAIRMAN AND CHIEF EXECUTIVE OFFICER

The UK Code states that on the board of directors, 'no one individual should have unfettered powers of decision' (Principle A.2).

To achieve this aim, there should be a clear division of responsibilities between the chairmanship of the board and the role of the chief executive.

- The chief executive is responsible for running the business, using powers delegated by the board, and for implementing the strategies decided by the board. The CEO is normally an employee of the company with a service contract.

- The chairman is responsible for leading the board, setting its agenda and making sure that it operates effectively. The chairman is usually a part-time non-executive appointment, although a substantial commitment in terms of time might be required (particularly in large public companies), and written into the letter of appointment. Major investors should be consulted before the appointment of a new chairman for a large public company, but the formal appointment of a new chairman is made by the board of directors, without any shareholder vote. (This is a provision in standard articles of association.) A chairman will have to submit themselves for re-election periodically as a director at the AGM, but not as chairman.

The UK Code states that the division of responsibilities between the chairman and chief executive should be clearly established and set out in writing (so that the division of responsibilities remains clear and does not become eroded over time) and agreed by the board. It also includes the following provisions:

- The role of chairman and chief executive should not be held by the same individual.

- On appointment, the chairman should meet the criteria for being independent. (Independence is explained later.)

- The chief executive should not subsequently go on to become the chairman. There would be a risk that the chairman, as former CEO, would have too much influence over the newly appointed CEO.

- If in exceptional circumstances a company wishes to appoint its CEO as the new chairman, the board should consult the major shareholders and set out its reasons to shareholders in advance and in the next annual report.

This aspect of the UK Corporate Governance Code has been challenged and criticised in a number of well-publicised cases, and there is a counter-argument that it can be damaging for a company and its governance to have two independent and strong-minded individuals as chairman and chief executive.

The Chairman of the Financial Reporting Council commented in a series of meetings with FTSE 100 chairmen in July 2006 that the Code provision that the roles of chairman and CEO should be held by different individuals is only an 'optional rule'. Under the 'comply or explain' regime, companies may appoint the same individual to hold both positions and simply have to give a good and convincing explanation for doing so.

However, the NAPF Corporate Governance Policy and Voting Guidelines (revised 2011) take a different view, stating that combining the roles of chairman and chief executive officer is acceptable 'only on rare occasions'. If a board of directors is considering combining the roles, the Guidelines suggest that there should be dialogue with the shareholders, who will want confirmation that external candidates have also been considered for the role.

---

CASE EXAMPLE
................
## BP

In 2006, the financial press reported on the future of Lord Browne, chief executive of BP. Many shareholders wanted Lord Browne to continue in his role after reaching the company's retirement age of 60 (in two years' time). However, the company chairman, Peter Sutherland, forced Lord Browne (reluctantly, apparently) to announce that he would be retiring at 60 and that planning for the succession would be put in hand.

Some shareholders felt that it was against the best interests of the company to let its successful chief executive go, and criticism was directed at the strong-minded chairman for insisting that this should happen.

---

CASE EXAMPLE
................
## BSkyB

In December 2007, Mr Rupert Murdoch announced his resignation as chairman of British Sky Broadcasting (BSkyB). The independent NEDs of BSkyB were given the task of recommending a new chairman for the company. They recommended Mr James Murdoch, the son of Rupert Murdoch and also the CEO of BSkyB. In the opinion of the BSkyB board this appointment would provide the company with the continuity that it needed. BSkyB's Senior Independent Director was quoted as saying: 'James will stand for re-election, so if shareholders are not happy, they have the chance to vote against him' (*Financial Times*, 10 December 2007).

---

CASE EXAMPLE
.................

## MARKS AND SPENCER

In 2004, Marks and Spencer resisted a takeover bid for the company from the financier Philip Green. The successful takeover defence was organised by the company's new chairman, Paul Myners, and chief executive, Stuart Rose.

During 2005 Kevin Lomax, the senior independent director, argued that the chairman and the chief executive were too close to each other, and that there was insufficient independence between them. After strong pressure from Lomax, Myners agreed to step down as chairman and his successor Sir Terry Burns was appointed (initially as deputy chairman in 2005) to take his place. Critics argued that this change had broken up a highly successful working relationship between the company's chairman and CEO.

In 2008 CEO Sir Stuart Rose was also appointed as company chairman, for a limited period until a successor to the role of CEO could be identified and appointed. This attracted strong criticism from some institutional investors. Legal & General publicly criticised the decision, saying that it was an arrangement that made it difficult to appoint a successor to Sir Stuart as CEO. However, shareholders could not prevent the appointment of the new chairman because this was a decision of the board. Shareholders were able, however, to vote on the re-election of Sir Stuart Rose as director at the AGM in 2008; 22% of shareholders either opposed his re-election or abstained in the vote.

---

## 3 THE ROLE OF THE CHAIRMAN

Although the role of the CEO as head of the management team is fairly well understood, there may be some uncertainty about the role of chairman.

The role of the chairman is described in the UK Corporate Governance Code. The *Guidance on Board Effectiveness* states clearly that 'good boards are created by good chairman'. Table 5.1 sets out the chairman's chief responsibilities.

The chairman is also responsible for the annual performance review of the board, its committees and the individual directors. They are therefore also responsible for ensuring that new directors are given the induction they need and for the development of individual directors in their role.

**Table 5.1** The role of the chairman

| UK CORPORATE GOVERNANCE CODE | GUIDANCE ON BOARD EFFECTIVENESS |
|---|---|
| Leading the board and ensuring its effectiveness. Setting the board's agenda and ensuring that sufficient time is available for discussion of all agenda items (in particular strategic issues). | Demonstrating ethical leadership. Setting a board agenda which focuses primarily on strategy, accountability, performance and value creation. Ensuring that issues relevant to this objective are reserved for board consideration. Making sure that an effective decision-making process is in place in the board and that the board committees are properly structured with appropriate terms of reference. Making sure that the board takes into account the nature and extent of the risks associated with implementing strategy. |
| Promoting a culture of openness and debate, by ensuring that the NEDs are given the opportunities to contribute effectively to the board, and that the relations between the executive directors and NEDs are 'constructive'. | Encouraging the active participation of all board members. Fostering effective relationships based on mutual respect and open communication, inside and outside the boardroom, between the NEDs, the CEO and executive directors. Consulting with the senior independent director in appropriate circumstances. Consulting with the SID as necessary. |
| Ensuring effective communication with shareholders. | Ensuring effective communication with shareholders and other stakeholders and making sure that directors are aware of the views of major shareholders. |
| Ensuring that all board members receive accurate and timely information. | Ensuring the timely flow of high-quality supporting information. |
|  | Regularly considering succession and board composition. |
|  | Taking the lead on director development and acting on the results of board evaluation. |

## A short checklist for an effective chairman

The responsibility of the chairman for ensuring that the board operates effectively has several practical implications. Other NEDs may judge the effectiveness of the board by reference to these issues.

- The agendas for board meetings should include forward-looking strategic issues. The board should not be simply a 'rubber stamp' for approving decisions already taken by the executive management.
- All directors should receive relevant, timely and clear information, to enable them to reach well-informed and well-judged opinions and views about matters that the board will decide on. This is critically important for the effectiveness of the NEDs.
- The chairman should allow sufficient time for decisions to be considered, especially decisions relating to complex or contentious matters. NEDs should not be given unrealistic deadlines for reaching an opinion.
- The chairman should encourage the participation of NEDs in board discussions.
- The chairman should make sure that the opinions of the shareholders are communicated to the board.

---

CASE EXAMPLE
................

# BSkyB and Barclays

Chairmen may be held to account for reputational risk of companies with which they are associated.

In April 2012, Mr James Murdoch resigned as chairman of BSkyB, (although he remained on the board as a NED) having previously resigned as chairman of News International following the 'phone hacking' scandal at the *News of the World* and the subsequent Leveson enquiry. He stated that his reason for resigning as chairman of BSkyB was to prevent the reputational damage to News International from spreading to BSkyB. The BBC reported him as saying: 'As attention continues to be paid to past events at News International, I am determined that the interests of BSkyB should not be undermined by matters outside the scope of this company.' He added: 'I am aware that my role as chairman could become a lightning rod for BSkyB and I believe that my resignation will help to ensure that there is no false conflation with events at a separate organisation' (BBC).

In July 2012, Mr Marcus Agius resigned as chairman of Barclays following admission by the bank that some of its traders had been involved in manipulating the LIBOR money market rates, accepting responsibility for the consequent damage to the reputation of the bank.

## 4 THE SIZE AND COMPOSITION OF THE BOARD

In a unitary board system, good governance requires that the board should not be dominated by one individual, or by a small group of individuals. This is to prevent the dominant individual or group from running the company in their own self-interest, rather than in the interests of the shareholders.

*Note*

Two-tier board structures are used in some European countries, notably Germany and the Netherlands (although an amendment to the Dutch Civil Code from January 2013 provides a legal basis for single-tier boards). In a two-tier board structure, consisting of a supervisory board of non-executives and a management board of executives, it should be possible for the supervisory board (led by the chairman) to act as a 'check' on the CEO and management board.

CASE EXAMPLE
................

## DOMINANT PERSONALITY

In the UK, public recognition that a dominant leader could be harmful for shareholders and employees was strengthened by the scandal surrounding the death of Sir Robert Maxwell in 1991 and the subsequent collapse of his media empire.

Mirror Group Newspapers was a part of the Maxwell 'empire'. After Sir Robert Maxwell's death, it emerged that the Mirror Group's debts were much larger than its assets, and £440 million was missing from the company's pension funds.

In 1996, after an eight-month trial, Maxwell's sons Kevin and Ian and another man, Larry Trachtenberg, were cleared of conspiracy to defraud Mirror Group pensioners.

In 2001 the Department of Trade and Industry released a report into the Maxwell affair which said 'primary responsibility' for the collapse of the Maxwell business empire lay with its founder, Sir Robert. A conclusion was that Maxwell had been allowed to run the group in the way that suited his own best interests, and as a consequence both shareholders and employees (members of the pension fund) had suffered.

After Maxwell's death, a three-year campaign for compensation for the Mirror Group pensioners resulted in some success. The government made a payout of £100 million, and there was a £276 million out-of-court settlement with City institutions and the remnants of Maxwell's media group.

## The UK Corporate Governance Code on the balance of power

The UK Code states that 'the board and its committees should have the appropriate balance of skills, experience, independence and knowledge of the company to enable them to discharge their respective duties and responsibilities effectively' (Principle B.1). The *Guidance on Board Effectiveness* comments that boards are more likely to make good decisions and maximise opportunities for long-term success if their members collectively have the right balance of skills, experience, knowledge and independence.

- The board should include an appropriate combination of executive and non-executive directors (and in particular independent non-executive directors) such that no individual or small group of individuals can dominate the board's decision-making (Principle B.1).
- The board should be sufficiently large that the requirements of the business can be met and changes to the composition of the board can be managed without undue disruption. However, the board should not be so large as to be unwieldy.
- When deciding on the chairmanship and membership of board committees, undue reliance should not be placed on particular individuals. In addition, committee membership should be kept 'refreshed'.
- No one except the chairman and members of the nomination, audit and remuneration committees is entitled to attend the meetings of those committees, although other individuals can attend if invited by the committee. This is to protect committee meetings from undue influence by non-committee members.

## Other provisions of the UK Corporate Governance Code on board membership

The UK Code makes the following additional provisions about membership of the board:

- Except for smaller companies, at least half the board (excluding the chairman) should be independent non-executive directors.
- Small companies (companies outside the FTSE 350) should have at least two independent non-executive directors (Provision B.1.2).

## 5 ROLE OF THE SENIOR INDEPENDENT DIRECTOR (SID)

The UK Corporate Governance Code states that the board should appoint one of the independent NEDs to be the senior independent director or SID (Provision A.4.1).

The role of the SID has three broad aspects:

(1) **For shareholders**. The SID should be available to shareholders if they have concerns that have not been resolved through contact with the chairman, CEO or other executive directors, or where contact through these individuals would be inappropriate. To develop an understanding of investor interests and concerns, the SID is usually expected to attend some of the regular meetings between the company and its major shareholders and financial analysts.

(2) **For the chairman**. The SID should normally provide support for the chairman, but should be prepared to respond to situations where the chairman does not appear to be acting in a way that seems satisfactory to the rest of the board, particularly the NEDs. The UK Code states that the SID should provide a 'sounding board' for the chairman and act as an intermediary for other directors 'when necessary'. In addition, the SID should lead the rest of the non-executive directors in carrying out the annual performance appraisal of the chairman, in a meeting without the board chairman present.

(3) **For the other non-executive directors**. The SID provides leadership to the non-executive directors on occasions when this is required. The UK Code states that the SID should lead the NEDs in meetings without the chairman present on occasions that are 'deemed appropriate'.

The SID is the 'leader' of the NEDs, in the sense that they can act as an effective channel of communication for the NEDs as a group, and can organise the activities of the NEDs on matters such as the annual review of the chairman's performance (see Chapter 10).

In some companies, the SID may be given the formal title of Deputy Chairman.

The role of the SID is described in the UK Corporate Governance Code, and in more detail in the *Guidance on Board Effectiveness*. The SID's responsibilities are set out in Table 5.2.

The SID is therefore a channel of communication between the company and its shareholders when normal channels don't work. This situation may arise, for example, when major shareholders are strongly opposed to a proposed strategy of the board, championed by the CEO and chairman, and want to make the NEDs aware of their responsibility to judge strategy proposals critically. The SID may also be a channel of communication when major shareholders are dissatisfied with the chairman and CEO and are looking for a change 'at the top' of the company.

| UK CORPORATE GOVERNANCE CODE | GUIDANCE ON BOARD EFFECTIVENESS |
|---|---|
| The SID should provide a sounding board for the chairman, and as such may act as an intermediary through whom the other NEDs can express their views and concerns to the chairman. | Provide support for the chairman. |
| The SID should also 'be available to shareholders if they have concerns which contact through the normal channels of chairman, chief executive or other executive directors has failed to resolve, or for which such contact is inappropriate'.<br>In addition, if the chairman fails to pass on the views of the institutional shareholders to the NEDs, there should be another channel of communication that could be used instead. | Ensure that any concerns expressed by shareholders or NEDs are addressed by the CEO or chairman.<br><br>Intervene when the company is undergoing a period of stress, to maintain board and company stability. The SID should work with the chairman, other directors and shareholders to resolve significant issues, such as a dispute between the chairman and CEO, or decisions being taken without the approval of the full board. |
| | Ensure that the chairman is giving sufficient attention to succession planning. |
| Lead the evaluation of the performance of the chairman, at least annually. | Lead the evaluation of the performance of the chairman. |

**Table 5.2** The role of the senior independent director

A senior independent director may also fulfil a valuable role in other unusual circumstances.

- If the board chairman is also the CEO or is a former CEO (contrary to the UK Code principles), or for some other reason was not independent when first appointed, the SID should provide independent leadership for the board and act as a strong spokesman for the independent NEDs.
- Even when a chairman is independent when first appointed, their role is likely to bring them closer over time to the views of the CEO and executive management, and their independence will inevitably be eroded to some extent. The SID should provide leadership to the independent members of the board when this situation creates a problem.

---

CASE EXAMPLE
................
## ROLES OF THE SID

Listed companies issue formal statements about the roles of the chairman, CEO and SID. These are generally based on the UK Code requirements, but sometimes provide interesting additional details. A formal statement of the role of its SID published by Babcock International in 2012 included the following roles for the SID:

- 'Be ready to take responsibility for an orderly succession of Chairman if necessary;
- Be ready to intervene and work with the Chairman and other directors and/or shareholders as appropriate in order to maintain Board and company stability should circumstances arise that give rise to stresses in the proper functioning of the board, for example, if:
  - there is a dispute between the Chairman and the Chief Executive;
  - shareholders or non-executive directors have expressed concerns that are not being addressed by the Chairman or the Chief Executive;
  - the strategy being followed by the Chairman and the Chief Executive does not have the support of the entire Board;
  - decisions are made by the Chairman and the Chief Executive without the required approval of the full Board; or
  - succession planning is not being addressed.'

---

In its formal statement on the role of the SID (2012), BG Group included an indication of the amount of time that the SID would be expected to commit to the role – at least three to four days per year, but 'significantly more in exceptional circumstances', in addition to the time required in the individual's capacity as NED.

## 6 THE BOARD COMMITTEES

A board of directors will often operate with a number of different committees. Each committee is required to consider a particular aspect of the board's affairs, and make recommendations to the full board. The role of NEDs on board committees varies according to the nature of the committee's responsibilities.

The UK Corporate Governance Code has given prominence to the roles of:

- the nomination committee;
- the audit committee; and
- the remuneration committee.

The Code also refers to the possibility that there may be a board risk committee, which may be particularly beneficial for financial services companies such as banks. (A risk committee of the board should not be confused with a risk executive management committee, consisting of executive management and risk officers, which is a part of the executive management structure in companies where such committees have been established.) The roles of these major board committees are described in later chapters.

There may also be other board committees, such as:

- a general purpose or finance committee, which may be given the powers to approve the opening of new bank accounts, or to recommend the allotment of shares under employee share plans; and
- a business practices committee or corporate social responsibility committee, which may have oversight of matters such as health and safety, the environment, and community and ethical issues.

There may be an executive committee (Excom), led by the CEO and consisting of executive directors and other senior executives. However, this is not a committee of the board, and it is constituted as a decision-making body for important management issues, such as:

- developing and reviewing budgets;
- reviewing internal controls; and

- examining all major proposed capital investment projects before submitting any proposal to the board of directors.

## 7 THE ROLE OF THE COMPANY SECRETARY

The Companies Act 2006 states that public companies must have a company secretary, but private companies are not required to have one (although they may choose to do so). The efficiency and effectiveness of a board may be greatly improved by a competent and knowledgeable company secretary.

A company secretary may have a range of duties, which should include providing advice and assistance to the chairman, acting as secretary to the board (and probably also the board committees) and giving advice on corporate governance matters to the board and individual directors.

NEDs may find a company secretary particularly useful as a first point of contact when they need information or professional advice, or need something done (such as arranging to attend a meeting with shareholders, or arranging a site visit).

The *Guidance on Board Effectiveness* states that the company secretary should play a leading role in good governance by supporting the chairman and helping the board and its committees to function efficiently. It also suggests that the company secretary should:

- report to the chairman on all board governance matters and, where appropriate, have their remuneration determined by the remuneration committee;
- ensure the presentation of high-quality information to the board and its committees;
- add value by fulfilling the requirements of the UK Corporate Governance Code, in particular in relation to director induction and development;
- with the chairman, periodically consider whether the board and the company's governance processes are fit for purpose, and consider any improvement initiatives that could strengthen the company's governance.

## 8 MATTERS RESERVED FOR THE BOARD

The constitution of a company normally gives almost unlimited powers to the board of directors, and allows the directors to delegate many of these powers to the executive management (led by the managing director or CEO).

This raises the issue of the division of powers:

- Which powers are delegated to the executive management, led by the CEO?
- Which powers are retained by the board of directors for collective decision-making?

A company is badly governed when the board of directors gives too many powers to the executive management.

However, a company is also badly governed if the board of directors retains too many powers, and (as a collective group) is too much involved in the day-to-day running of the company's operations.

There has to be a balance between powers retained by the board and powers delegated to the executive management. Executive management should be accountable to the board for the powers that have been delegated to them, and the board of directors must, as one of its responsibilities, monitor the performance of the executive management.

The UK Corporate Governance Code therefore contains a provision that the annual report should include a statement of how the board operates: this should include a 'high-level' statement of which types of decision are reserved for board decision and which are delegated to executive management (Provision A.1.1).

### ICSA Guidance Note on Matters Reserved for the Board

ICSA has issued a guidance note, listing the matters that might be reserved for decision by the board, and which might therefore make up the formal schedule referred to above (see Directory). Some of the items in the ICSA list are summarised below.

- Matters that the board of directors must by law reserve for its own decision. For example, the board of directors is required by law to approve the annual report and accounts and the board collectively must make appointments to the board.
- Requirements of the UK Listing Rules, such as the requirement for the board to approve circulars before they are sent out to shareholders.
- Recommendations of the UK Corporate Governance Code, such as reviewing the performance of the company and approving the terms of reference of board committees.
- Matters that the board should delegate to committees (the nomination, audit and remuneration committees), as recommended by the UK Code.
- Items that are not specified by law or by the UK Code, but that a board of directors would typically be expected to retain for its own decision-making,

such as deciding the long-term objectives and strategy of the company, the approval of major capital expenditures and other large contracts (such as large bank borrowings and major asset disposals), and oversight of management and the group's operations.

- When the board has a nomination committee, remuneration committee and audit committee, decision-making powers are not fully delegated to these committees. The committees are asked to make recommendations to the board, and the final decision on the matter is taken by the board.
- The ICSA's guidance note suggests that the board should approve in advance, before the company is contractually committed, all contracts that are material, either strategically or for reasons of their size, and in the ordinary course of the company's business.

## 9 THE CONDUCT OF BOARD MEETINGS

The effectiveness of a board depends largely on how board meetings are conducted, and the success of the chairman in getting board members to reach well-considered decisions, and ensure that these decisions are implemented and subsequently reviewed.

The conduct of board meetings is the responsibility of the chairman, supported by the company secretary (if there is one) or a senior administrator. Meetings should be held with sufficient frequency to enable the board to carry out its responsibilities, and enough time should be allocated to meetings to enable the agenda items to be discussed – without getting into the problem of wasting too much time.

Regular board meetings should be scheduled well in advance, possibly for the entire financial year. Alternatively, at the end of each board meeting, the date of the next meeting may be agreed and scheduled. Additional non-scheduled meetings may be called as necessary. For non-scheduled meetings, every effort should be made by the chairman/company secretary to enable as many board members as possible to attend.

Meetings should be structured around the agenda and board papers. A typical agenda will consist of:

- apologies for absence;
- approval of minutes of the previous meeting;
- matters arising from minutes of the previous meeting;
- agenda items, both regular and 'one-off' matters for discussion; and
- any other business.

Minutes provide a formal record of what has been discussed and decided at each meeting. Well-written minutes will also flag the decisions that have been taken and 'action points' that indicate who has the responsibility for implementing the decision.

A discussion of matters arising from the minutes of the previous meeting allows the board to review decisions that were taken and to check that individuals have acted on the action points.

Agenda items will include topics that come up regularly, such as a review of the management accounts for the most recent period. Each year the board should also discuss the draft budget at one or more meetings and then formally approve the budget for the following financial year.

Board members should be provided with papers relating to each agenda item in advance of the meeting. Minutes of the board meeting should be distributed as soon as possible after the meeting, to reduce the risk that board members will forget the details of what was discussed and agreed.

'Any other business' (AOB) gives board members an opportunity to raise issues that have not been included on the agenda, and for which board papers are not required.

### Role of the chairman at board meetings

The chairman is the leader of the board but should not dominate it. Their role at board meetings is to work through the agenda within an appropriate time frame, encouraging all board members to contribute to the discussions. NEDs should be encouraged to provide 'constructive challenge', particularly on matters relating to strategy and performance.

- Sufficient time should be allowed for debate.
- The chairman should bring discussion of issues to a 'timely closure'. This means reaching agreement, or deciding on the next steps to be taken when there is still some disagreement or uncertainty. In some cases, matters on which there is continuing disagreement may be taken to a vote.
- Discussions should be constructive, and the chairman should provide a calming influence when board members disagree strongly, and tempers may be raised.
- Decisions should be clear and properly minuted, so that executives will be able to understand the actions that are expected from them.

The articles of association are likely to state that boards should reach their decisions by majority vote, with the chairman having a casting vote in cases where the decision is divided 50:50. However, split decisions should be unwelcome and the aim should always be to reach a consensus, with all directors agreeing on a collective decision. The performance of the chairman can often be judged by their ability to steer the board towards a consensus view.

If a director is in the minority when a decision is taken and on reflection cannot agree with the views of the majority, they may wish to consider resignation, particularly if the disagreement is on an important matter.

## 10 BOARDROOM BEHAVIOUR AND DECISION-MAKING

The effectiveness of board meetings depends not only on the structure and organisation of meetings, but also on the behaviour of the board members, and how they work together. The *Guidance on Board Effectiveness* is clear that high-quality decision-making is critical for the effective operation of boards and does not happen by accident: directors should minimise the risk of poor decision-making by taking time to design their decision-making policies and procedures.

However, decision-making can be adversely affected by problems such as:
- the effects of a dominant personality or group on the board;
- insufficient attention to risk and how risk affects decision-making;
- a reluctance to involve NEDs;
- matters being brought to the board for sign-off rather than debate;
- complacent or intransigent attitudes; or
- weak organisational culture.

The *Guidance* also identifies that good decision-making can be facilitated by:
- high-quality board documentation;
- obtaining expert opinion when necessary;
- allowing time for debate and challenge;
- achieving timely closure; and
- providing clarity on actions, timescales and responsibilities.

Boards are also encouraged to review and evaluate past decisions.

## 11 REPORTING ON HOW THE BOARD OPERATES

The Higgs Report recommended that the annual report should include information about how the board of directors operates. 'A greater understanding of how a board operates is likely to create greater confidence amongst shareholders and others in the leadership and governance of the company.' This recommendation has been adopted in the UK Corporate Governance Code, which includes a provision that the annual report should:

- include a statement of how the board operates;
- identify the chairman, deputy chairman (if there is one), chief executive, the senior independent director and the chairmen and members of the nomination, audit and remuneration committees; and
- set out the number of meetings of the board and these committees and individual attendances by each of the directors.

Some companies provide extensive information about how the board operates. The following example is a lengthy extract from a publication by BP plc of its Board Governance Principles. This is quoted extensively because it provides an excellent example of compliance with the UK Code requirements and a useful insight into how the board of a major global company actually operates at a time when it has come under scrutiny pressure in the US about its compliance with environmental and health and safety regulations.

---

CASE EXAMPLE

................

## BP: THE BOARD AND ITS PROCESSES

*Shareholders*
The Board is committed to promoting the success of BP. It represents the interests of all shareholders and seeks to act fairly between them. The Board will engage in an appropriate dialogue with shareholders and seek to obtain the view of the shareholders as a whole.

*Board Meetings*
The Board will determine the key items for its consideration for the coming financial year. The agenda will be set by the Chairman in consultation with the Group Chief Executive (GCE) and with the support of the Company Secretary. A similar process will be used for meetings of Board Committees.

Discussion at Board meetings will be open and constructive. All discussions of the Board and their record will be maintained in confidence unless there is a specific decision or legal requirement to make disclosure.

In participating in Board discussions, Executive directors are expected to discharge their responsibilities as directors of BP and not to act solely as the representative of that activity for which they bear executive responsibility ...

---

## Board Composition

The Board will comprise a mix of individuals that ensures an appropriate range of knowledge, views and experience. The Nomination Committee will keep under review this mix of skills and make recommendations as appropriate ...

The Board should be of a size which enables the full engagement of all the directors.

The number of directors will not normally exceed 16.

The Board will maintain plans for the succession of the Executive and Non-Executive directors.

All directors will stand for re-election by shareholders each year ...

## Other Directorships

Membership of the Board represents a significant time commitment and Non-Executive directors must be prepared to give sufficient time for the discharge of their BP responsibilities.

All directors should regularly inform the Board through the Company Secretary, of other directorships they hold. The Nomination Committee will keep under review the commitments of Non-Executive directors and make recommendations to the Board if the Committee concludes that a director's other commitments are inconsistent with those required by BP ...

## The Chairman and Deputy Chairman

The Board will appoint from among their number a Chairman and a Deputy Chairman neither of whom will be employed executives of the Group ...

The Chairman will provide leadership of the Board and will act as facilitator for meetings.

The Chairman has authority to act and speak for the Board between meetings on all matters relating to the Board Principles and will engage with the GCE on behalf of the Board as required. The Chairman is empowered to make any decision, establish any policy, take any action or enter into any obligation which is consistent with the Board Principles and, in so doing, may interpret the Board Principles in any reasonable manner.

The Chairman will report to the next meeting of the Board on any material or sensitive exercise of this authority.

The Chairman will ensure that systems are in place to provide directors with accurate, timely and clear information to enable the Board to consider properly all matters before it.

The Deputy Chairman shall act for the Chairman in his absence or at his request.

The Deputy Chairman will normally serve as the Board's Senior Independent Director and will be available to shareholders who have concerns that cannot be addressed through normal channels.

## Board Committees

The Board may at any time establish Committees of the Board to assist it in carrying out its responsibilities. Any Committee will be subject to the Board Principles and will speak or act for the Board only when and to the extent so authorised.

The permanent Committees of the Board include the Chairman's Committee, the Safety, Ethics and Environment Assurance Committee (SEEAC), the Remuneration Committee, the Audit Committee, the Results Committee and the Nomination Committee. Regular meetings of the permanent Committees will be scheduled annually ... With the exception of the Results Committee, all Committee members, including the chairman of each Committee, shall be Non-Executive directors. The main responsibilities and requirements for the composition of the permanent Committees are set out in the Appendix.

## The Company Secretary

All Board members will have access to the advice and services of the Company Secretary. The Company Secretary reports to the Chairman and is responsible to the Board ...

The Company Secretary is responsible for advising the Board and the Committees on all governance matters, ensuring that Board procedures are followed, that the applicable laws and regulations for the conduct of the affairs of the Board are complied with and for all matters associated with the maintenance of the Board or otherwise required for its efficient operation.

## Delegation to the GCE

The Board is responsible for reviewing and, where appropriate, determining the Strategy and the monitoring of risk and performance. It delegates to the GCE authority for the executive management of BP consistent with the BP Goal and the Executive Limitations.

The Board will hold the GCE accountable for the discharge of this authority.

# 12 CHECKLIST FOR AN EFFECTIVE BOARD

The following checklist sets out some of the questions that should be asked when assessing the effectiveness of the board.

## 1. Board structure: skills and experience

1.1 Does the board collectively have a suitable mix of skills and experience to take the company forward? ☐

1.2 Is the structure of the board and its committees appropriate? ☐

1.3 Do the NEDs give the time to the company that is needed? ☐

1.4 Are board members given sufficient induction and relevant training? ☐

## 2. Focus

2.1 Does the board have a clear sense of purpose? ☐

2.2 Does the board have clear objectives for the company? ☐

2.3 Does the board have sensible strategies for the achievement of those objectives? Does it measure its progress against key strategic targets? ☐

2.4 Does the board receive information about key performance indicators for the business, including financial data? ☐

2.5 Are the matters reserved for collective decisions by the board clearly defined? ☐

2.6 Is the board focusing its attention on the relevant/correct areas? Is there an appropriate balance between short-term and long-term issues? ☐

2.7 Have decisions by the board proved successful? What could have been decided differently that would have been better? ☐

2.8 Is the chairman effective as a leader of the board? ☐

## 3. Board meetings

3.1 Does the board meet often enough to carry out its responsibilities properly? ☐

3.2 Does the board have occasional longer meetings, away from the office, to discuss strategy? ☐

3.3 Is sufficient time given in board meetings for all important issues to be discussed fully before a decision is reached? ☐

3.4 Do the non-executive directors challenge the executive directors, while still remaining supportive? ☐

3.5 Do board members receive board papers in good time before meetings? ☐

3.6 Are there clear and concise papers on each agenda topic? Do these papers set out the issues properly and identify alternative courses of action where appropriate? ☐

3.7 Are these papers of a suitable length? Is the information clear and comprehensible? ☐

3.8 Are directors well-prepared when they come to board meetings? ☐

3.9 Is there a high attendance at board meetings? ☐

3.10 Do all board members contribute sufficiently to the discussions at meetings? ☐

3.11 Is the board too large for meetings to be effective? ☐

# CHAPTER SIX

# The nomination committee

....................

## OVERVIEW

A nomination committee, as a committee of the board, should be responsible for identifying individuals for appointment to the board and for making recommendations to the board about new appointments.

The committee should also make recommendations to the board on succession planning for both executive and non-executive directors.

In its search for a new chairman or NED, the nomination committee is normally expected to use either open advertising or the services of an external search agency. A chairman should be considered independent on first appointment. Any appointment of a chairman or NED that does not comply with these requirements in the UK Corporate Governance Code should be disclosed and explained in the annual report and accounts.

## 1   PURPOSE OF THE NOMINATION COMMITTEE

The UK Corporate Governance Code (Principle B.2) states that there should be a 'formal, rigorous and transparent procedure' for the appointment of new directors to the board.

The board itself should also satisfy itself that plans are in place for an orderly succession of new appointments to the board and senior management positions in the company. (The Code does not specify what it means by 'senior management', but this could include senior executive management positions below board level, as well as executive directors.)

The process for making board appointments should be led by a nomination committee, a sub-committee of the board, which should make recommendations to the full board (Code Provision B.2.1).

Some smaller listed companies may not have a nomination committee, perhaps because their board is too small. In such cases, they are non-compliant with the UK Code and are required to explain their non-compliance in their annual report and accounts.

## 2 COMPOSITION OF THE NOMINATION COMMITTEE

The UK Code states that a majority of the members of the nomination committee should be independent NEDs.

The chairman of the committee should be either the company chairman or an independent NED. (If the committee chairman is the company chairman, he/she should not chair the committee when the succession to the company chairmanship is being discussed.)

Except for allowing the possibility that the board chairman may also chair the nomination committee, the UK Corporate Governance Code does not say anything specific about the chairman's responsibilities for the make-up of the board or appointments to the board. The FRC's Guidance on Board Effectiveness (2011) on the other hand states that the chairman's role includes 'regularly considering succession planning and the composition of the board'.

Since both the chairman and the nomination committee have responsibilities for the size and composition of the board, it could make good sense to appoint the board chairman as chairman of the nomination committee; this is fairly common practice.

A majority of independent NEDs on the committee should prevent the chairman or CEO from having excessive influence over appointments to the board. The existence of executive directors on the board should add balance to the committee's assessments, and their knowledge and expertise may be particularly important for the process of appointing new executive directors.

No one should be allowed to attend meetings of the nomination committee, other than the committee members, unless they are invited to do so by the committee. This means for example, that the chief executive officer does not have a right to attend, unless they are also a committee member.

## 3  ROLE OF THE NOMINATION COMMITTEE

Listed companies are required by the UK Code (Provision B.2.1) to make available the terms of reference of their nomination committee, for example, on the company's website.

The ICSA has issued guidance on the terms of reference for a nomination committee, including model terms of reference. These can be downloaded from the ICSA website (see Directory). The guidance includes the following provisions.

- Appointments to the nomination committee should be made by the board, for periods of up to three years. The board should also appoint the committee chairman, who should be either the chairman of the board or an independent NED.
- Only committee members have a right to attend committee meetings, but the committee may choose to invite other people to attend, such as the CEO, head of human resources and external recruitment advisers, as and when appropriate.
- The terms of reference should specify the number of regular meetings of the committee each year. The ICSA guidance suggests two meetings a year to conduct routine business, although additional meetings may be required when a new appointment to the board is being made.
- Committee meetings should be called by the committee secretary (who may be the company secretary) at the request of the committee chairman.

The duties of the nomination committee should be:

- to review regularly the structure, size and composition of the board and make recommendations (to the board) for changes;
- to review the results of the annual process of board performance evaluation that relate to the composition of the board;
- to keep under review the leadership needs of the company;
- succession planning for directors and senior executives of the company;
- to identify candidates to fill vacancies on the board of directors, as and when these arise, and from the candidates who have been identified, nominating individuals for appointment, for approval by the full board;
- to recommend (to the board) appointments to the board committees;

- to recommend whether non-executive directors should be reappointed on the expiry of their current term of appointment (having regard to the need for continual refreshing of the board membership);
- to recommend whether the board should propose any director retiring by rotation (in accordance with the company's articles of association or the UK Corporate Governance Code) for re-election by the shareholders at the next annual general meeting;
- to arrange a periodic review of its own performance and recommend to the board any changes that it considers necessary; and
- to produce a report about the activities of the committee in the annual report to shareholders.

### An example of terms of reference for a nomination committee

Although the ICSA has provided model terms of reference for a nomination committee, terms of reference in practice vary in the amount of detail provided. An example is shown below.

---

CASE EXAMPLE

·················

## HAYS PLC, THE RECRUITMENT SPECIALISTS

*Terms of reference for the nomination committee*
To lead the process for Board Appointments and make recommendations to the Board.

*Constitution*
The majority of the members should be Independent Non-Executive Directors and chaired by the Chairman. The quorum shall be three. For specific assignments the Chief Executive may be a member of the Committee. The Company Secretary will act as Secretary to the Committee, ensuring papers are distributed and minutes of decisions are maintained.

*Duties*
Prior to appointment evaluate the balance of skills knowledge and experience and prepare an appropriate description of the role and capabilities for a particular appointment.

---

Be responsible for identifying and nominating for Board approval, suitable candidates to fill Board vacancies, taking into consideration the benefits of diversity on the board, including gender.

Annually review the structure size and composition of the Board and make recommendations of any changes required.

Review the succession plans for the Board so as to maintain an appropriate balance of skills and experience on the Board, to ensure progressive refreshing of the Board.

Make recommendations to the Board on the membership of the Remuneration and Audit committee, including chairmanship thereof.

Recommend to the Board re-election of Directors either when required by rotation or at the completion of the term of office for a Non-Executive Director.

Consider the time commitment that any Non-Executive Director will need to give to the Company on appointment.

Review formal appointment letters for Non-Executive Directors.

Prepare an annual statement of activities of the Committee for inclusion in the Annual Report.

## Changing the structure and composition of the board

The nomination committee is responsible for keeping under review the balance of skills and experience of board members, and ensuring that new appointments will help to achieve or maintain a balance that is appropriate for the needs of the company.

To comply fully with the UK Corporate Governance Code, nomination committees should carry out regular reviews of the structure and composition of the board, and recommend changes to the main board. The emphasis of the UK Code is on regular refreshment of the board.

This proactive approach is in contrast to a reactive committee, whereby the committee begins a search for a new board member only when asked to do so by the board, or only when a vacancy occurs.

Although the nomination committee is given the responsibility to make recommendations for new appointments or other changes to the board, it should be expected to listen to the views of some non-committee members. In particular, if the board chairman is not a committee member, their input may be valuable. The *Guidance on Board Effectiveness* comments:

'The chair's vision for achieving the optimal board composition will help the nomination committee review the skills required, identify the gaps, develop transparent appointment criteria and inform succession planning.'

The *Guidance on Board Effectiveness* also suggests that diversity of personal attributes is also important and that directors should have the ability to listen carefully, forge relationships and develop trust. Diversity is important to ensure that a board is not composed solely of like-minded individuals.

### Filling vacancies on the board

Planning for the continual refreshing of a board of directors should be seen more as a process of maintaining an effective board by bringing in new skills and experience, rather than getting rid of ineffective board members. It should be a natural process of change and development.

The need for diversity in board membership is explained in Chapter 3, but diversity does not simply mean greater representation by women.

There are various factors to consider when planning board succession and changes to the board size and composition.

- NEDs should be appointed because they will bring particular skills and experiences to the board, but they are typically appointed for a fixed three-year term, which may then be renewable at the end of each three-year period. However, they should not necessarily expect a renewal of their contract at the end of its term: they need to be aware that their appointment may well be terminated in order to bring new ideas and new experiences to the board, with new appointments.
- The skills and experience required from board members may change as the company grows. For example, if a UK-based company expands overseas, it might be appropriate for the board to consider new appointments of NEDs with knowledge of the overseas business and its environment.
- The requirement to increase the proportion of women on the board should also be taken into consideration in planning board composition over the next few years.
- In some cases, NEDs may be replaced because they are not contributing enough to the work of the board. However, this is not the main purpose of a review of board composition.

## 4 APPOINTING A COMPANY CHAIRMAN

For the appointment of a company chairman, the UK Corporate Governance Code states that the nomination committee should prepare a job specification (Provision B.3.1). This should include an assessment of the time commitment expected, recognising the need for the chairman to be available in the event of any crisis.

When an individual is recommended by the committee for appointment as chairman, his/her other significant commitments should be disclosed to the board (and included in the company's next annual report).

## 5 REPORTING THE WORK OF THE COMMITTEE: THE USE OF ADVERTISING AND EXTERNAL SEARCH AGENCIES

The UK Corporate Governance Code states that a separate section of the annual report should describe the work of the nomination committee. This should include a description of the process used by the committee in relation to board appointments.

More specifically, the description of the appointment process should include an explanation if neither open advertising nor the services of an external search agency has been used in the appointment of a chairman or a non-executive director. It therefore applies a 'comply or explain' requirement specifically to the use of advertising or an external search agency.

By including this provision, the Code is trying to ensure that the search by the nomination committee for candidates for appointment to the board will be open and based on merit.

The 2012 revision of the UK Code introduced a specific reference to the board's policy on diversity. The provision of the Code (B2.4) dealing with the nomination committee's report on appointments to the Board now states:

> 'A separate section of the annual report should describe the work of the nomination committee, including the process it has used in relation to board appointments. This section should include a description of the board's policy on diversity, including gender, any measurable objectives that it has set for implementing the policy, and progress on achieving the objectives.'

### Appointments that do not comply with the UK Code

Appointments to the board might not comply with the requirements of the UK Code. For example:

- the same individual might be appointed as both chairman and CEO of the company;
- a former CEO of the company may be appointed as the chairman;
- a FTSE 350 company might not have a majority of independent NEDs on the board.

The UK Listing Rules require companies to explain any non-compliance with the UK Code. Non-compliance is acceptable, but should be justifiable. Although the responsibility for appointments to the board rests with the board as a whole, the process used by the nomination committee in making its recommendations will inevitably come under public review.


## 6   SUCCESSION PLANNING

The nomination committee will usually be given responsibility for making recommendations about succession planning. A supporting principle in the UK Corporate Governance Code states that:

> 'The board should satisfy itself that plans are in place for orderly succession for appointment to the board and to senior management, so as to maintain an appropriate balance of skills and experience within the company and on the board, and to ensure progressive refreshing of the board.'

'Progressive refreshing of the board' calls for succession planning, and identifying in advance the type of person who would improve the balance of skills and experience on the board.

Succession planning is commonly associated with planning for the eventual replacement of key board members – the chairman, chief executive officer and finance director. However, succession planning should involve a review of the entire board, including NEDs.

The board should be refreshed regularly, and this is achieved by appointing a new NED to replace an existing NED whose term of appointment has reached its end (and will not be renewed). The nomination committee may recommend the reappointment of a NED at the end of their first three-year term, but termination of an appointment after six years may be more usual, when the NED's second three-year term ends.

The committee should also 'keep under review' the leadership needs of the company, both executive and non-executive, in order to ensure that the company will continue to compete effectively in its market place.

## 7 CHECKLIST FOR A NOMINATION COMMITTEE

The following checklist sets out examples of the requirements for selecting an independent NED and for succession planning.

### 1 Appointing an independent NED

1.1 New appointments are planned in advance, and are not a reactive response to vacancies that occur. ☐

1.2 The board and the committee have a policy on diversity, including gender, and apply this policy to the appointment of new directors. ☐

1.3 When appointing a NED, there should be a rigorous and formal process for drawing up a profile of the type of individual required. ☐

1.4 The committee should select a panel of suitable candidates who seem to fit this profile. ☐

1.5 When choosing individuals for the panel, the committee should draw from a pool of talented individuals other than individuals who are known to the chairman, CEO or other board members. ☐

1.6 Executive directors should not give any lead, directly or indirectly, in the choice of a NED. ☐

1.7 The person appointed must confirm that they can commit the necessary time, including time for induction and training. ☐

### 2 Succession planning for CEO

2.1 Succession planning should recognise the qualities required from the next CEO, given the strategic direction that the company is taking. ☐

2.2 The current CEO should be asked to provide input into the succession planning process. ☐

2.3 Succession planning should involve the entire board. ☐

2.4 A search for the next CEO should recognise company tradition in making such appointments from internal or external candidates. When an external appointment is made, there is a risk of losing existing senior executives who feel they have reached a glass ceiling and will never advance higher in the company. ☐

2.5 When an internal appointment is made for the next CEO, it might be appropriate to arrange for the selected individual to broaden their experience within the company. This can be done by moving the individual to different senior positions within the company, to 'groom' them for the future role as CEO. ☐

2.6 There should be a contingency plan for the appointment of a new CEO in the event that the current CEO leaves the company sooner than expected (for example, through dismissal due to poor performance). ☐

# CHAPTER SEVEN

# The remuneration committee

....................

## OVERVIEW

The remuneration of executive directors and other senior executives is an important and emotive aspect of corporate governance. Several issues are involved.

Senior executives should not be allowed to decide their own remuneration; therefore a provision in the UK Corporate Governance Code is that their remuneration should be decided by a remuneration committee of independent NEDs.

The remuneration package for a senior executive should be sufficiently attractive to persuade talented individuals to work for the company and should also provide incentives for achieving specified performance targets (which should be targets that will enable the company to satisfy the expectations of its shareholders).

A balance needs to be struck in a remuneration package between basic salary, short-term incentives and long-term incentives. The remuneration committee should also consider all aspects of remuneration, including pension rights and the entitlements of any individual who is removed from office for poor performance.

Institutional investors monitor closely the remuneration policies of companies and individual executive remuneration packages, and when they disapprove strongly of any aspect of remuneration, they may vote against the board of directors on a selected issue at the AGM. Concerns of the institutional investors have included 'rewards for failure', high (and hidden) pension benefits for senior executives and the high rates of annual increase in the basic pay and bonuses of senior executives.

Remuneration committees should be able to justify their decisions, and may seek the advice of specialist remuneration consultants (as a way of demonstrating objectivity and due care).

Disclosure by companies of their remuneration policy and details of the remuneration of individual directors has now gained acceptance in the UK and the USA. UK quoted companies are required to include a remuneration report in their annual report and accounts.

Remuneration for senior executives remains a contentious issue in the UK. The main concerns currently appear to have been lack of transparency in executive remuneration, the absence of a clear link between performance and rewards, and insufficient shareholder influence over remuneration policy.

## 1 REMUNERATION AS AN ISSUE IN CORPORATE GOVERNANCE

The remuneration of executive directors and senior executives has been recognised in the UK since the 1990s as a problem for good corporate governance. The remuneration of NEDs tends not to be a contentious governance issue, but NEDs may be members of the board remuneration committee, and as such need to be aware of issues involved with the remuneration of executive directors and other senior company executives.

In the public mind, the remuneration of executive directors and senior executives has been associated with:

- the high rewards paid to 'fat cat' directors: this term was widely used in the UK media following the privatisation of many utility companies in the 1990s, when senior executives were awarded large increases in remuneration for doing the same job as before; and
- 'rewards for failure', and the large severance payments to senior executives who are dismissed by the company for poor performance.

There has also been some recognition of the problem in the USA. In 2002, Alan Greenspan (then the chairman of the US Federal Reserve Board) accused many senior executives in the USA of 'infectious greed', and the President of the Federal Reserve in the same year condemned the high level of remuneration for CEOs as 'morally dubious'.

## Source of guidance on remuneration

In the UK, the main source of guidance on remuneration for directors and senior executives is the UK Corporate Governance Code, although the rules on disclosure of remuneration details are in the Companies Act 2006.

The European Commission issued recommendations about the remuneration of directors in listed companies in 2004, and supplemented these with further recommendations in 2009. The 2009 recommendations provide guidelines on the proportionality of a director's remuneration package (relative to other executive directors and senior executives in the company), and the balance between fixed and variable elements of pay and between long-term and short-term performance criteria. Existing UK guidelines are consistent with the European Commission recommendations.

## The level and make-up of remuneration

From a corporate governance perspective, the remuneration of executive directors and senior executives is not primarily an ethical issue. The UK Corporate Governance Code identifies the key issues about the level and make-up of remuneration for directors as follows (Principle D.1).

- Levels of remuneration should be sufficient to attract, retain and motivate directors of the quality required to run the company successfully. However, the company should avoid paying more than is necessary for this purpose.
- A significant proportion of the remuneration of executive directors should be linked to rewarding the individual for corporate and individual performance. However, there is no definition or specification of just what a 'significant' proportion should be.
- The performance-related elements of remuneration should be 'stretching' and designed to promote the long-term success of the company.

The problem lies in devising a reward scheme that provides a suitable and effective incentive. How large should the incentive be? What should the specific incentives be, so that the incentive element in each remuneration package achieves its intended purpose? And how should the remuneration packages for individual executives be formulated within a consistent remuneration policy?

## 2 THE NEED FOR A REMUNERATION COMMITTEE

The need for a remuneration committee in listed companies was recognised in the 1990s. The 1995 Greenbury Report on directors' remuneration reached the following conclusions.

- Formulating the remuneration packages of executive directors and other senior executives is a key issue for corporate governance.
- The system for remunerating executive directors and other senior executives is open to abuse whenever the executives are allowed to decide their own remuneration.
- Shareholders are not in a position to decide the remuneration of directors. However, they should be entitled to receive extensive information about their remuneration. (It is a key principle of good corporate governance that no individual should be able to decide their own remuneration.)
- The remuneration of executive directors and other senior executives should be decided by a remuneration committee, consisting entirely of independent NEDs.

These recommendations were adopted and were included in the Combined Code (from 1998) and now the UK Corporate Governance Code.

### UK Corporate Governance Code requirement for a remuneration committee

As a general principle, the UK Code (Principle D.2) states that there should be a formal and transparent procedure for:

- developing policy on executive remuneration; and
- deciding the remuneration package of individual directors.

No director should be involved in deciding their own remuneration.

The board should establish a remuneration committee consisting entirely of independent NEDs.

### Composition of the remuneration committee: advice to the committee

The committee should consist of at least three independent NEDs in larger companies (FTSE 350 companies) and at least two independent NEDs in smaller companies.

The chairman of the board may sit on the remuneration committee as a member, provided that they were considered independent on appointment, but should not be the chairman of the committee.

The board chairman, whether a member of the remuneration committee or not, should ensure that the company maintains contact with its main shareholders about remuneration.

In addition, the remuneration committee should consult with the board chairman and/or chief executive officer about their proposals for the remuneration of other executive directors.

The remuneration committee may also take advice from executive directors and other senior executives about remuneration. Executives may be able to provide insights into what fellow executives might expect to earn, and what specific performance targets might be appropriate for incentive schemes.

When it takes advice from executive colleagues, 'care should be taken to recognise and avoid conflicts of interest.'

It would also be appropriate for the remuneration committee to talk to the finance director about the potential impact of a proposed remuneration scheme on the company's reported profits.

### Remuneration consultants

Remuneration committees will often obtain professional advice on remuneration from a firm of remuneration consultants. The UK Code states that the remuneration committee should have the responsibility for appointing any such consultants, and where consultants are used, a statement should be 'made available' about whether they have any other connection with the company.

## 3 DUTIES OF THE REMUNERATION COMMITTEE

The terms of reference for the remuneration committee vary between different companies. The UK Corporate Governance Code states that the company should make the committee's terms of reference 'available'. (This requirement can be met by putting the information on the company's website.)

More specifically, the Code states that the delegated responsibilities of the remuneration committee should include the responsibility for:

- deciding the remuneration of all executive directors and the chairman, including pension rights and any compensation payouts: the committee should therefore be responsible for negotiating remuneration with these individuals;
- recommending and monitoring the level and structure of remuneration for senior management. The definition of 'senior management' should be decided by the board, but it will normally include the first layer of executive management below board level.

The UK Code states that there should be a procedure for developing policy on executive remuneration. It does not suggest what this procedure should be, or whether the remuneration committee should have the responsibility for recommending policy to the board. However, the ICSA model terms of reference for a remuneration committee include a provision that the committee should 'determine and agree with the board the framework or broad policy for the remuneration of the company's chief executive, chairman, the executive directors, the company secretary and such other members of the executive management as it is designated to consider.'

The committee may devise a new long-term incentive scheme for executive directors and senior management, but any such scheme (and, usually, any significant change to an existing scheme) should be submitted to the shareholders for their approval before being introduced.

## Model terms of reference for a remuneration committee

The ICSA has issued guidance on the terms of reference for a remuneration committee, including model terms of reference. These can be downloaded from the ICSA website (see Directory). The guidance includes the following provisions.

- Appointments to the nomination committee should be made by the board, for periods of up to three years, provided that they continue to meet the criteria for committee membership. The board chairman may be a member of the committee, provided that they were considered independent on first appointment, but may not be the committee chairman.
- Only committee members have a right to attend committee meetings, but the committee may choose to invite other people to attend, such as the CEO, head of human resources and external remuneration consultants, as and when appropriate.
- The terms of reference should specify the number of regular meetings of the committee each year. The ICSA guidance suggests at least two meetings a year, and one of these should be held close to the end of the financial year to review the directors' remuneration report.
- Committee meetings should be called by the committee secretary (who may be the company secretary) at the request of the committee chairman.

The duties of the remuneration committee, for the parent company, major subsidiaries or the group as a whole, as appropriate, should be:

- to agree the broad policy for remuneration of the board chairman, CEO, executive directors, senior executives and company secretary. (The remuneration of NEDs is a matter for the board chairman and executive directors to decide.)

- to determine the total individual remuneration package of board chairman, CEO, executive directors, senior executives and company secretary, including bonuses, incentive payments, share options and share awards. The committee should have full authority to appoint remuneration consultants, within the budgetary constraints set by the board.)
- to approve the design of any performance-related pay schemes, determine targets for those schemes and approve the total annual payments under these schemes;
- to review the design of share incentive plans, prior to their submission for approval by the board and shareholders;
- for any such share incentive plans, to decide each year whether any awards should be made and the amount of any such rewards (both in total and to individuals);
- to determine the policy for and scope of pension arrangements for executive directors and other senior executives;
- to determine contractual arrangements with directors for compensation on termination of office, and to avoid making excessive 'rewards for failure'; and
- to produce a report on the company's remuneration policy and practices for inclusion in the company's annual report, and to ensure that this is put to the shareholders for approval at the AGM.

## 4 REMUNERATION PACKAGE STRUCTURES

The remuneration package of executive directors and senior executives will typically consist of the following elements:

- basic salary;
- short-term incentive (often in the form of a bonus, although bonus payments may be deferred or payable over several years, and subject to clawback if actual performance in retrospect is found to be worse than initially measured);
- long-term incentive (often in the form of a share scheme); and
- pension arrangements.

Each element in a remuneration package has a purpose. When a remuneration committee considers the package for a director, it should consider:

- each separate element in the package; and also
- all the elements in the package as a whole.

For example, a director may be paid a median basic salary, but may have a very generous pension entitlement or an attractive incentive scheme.

A problem for remuneration committees is to decide not only on the size of rewards that should be offered to executives, but how the incentives should be divided between short-term and long-term, between cash and equity and between current pay and pension rights. The relative proportions can vary significantly between companies, although the incentive element should be high.

It is usual for remuneration committees (advised perhaps by a firm of consultants) to benchmark remuneration packages with those paid by other companies in a peer group. However, by setting remuneration levels and incentives in this way, there is a risk that remuneration will increase steadily over time as remuneration committees try to avoid being the worst payers in the peer group.

The UK Code states that the remuneration committee should judge where to position their company relative to other companies, but they should use comparisons with caution, in order to avoid an 'upward ratchet' of pay levels with no corresponding improvement in performance.

The UK Code also suggests that the company should be 'sensitive' to pay and employment conditions elsewhere in the group, especially when deciding annual salary increases. This is a reference to the need to recognise the possible adverse consequences of making large increases in the remuneration of directors and senior executives, when pay rises for all other employees are comparatively very modest.

### Short-term incentives: bonus

A senior executive incentive scheme will offer directors and other senior managers in the scheme an annual bonus (normally in cash) for meeting or exceeding target performance levels. The bonus scheme may be on a sliding scale, with a bonus for meeting target and higher bonuses for exceeding targets by a certain amount.

There may be a cap on the maximum bonus that any individual may earn. For example, an incentive scheme may provide for a bonus equal to 30% of basic salary for meeting performance targets, with a maximum bonus of 60% of salary for exceeding targets.

The bonus payments will be linked to one or more key performance indicators, possibly using a balanced scorecard approach. The targets may include performance indicators for the business as a whole (such as a target for earnings per share) and personal targets for the individual executive.

It is widely accepted that the nature and potential size of annual bonuses can drive the behaviour of senior executives, and that there is a risk of short-termism, with executives focusing on current year profits in order to earn a large bonus, possibly at the expense of the company's longer-term success.

### Long-term incentives: share plans

Long-term incentive schemes usually take the form of awards of either share options or fully paid shares in the company. A company might have several different share schemes, and individuals may participate in some or all of them.

Each scheme should have a set 'life', with a maximum number of shares or share options that can be awarded under the scheme. New schemes may be introduced before existing schemes reach the end of their life.

The award of shares or share options should be conditional on the director or senior executive meeting certain performance targets. For example, a scheme might award free shares to executive directors for achieving total shareholder return (TSR) targets over a three-year period, relative to comparator companies.

A company may also offer a deferred annual bonus scheme, whereby directors and other executives participating in the scheme are entitled to use some or all of their annual cash bonus entitlement to buy shares in the company. These may be held in trust for a number of years (typically, three years), after which the individual is entitled to the award of additional free matching shares from the company. The award of free matching shares at the end of the qualifying period may be subject to a minimum growth target. For example, the award of free matching shares may be subject to the condition that growth in earnings before interest, depreciation and amortisation (EBITDA) should be no less than the growth in the retail prices index over the qualifying period.

### Pension arrangements

Executive directors will also receive certain pension benefits. They may be members of a company pension scheme, possibly a defined benefits scheme. In addition, there may be 'unfunded' pension arrangements for individual directors.

The UK Corporate Governance Code states (in a supporting schedule) that only basic salary should be pensionable, not incentive payments. It also states that the remuneration committee should think about the consequences for pension costs of any increases in an individual's basic pay or pension rights, particularly when the individual is close to retirement (and so will have little time left to justify the pension increase).

## 5 LINKING REWARDS TO PERFORMANCE

In constructing a remuneration package with an incentive element, a key aim should be to link the rewards for the executive to company performance, so that executives are rewarded for achieving or exceeding agreed targets. In theory, this provides an incentive to the executive to make sure that the targets are achieved. This should link rewards for executives with benefits for the company and its shareholders, so that the directors have a mutual interest with the shareholders in the success of the company.

### Problems with linking rewards to performance

In practice, experience has shown that in many cases the remuneration of directors and the best interests of the company and its shareholders are not properly aligned. The Department for Business, Innovation and Skills (BIS) issued a discussion paper on Executive Remuneration in 2011 which commented:

> 'The structure of remuneration has become increasingly complex. This has led many companies, investors, remuneration and governance advisors and academics to question whether the symmetry between pay and performance has been lost.'

Here are some frequent criticisms of reward schemes.

- There may be disagreement about what performance targets should be. Should they be financial targets only, or should there be non-financial targets? Should there be just one target or several different targets? How can incentives and rewards for short-term targets be reconciled with incentives and rewards for longer-term targets?
- Executives may be rewarded with bonuses for meeting an annual profit target, regardless of the consequences that higher short-term profits might have for the longer-term performance of the company.
- Executives may have expectations that they will receive rewards, even when the company does not perform particularly well.
- Executives are often protected against the 'downside'. Like the shareholders, they benefit when company performance is good, but they do not suffer significantly when performance is poor.
- There may be a 'legacy effect' for new senior executives. For some time after a new senior executive is appointed, financial performance and competitive performance may be affected by decisions taken in the past by their predecessor. Rewards for the new executive may therefore be the result of past actions by another person.

- Occasionally, incentive schemes are criticised for rewarding an executive for doing something that ought to be a part of their normal responsibilities, such as rewarding a CEO who is planning their retirement for successfully identifying a successor.

The BIS discussion paper referred to above also commented on the growth in senior executive pay, which had been rising at a much faster rate than company profitability.

'Despite the efforts to link pay to company performance, the rate of growth of remuneration has greatly outstripped the growth in the total return received by investors. Some researchers have argued that the move towards more complex remuneration structures with a greater proportion of reward being deferred, has actually driven increases in overall remuneration because executives expect higher pay in reward for higher risk. In other words, the value of deferred pay may be discounted because of the possibility it will not be paid. It has also been suggested that complex schemes increase the likelihood that at least some elements will pay out, leading to higher overall pay awards.'

## 6 THE DESIGN OF PERFORMANCE-RELATED SCHEMES
The UK Corporate Governance Code provides some guidance on the design of performance-related remuneration schemes for executive directors.

- Short-term incentives. The remuneration committee should consider whether directors should be eligible for annual bonuses. If it decides that they should be eligible, the performance targets should be 'relevant, stretching and designed to promote the long-term success of the company'. There should be an upper limit to bonuses each year. There may be a case for paying a part of bonuses in shares of the company, and requiring the individual to hold them for a 'significant period' after receiving them.

- Long-term incentives. The committee should also consider whether directors should be eligible for rewards under long-term incentive schemes, such as share option schemes or the vesting of shares in the company. If share options are granted, they should normally not be exercisable for at least three years from the date they were granted. Directors should be encouraged to hold the shares for a further period after they have been vested or after the options have been exercised, subject to the need of the director to finance the costs of acquiring the shares or meet any tax liabilities in connection with receiving the shares.

Any proposed new long-term incentive scheme should be submitted to the shareholders for approval. Any new scheme should form a part of a well-considered overall remuneration plan that incorporates all other existing incentive schemes (and may replace an 'old' existing scheme). The total rewards that are potentially available to directors should not be excessive.

Grants under executive share option schemes and other long-term incentive schemes should normally be phased, rather than awarded in a single large block.

- Performance criteria. Payments or grants under all incentive schemes should be subject to 'challenging performance criteria' that reflect the company's objectives.

## 7  SHARE OPTION SCHEMES AND RESTRICTED STOCK AWARDS

Share option schemes and the award of shares to senior executives can be used to align the long-term interests of the individual directors and senior executives with the long-term interests of shareholders, because both the director/executive and the shareholders will benefit from increases in the share price.

However, there are some potential problems with schemes, some of them referred to earlier, although these problems can be overcome.

- When options are granted in large blocks, there will be a temptation for the director or executive to do their best to make sure that the share price is as high as possible at the date that the options become exercisable. What happens later is of much less importance. A director may therefore seek to maximise profits (and so boost the share price) at the time that the options can be exercised, even if this means that longer-term performance will be adversely affected. To overcome this problem, it is recommended that share options should be granted to individuals as a phased grant over a period of years, rather than in a single large block. This will encourage the individual to think about performance of the share price over a longer term.
- It has also been argued that there should be a restriction on sales of shares by directors or executives after they have been awarded shares or have exercised share options. These are commonly set out and agreed in the form of share ownership guidelines. The restriction may, however, be in the form of a minimum retention ratio. This would require the individual to retain a minimum percentage of the shares acquired, and not to sell them

before the end of a specified minimum period. For example, a share option scheme might require an individual to retain at least, say, 25% of the shares obtained by exercising share options, for at least five years after the shares have been acquired. The purpose of a minimum retention ratio would be to ensure that the individual continues to have a personal interest in the share price for a period of time after the options have been granted.

- This same argument applies to the award of shares to executives. When executives are given shares in their company, they may be required to retain them for a minimum number of years before they are able to sell them or dispose of them in any other way.

- The option exercise price. Individuals receiving share options will stand to make a bigger gain if the exercise price for the share options is lower. The UK Code states that share options should not be issued with an exercise price that is at a discount to the current share price. For example, if the current share price is £6, share options should not be issued with an exercise price less than £6.

- The size of option awards. It is also recognised that there should be a limit to the quantity of share options that is granted, because share options dilute the interest of existing shareholders in the company, when the options are exercised. Under the Listing Rules, shareholders' approval is required for the issue of shares for employee share schemes. This means that shareholders can limit the total amount of share options granted by setting a limit on the number of new shares that the company can issue for cash. Typically, investment institutions may agree to a limit of up to 5% of the company's issued share capital for executive schemes and 10% for all schemes.

Note: When the share price falls below the exercise price for share options, the options are said to be 'under water'. There have been instances in the past where a company has cancelled share options that are under water, and reissued new options to the option holders with a strike price at the new, lower market price. This has been criticised as an abuse of share option schemes that rewards directors and executives even though the shareholders have suffered a loss.

## 8  EQUITY INCENTIVE SCHEMES: THE ACCOUNTING PROBLEM

The remuneration committee and the board as a whole need to be aware of the potential consequences of equity incentive schemes for the company's accounts.

Share option schemes and awards of shares will affect the company's reported profits each year, and this could have some impact on the share price.

International Financial Reporting Standard 2 (IFRS2 *Share-based payments*) requires companies to recognise the award of share options as an expense in the company's annual income statements, from the time that the share options are granted.

## Why are share options an expense?

The reason for treating share options as an expense is that share options represent a reward to employees, and benefits to employees should be recognised as an employment cost.

When a company issues share options, it incurs an expense. It gives employees the right to subscribe for new shares at a future date, at a price that is expected to be lower than the market price of the shares when the options are exercised.

Share options therefore have a value. When share options are awarded to an employee, the employee is therefore given something of value (a cost) in return for the benefit.

## Accounting for equity-settled share-based payment transactions

IFRS2 states that for share-based payment transactions, such as the award of share options, the cost of the services received (the employees' labour) should be recognised when the transaction is made. A company should measure this cost at fair value.

When share options are granted to an employee, the fair value of the employment services provided in return for the options cannot be measured reliably; therefore the cost of the services should be measured as the fair value of the share options, using a share option pricing model.

In the case of share options to employees, the cost of the options should be calculated at the grant date. This is the date that the options are awarded to the employee, not the date that they can be exercised (which may be three or more years later). This cost of options is then amortised over the period from their grant to the time that they 'vest'. This creates an annual charge in the income statement (profit and loss account).

The fair value of the options at the date of the grant of the options is used to account for the transaction. The fair value of the options at subsequent year-ends is not relevant: in normal circumstances, the share options are not revalued each year.

---

CASE EXAMPLE
·················
## ACCOUNTING FOR SHARE OPTIONS

A simplified example may help to show how the cost of share options is accounted for.

An employee is granted 60,000 share options and a vesting condition is that the employee should work for three more years in order to earn the right to exercise the options.

- At the end of Year 1, the number of options taken into consideration in measuring the cost of the share options is 20,000 (60,000 × 1 year/3 years).

- At the end of Year 2, the number of options taken into consideration in measuring the cost of the share options is 40,000 (60,000 × 2 years/3 years).

- At the end of Year 3, the number of options taken into consideration in measuring the cost of the share options is the actual number of options for which the exercise rights are vested. This is 60,000.

The amount charged as an employment cost in the income statement each year is the difference between:

- the accumulated cost of the options as at the end of the current year, and

- the accumulated cost of the options as at the end of the previous year.

---

In this example, if the value of a share option obtained from an option pricing model was £4 when the options were granted, the charge in the income statement will be £80,000 in the first year (20,000 × £4), £80,000 in the second year (40,000 × £4 – £80,000) and £80,000 in the third year.

Note: The cost of the share options is treated as an expense in the income statement each year. This might seem odd, since the company does not actually have to make any payments. What actually happens is that share options are accounted for by charging an expense in the income statement, but adding the amount of this charge to a revenue reserve in the balance sheet. The share option expense therefore reduces the reported annual profit, but does not reduce the company's total reserves.

# 9 TERMS OF EMPLOYMENT AND COMPENSATION FOR LOSS OF OFFICE

## Service contracts

Issues that often raise concerns about the service contracts of executive directors and senior executives are the amount of remuneration payable (including the nature of incentive arrangements), the notice period or term of the contract and the amounts that might be payable as compensation to the individual in the event of their dismissal.

The amount of compensation payable and the length of the notice period or service contract are connected. The amount payable to an individual will usually depend to some extent on the period of notice that the company is contractually required to give, or the remaining unfinished term of a fixed-term contract.

The UK Corporate Governance Code therefore specifies that notice periods or contract periods should be set at one year or less. This requirement is fully supported by the National Association of Pension Funds and the Association of British Insurers.

## Compensation commitments

A principle of good corporate governance is that individual directors and senior executives should not be rewarded for poor performance. The UK Code therefore seeks to minimise payments of compensation to directors for loss of office.

Companies are obliged by law to honour the terms of service contracts with their executives. If an executive is dismissed, the company may therefore be obliged to make payments to buy itself out of the contract, and there may be additional compensation payable under employment law, for unfair dismissal.

In order to limit payments of compensation on loss of office, it is therefore essential to make suitable provisions in the individual's service contract, when this is first negotiated by the remuneration committee.

The UK Code states that when it negotiates the terms of a service contract with a new director, the remuneration committee should consider what the compensation payments might be in the event that the individual is dismissed. The aim of the committee should be to avoid rewarding poor performance. To this end, the committee should take a 'robust line on reducing compensation to reflect departing directors' obligations to mitigate loss'.

An individual dismissed by a company is required to try to mitigate the losses they suffered as a result of the dismissal. They can do this, for example, by finding new employment as soon as possible. A service contract may therefore provide for the total compensation on loss of office to be payable in stages (instead of in full at the time of dismissal) and for these payments to be halted if the individual finds new employment elsewhere.

## 10 REMUNERATION AND SHAREHOLDER ATTITUDES

Shareholders, particularly institutional investors, have shown a strong interest in remuneration as an issue in corporate governance. The views of insurance companies and pension funds are most often expressed by their trade associations, the Association of British Insurers and the National Association of Pension Funds. A role of the institutional representative bodies is to guide and possibly co-ordinate the decisions of their members.

The Association of British Insurers has issued guidelines for its members on executive remuneration (Table 7.1). These are consistent with the principles and provisions of the UK Corporate Governance Code, but are more specific in detail. It is useful for directors to check the conformity of their company with the following ABI guidelines.

**Table 7.1** The ABI guidelines on executive remuneration, 2011

| ABI guideline | DOES THE COMPANY CONFORM? | |
| --- | :-: | :-: |
| | Y | N |
| The board of directors as a whole is accountable to shareholders for remuneration policy, but the main responsibility for senior executive remuneration lies with the remuneration committee. The committee should therefore maintain a 'timely and constructive dialogue' with the company's major shareholders and with the ABI, on matters such as changes in remuneration policy and incentive schemes. | ☐ | ☐ |
| Boards should be able to demonstrate that remuneration arrangements for senior executives are linked to the company's business objectives and strategies, taking risks into account. | ☐ | ☐ |
| Remuneration arrangements should be reviewed regularly, to ensure that they remain linked to corporate objectives and business strategy, taking risks into account. | ☐ | ☐ |

| ABI guideline | DOES THE COMPANY CONFORM? | |
|---|:---:|:---:|
| | Y | N |
| The company should maintain a 'constructive and timely dialogue' with the company's shareholders on matters relating to senior executive remuneration, such as changes in remuneration policy and share incentive schemes. | ☐ | ☐ |
| Executive remuneration should be linked to individual and corporate performance through graduated targets that align the interests of the executives with those of shareholders. | ☐ | ☐ |
| Executives must not receive rewards unless they are justified by performance. | ☐ | ☐ |
| The remuneration committee should guard against the possibility of unexpected windfall gains for individuals when designing share-based incentive schemes. | ☐ | ☐ |
| The remuneration committee should pay particular attention to the remuneration of senior executives who are not directors. The chairman and NEDs should not receive incentives geared to share price performance, since this could affect their ability to 'provide impartial oversight and advice'. | ☐ | ☐ |
| Any material ex gratia payments to an executive must be fully explained and justified, and should be subject to shareholder approval before they are paid. | ☐ | ☐ |
| Any payment of a bonus for the completion of a transaction should be subject to shareholder consent. (Shareholders should not normally support 'transaction bonuses'. These are bonuses that are paid on the successful completion of a particular transaction, such as the completion of a takeover.) | ☐ | ☐ |
| Remuneration committees should review share incentive schemes regularly, to make sure that they remain effective. | ☐ | ☐ |
| Substantial amendment to any share incentive scheme should be submitted to shareholders for approval. The cost of a share incentive scheme should be disclosed at the time that shareholder approval for the scheme is sought. | ☐ | ☐ |
| There should be limits to the dilution of shareholdings as a result of share incentive schemes. | ☐ | ☐ |
| The phasing of the award of shares and granting of share options 'is encouraged'. This will lessen the likelihood of problems with 'under water' options. | ☐ | ☐ |

## Severance payments for loss of office: attitudes of institutional investors

The investment institutions are also clear about their attitude to severance payments for loss of office. A joint statement by the ABI and NAPF (2008) commented:

'It is unacceptable that failure, which detracts from the value of an enterprise and which can threaten the livelihood of employees, can result in large payments to its departing leaders. Executives, whose remuneration is already at a level which allows for the risk inherent in their role, should show leadership in aligning their financial interests with those of their shareholders.'

## The significance of shareholder attitudes

Shareholder views on remuneration packages can be important. Institutional investors are now being encouraged to use their votes at general meetings.

The power of individual shareholders in large companies is usually restricted. Even the largest shareholders usually do not own a large proportion of the shares in their company, and it is very difficult for shareholders to act in unison to achieve a majority of votes against or for a resolution at any general meeting of the company.

However, institutional investors are increasingly active, and remuneration committees need to be aware that proposed incentive schemes, or the remuneration package of a senior executive such as the CEO, may arouse strong opposition.

Shareholders can express their displeasure with remuneration policy and remuneration packages by voting collectively in any of the following ways:

- to vote against a proposed new incentive scheme;
- to vote their disapproval of the remuneration report (see later); or
- to vote against the re-election of a director who is retiring by rotation, particularly if the director is a member of the remuneration committee or is a beneficiary of a generous remuneration package.

---

CASE EXAMPLE
................

## SHAREHOLDERS AND REMUNERATION

At the company's AGM in May 2009, shareholders of Royal Dutch Shell voted against an executive pay plan by voting down the remuneration report with a majority of 59%. The shareholders were objecting to a discretionary pay award to directors for performance in 2006–08, even though the performance targets were not met. The vote against a remuneration report is not binding, but in

---

response to the vote, the chairman said he would be talking to major share-holders. At the same AGM, the only member of the remuneration commit-tee up for re-election was re-elected with a large majority (only 5% against), but following investor pressure the chairman of the remuneration committee resigned later in the year. In February 2010, the company sent a letter to share-holders announcing changes to the executive remuneration arrangements.

In 2009, a 55% majority of shareholders of Punch Taverns voted against the remuneration report at the AGM. Shareholders were expressing their dis-approval of large pay awards to senior executives in a year when the group's reported losses had quintupled to over £400 million and dividend payments were suspended. The ABI had issued a red top alert to its members, advising them to vote against the remuneration report.

In 2102 54% of shareholders at the AGM of Aviva voted against the remu-neration report – only the fourth time that this ever had happened in a FTSE 100 company. The following week, Aviva's CEO left the company with £1.75 million in severance pay. During the CEO's five-year tenure in office, the com-pany's share price had fallen by 60%. The chairman of the remuneration com-mittee is reported to have commented: "We could and should have done more to engage with shareholders'.

## 11 THE REMUNERATION REPORT

Quoted companies are required by the Companies Act to prepare a directors' remuneration report each year, which must be approved by the board. This report is normally issued as part of the annual report and accounts, and may include the report on the work of the remuneration committee.

Shareholders must vote at the annual general meeting on a resolution to approve the report. The vote is advisory only, and shareholders do not have the power to reject the remuneration package for any individual director.

The report must include extensive disclosures about remuneration policy, the incentive arrangements for individual directors and the total remuneration of each individual director for the year, analysed into its component parts.

Some of the information in the report is subject to audit by the company's exter-nal auditors.

Although the vote on the remuneration report is advisory only, the shareholders can express their opposition to the company's remuneration policy and practices by voting not to approve the report – and sometimes they do.

In its Corporate Governance Policy and Voting Guidelines the NAPF recommends that voting against the remuneration report is generally an appropriate way for shareholders to register their concern about a company's remuneration practices. However, where 'severe and persistent infringements of good practice' occur, and there is evidence that the company's remuneration policy is not aligned with the interests of the company's shareholders, shareholders may also vote against the re-election of the chairman of the remuneration committee or any remuneration committee member.

### Proposal for legislative changes on senior executive remuneration

The UK government has now accepted the view in 2012 that shareholders should be given greater influence over their company's remuneration policy and that there should be more transparency and comparability (between companies) in reports on remuneration.

In 2013, the government introduced new legislation, effective from 1 October 2013. The Enterprise and Regulatory Reform Act 2013 amends the Companies Act for directors' remuneration in quoted companies. Shareholders in quoted companies should have a binding vote on pay policy at the AGM every three years. This should be a vote on a forward-looking remuneration policy report.

- Once a pay policy has been approved by the shareholders, the company cannot make payments that are outside the permitted scope of the policy.
- Any proposed change in the policy within the three-year period must be put to the shareholders in a binding vote.
- If any payment is made without the required approval, any directors who authorised the payment may be jointly and severally liable to indemnify the company for any loss that it incurs as a result.

As part of this pay policy, companies must explain their approach to exit payments (severance payments) on the departure of a senior board member. This should also be subject to the binding shareholder vote. When a director leaves, the company will immediately have to publish a statement of the exit payment that has been agreed: this cannot be outside the permitted scope of the remuneration policy approved by the shareholders.

New regulations have also been issued setting out the required content of a directors' remuneration report for large and medium-sized quoted companies.

These are the Large and Medium-Sized Companies and Groups (Accounts and Report) Regulations 2013.

Among the required disclosures, companies have to report a single figure for the total pay that each director receives each year. This figure will include all rewards, including bonuses and long-term incentives. The aim is to create a reporting that improves the comparability between companies on directors' pay.

### Directors' remuneration and smaller quoted companies

The Quoted Companies Alliance (QCA) issued a Remuneration Committee Guide for Smaller Quoted Companies in 2012. This guide covers issues such as the objectives of the remuneration committee in smaller quoted companies, factors to consider when setting policy for directors' remuneration, communicating with shareholders and the membership and functions of the remuneration committee.

## 12 CHECKLIST FOR A REMUNERATION COMMITTEE

The following checklist sets out requirements for linking remuneration to performance.

**Linking remuneration to performance**

| | | |
|---|---|---|
| 1.1 | Is the company policy on remuneration consistent with the principles and provisions in the UK Corporate Governance Code and with the guidelines of investment institutions on remuneration? | ☐ |
| 1.2 | Do the main institutional shareholders in the company support the company's remuneration policy? | ☐ |
| 1.3 | Is there an appropriate balance between basic pay, short-term incentives and longer-term incentives? | ☐ |
| 1.4 | Are members of the remuneration committee satisfied that the performance targets for executives are appropriate and closely linked to achieving the company's objectives? | ☐ |
| 1.5 | Do the performance targets offer high rewards to executives only for exceptionally good performance? Or could an executive receive high rewards for only moderate performance? | ☐ |
| 1.6 | Is the remuneration committee satisfied that the pension rights in the remuneration package of each executive are appropriate, and can be justified to institutional shareholders? | ☐ |

## Linking remuneration to performance

1.7 Have the pay and performance targets for executives been compared objectively □ with the pay and performance targets for executives in a suitable peer group of other companies?

1.8 Does the remuneration committee check carefully that performance targets have □ been met before approving the payment of rewards?

1.9 Do the remuneration packages of executives ensure that the company does not □ give 'rewards for failure' in the event that the executive is dismissed for poor performance?

1.10 Do any executives have a contract with a notice period in excess of 12 months? □ If so, how is this justified?

1.11 Is the remuneration committee satisfied that the remuneration policy of the □ company and the remuneration for individual directors are transparent and clearly presented to shareholders and the public?

# CHAPTER EIGHT

# Financial reporting, auditing and the audit committee

....................

## OVERVIEW

The board of directors collectively has a responsibility for reporting to shareholders. The board must account to shareholders for their stewardship of the company, and it is essential that the report and accounts should be reliable and clear. Responsibilities for financial reporting are among the most important responsibilities of all directors, and especially for the NEDs on the audit committee.

The need for best practice guidelines in corporate governance was first recognised as a result of scandals involving misleading financial reporting and doubts about the reliability of published company accounts and even the reliability of external auditing.

Rightly or wrongly, external auditors have sometimes been suspected of caving in to the arguments of a client company's executives – on matters such as accounting policy and accounting estimates – to avoid the risk of losing the favour of the company's decision-makers and losing their audit (and non-audit) work. However, the directors of a company have the legal responsibility for financial reporting, and it is wrong to assume that the external auditors have a responsibility for the preparation of 'true and fair' accounts.

The UK Corporate Governance Code recommends that there should be an audit committee of independent NEDs, with a range of responsibilities. These include making sure that the external auditors remain independent and the relationship between the auditors and the company's executives does not become too close or dependent. The audit committee's responsibilities should also include monitoring the process of preparing the financial accounts and reviewing the quality of the audit, including recommending a change of auditors where appropriate.

The chairman of the audit committee should have recent relevant financial experience, and the other members of the audit committee should have a suitable level of financial literacy. The skills of audit committee members should be sufficient to enable them to perform a monitoring role.

The work of the audit committee can be demanding, and there are growing pressures on committee members to give more time to their work.

## 1 CORPORATE GOVERNANCE, FINANCIAL REPORTING AND AUDITING

### The accountability of directors to shareholders: the annual report and accounts

The directors of a company are in effect agents acting on behalf of the shareholders. As such, they are accountable to the shareholders for their 'stewardship' of the company's assets, and for the company's performance.

A critical aspect of accountability is the presentation of the annual report and accounts to the shareholders for approval. The annual report and accounts is the most important document for the delivery of information to the shareholders about the financial position and financial performance of the company. The information may be used by shareholders and other investors to make investment decisions, about buying or selling shares.

For NEDs, financial reporting and auditing are important areas of responsibility, because:

- all directors have legal responsibilities for the information presented in the annual report and accounts; and
- independent NEDs make up the audit committee of the board.

## 2 FINANCIAL REPORTING: THE DUTIES AND RESPONSIBILITIES OF DIRECTORS

The directors of companies have certain legal requirements with regard to financial reporting:

- They have a duty to prepare annual financial statements, which must be approved by the board and signed by a board member on behalf of the board. Public companies must submit the annual accounts to the shareholders for approval and file a copy with the Registrar of Companies within seven months of the end of the financial year (Companies Act 2006 requirement).
- They must prepare a directors' report, which must also be approved by the board and signed on their behalf by a board member or the company secretary.
- The directors of a quoted company must publish a directors' remuneration report, which must also be approved by the board as a whole and signed on their behalf by a board member or the company secretary.
- The directors must submit the report and accounts to the shareholders for approval at the annual general meeting of the company, and shareholders must also be invited to approve the directors' remuneration report (in an advisory, non-binding vote).

### The role of the external auditors

The role of a company's external auditors is to review the annual financial statements and make a report to shareholders, giving their opinion about whether the financial statements give a 'true and fair view' of the financial position and financial performance of the company.

The report by the external auditors, included within the published annual report and accounts, is intended to provide reassurance to the shareholders that they can rely on the information in the financial statements.

### The UK Corporate Governance Code and responsibilities of the directors for financial and business reporting

The UK Code states that the board has a responsibility to present a fair, balanced and understandable assessment of the company's position and prospects.

- Provision C.1.1 states that the directors should explain in the annual report their responsibility for preparing the annual report and financial statements.
- They should state that they consider the annual report and accounts, taken as a whole, to be fair, balanced and understandable and that it provides the information necessary for shareholders to assess 'the company's performance, business model and strategy'.
- There should also be a statement by the auditors about their reporting responsibilities.

Provision C1.2 goes on to clarify the meaning of 'business model'. It states that the directors should include in the annual report a statement of how the company generates value or preserves value over the longer term, and indicates that this is the meaning of the business model. The statement should also explain the board's strategy for delivering its objectives.

It should be apparent that the board's 'traditional' responsibility for financial reporting has been extended to include business reporting as well.

There is often a certain amount of confusion and misunderstanding about responsibilities for financial reporting. A commonly held view is that the external auditors are in some way responsible for making sure that the financial statements are reliable, and that if the financial statements prove to be misleading, the auditors must be negligent and liable to the shareholders of the company. High levels of expectation about what auditors should do may lead to legal action against auditors if this level of expectation is not met.

In reality, the board of directors are responsible for the financial statements. If these are misleading or materially incorrect, the directors themselves may be liable.

### Responsibilities of management (directors) and auditors for fraud and error

Management is responsible for preparing financial statements that show a 'true and fair view'. This role is reinforced by principles of good corporate governance, which require management to set up appropriate reporting systems and internal controls.

- Management is therefore responsible for the prevention and detection of fraud and error in the accounting system.

- The auditors' responsibility is to obtain reasonable assurance that the financial statements, taken as a whole, are free from material misstatement, whether caused by fraud or error.

It is not the primary responsibility of auditors to prevent or detect fraud or error, although the audit may act as a deterrent to fraud. Auditors may also discover error or fraud during the course of their audit work, but they are by no means certain to do so whenever error or fraud has occurred. Auditors may also be potentially liable for failing to detect fraud during an audit when it should have been within their professional competence to do so. (The law on auditor liability for failure to detect fraud may vary between countries.)

## 3 FINANCIAL REPORTING: POTENTIAL PROBLEMS

Financial reporting is a central issue in corporate governance. The report and accounts allow the shareholders to assess whether the company has been governed in the interests of the shareholders. However, shareholders can do this only if the financial statements are reliable. The reliability of financial statements depends on:

- the honesty of the company in preparing the report and accounts;
- the choice of accounting policies by the company in presenting the financial results;
- the care used by the directors in satisfying themselves that the accounts provide a true and fair view and that everything of relevance has been properly reported;
- the opinion of the external auditors, which shareholders should be able to rely on as the opinion of independent professionals.

In the UK, the Cadbury Code on corporate governance was issued in 1992 as a direct consequence of deep concerns about the quality of financial reporting and doubts about the ability of the auditing profession to provide sufficient assurances to investors about the reliability of company financial statements. Similar concerns emerged in the US from the end of 2001 with the collapse of major corporations such as Enron. Misleading financial reporting may be the result of dishonesty and fraud, but more often is likely to be the result of aggressive accounting policies.

On occasion, some companies may want to report strong growth in revenues and profits, or even to improve the look of the balance sheet by 'hiding' debts or other liabilities. The company could probably succeed in presenting an excessively favourable picture of its performance for a number of years, particularly when the economy is strong and business is growing. Eventually, however, it becomes impossible to 'massage' the figures any further. Unless the business can sustain a strong 'real' growth in its operations, it cannot achieve strong profits growth indefinitely. Eventually, a company that uses 'creative accounting' methods will have to report declining profits or re-state the accounts for previous financial years and disclose hitherto hidden losses.

### FRC report on Effective Company Stewardship

In 2011, the Financial Reporting Council produced a report: 'Effective Company Stewardship: Enhancing Corporate Reporting and Audit'. This report followed a review by the FRC into the lessons that could be learned for financial reporting and audit by the global financial crisis in banking in 2007–09. The report referred to several studies that had been published, criticising the quality of company reporting.

- A 2011 report by Deloitte stated that company reports and accounts for listed companies were 41% longer than in 2005 and on average were over 100 pages long.
- Another report by Black Sun (2009) found that 40% of companies failed to report any non-financial Key Performance Indicators, and although the quantity of reporting on corporate social responsibility had increased, the quality of the material was generally poor since it did not explain how CSR was an integral part of the company's business.
- Black Sun also found that most narrative reporting on risk was a list of 'boilerplate disclosures' that did not provide meaningful information about the potential impact of risks or what the company was doing to mitigate them.
- Narrative reporting on corporate governance was also mainly a 'box-ticking exercise'.

The FRC report went on to state its aims with regard to financial and business reporting.

- There should be higher quality narrative reporting, particularly on business strategy and risk management. The annual report should communicate high-quality and relevant narrative and financial information.
- Directors should take full responsibility for ensuring that the annual report, viewed as a whole, provides a fair and balanced report on their stewardship of the business.
- Directors should describe in more detail the steps that they take to ensure the reliability of the information on which the management of their company is based.

The report also recognised the problems directors face with the complexity of financial reporting. Financial reporting by many companies has moved a long way from the traditional approach of reporting assets and liabilities at their historical cost. Some assets and liabilities are reported at their market value, rather than at cost. Although this change has improved the potential value of accounts – historical numbers are easy to obtain but often meaningless – it has increased their complexity and requires companies and auditors to exercise significantly greater judgement. As a result, the reliability of financial statements is now more dependent on:

- the approach that the company takes to establishing the current values of assets and liabilities; and
- the quality of the external audit.

---

CASE EXAMPLE
................

# ENRON

The collapse of US energy corporation Enron is one of the most notorious examples of misleading financial reporting. Enron used accounting policies that increased its reported income and asset values, and took liabilities off its balance sheet. In one transaction, for example, it recorded about $200 million of project expenses as assets, even though the projects had effectively been cancelled. This was justified on the grounds that the projects had not yet been cancelled officially. Capitalising expenses in this way means that expenses are not charged against profits, but add to the reported value of the company's assets. Another technique used extensively by the company was to set up special purpose entities in order to take liabilities off the balance sheet and avoid having to report losses. After allegations of misleading financial reporting by a whistleblower, initially rejected by the company, the company had to re-state its financial statements for the previous four years. This reduced the reported value of the company's equity by 10%. The company collapsed towards the end of 2001.

Enron's auditors did not express any concerns about the company's accounting policies. The auditors were the Houston office of Arthur Andersen, at the time one of the five largest audit firms in the world. It was subsequently alleged that the Houston office of the firm was not independent from the company, because it relied on Enron for over 25% of its annual income for audit and

---

non-audit work. When the Securities and Exchange Commission announced an investigation into the collapse of Enron, Andersen tried to cover up evidence of inadequate audit work by shredding several tons of documents and deleting thousands of e-mails and computer files.

---

CASE EXAMPLE
················

# CONNAUGHT

UK property service group Connaught was a FTSE 250 company. In June 2010 the company issued the first of two profit warnings and announced that its accounting practices were being independently reviewed by Deloitte (who were not the company's external auditors). The problem was reported to be connected with aggressive accounting policies relating to when and how the company booked revenue and costs for its long-term contracts. In August 2010, it was rumoured that the accountancy issues were more widespread than originally thought, and were not just restricted to contracts in its social housing maintenance division. Over a period of less than three months, the company's shares collapsed in price and lost most of their value, and in mid-August its total equity market capitalisation was just £20 million. In September the largest of the group companies went into administration.

The profit warnings by the company and the independent review of its accounting practices undermined the perceived reliability of the company's financial reporting. This in turn suggested serious problems with corporate governance.

---

## 4  GOING CONCERN STATEMENT

The going concern assumption in financial reporting is that the company (reporting entity) will be able to continue in business for the foreseeable future; therefore assets in the financial statements can be valued on a going concern basis rather than a 'break-up' basis.

'A company is judged to be a going concern if, for the foreseeable future, there is a high level of confidence that it will have the necessary liquid resources to meet its liabilities as they fall due and will be able to sustain its business model, strategy and operations and remain solvent, including in the face of reasonably predictable internally or externally-generated shocks' (FRC Guidance).

Various regulations and accounting standards require the directors of companies to make a going concern statement in the annual report. This is a statement giving their opinion about whether the company is a going concern and will continue to be so for the foreseeable future (for at least the next year from the date of the statement).

- The UK Corporate Governance Code includes a provision (Provision C.1.3) that the directors should report in the company's annual and half-yearly financial statements that the business is a going concern, 'with supporting assumptions and qualifications as necessary'.
- The UK Listing Rules also require the directors to make a statement in the report and accounts that the company is a going concern, together with supporting assumptions and qualifications as necessary.
- Other (non-listed) companies may be subject to the requirements of international accounting standards (IAS1) or UK accounting standards and UK generally accepted accounting practice that the directors should satisfy themselves that it is reasonable for them to conclude that the company is a going concern.

There are two purposes of going concern reporting:

(1) **Stewardship purpose** – The board should provide information to stakeholders about the company's economic and financial viability, helping to demonstrate the board's stewardship and governance of the company.

(2) **Financial reporting purpose** – The statement should disclose reliable information about going concern that is needed for the financial statements to give a true and fair view.

The ability of a company to continue in business for the foreseeable future is often a question of cash flow (liquidity) rather than profit or loss. A loss-making company can continue in business if it has the cash to pay what it owes, but a company cannot continue as a going concern if it runs out of cash.

The Financial Reporting Council has issued guidance on the preparation of going concern statements, significantly titled *Going Concern and Liquidity Risk: Guidance for Directors of UK Companies* (2009). This guidance states that directors should carry out their assessment carefully, with a view to reaching one of three possible conclusions:

- There are no material concerns about the ability of the company to continue as a going concern.
- There are material concerns, but the use of the going concern basis for accounting remains appropriate. Suitable disclosures should be made in the going concern statement about the concerns that the directors have.

- The company will have no alternative but to cease trading or go into liquidation, therefore use of the going concern assumption to prepare the financial statements is inappropriate.

In the past, a typical going concern statement within a corporate report might have been as follows:

'The directors, on the basis of current financial projections and facilities available, have a reasonable expectation that the company and group have adequate resources to continue in operational existence for the foreseeable future. The directors accordingly continue to adopt the going concern basis in the preparation of the group's financial statements.'

Going concern statements should now be more informative, explaining the reasons why the directors have arrived at their view. The following examples are based on illustrative going concern statements in the FRC's 2009 guidance:

---

**CASE EXAMPLE**
...............
## GOING CONCERN STATEMENTS

**A small company that complies with the UK accounting standard for small companies**

'There has been a significant reduction in requests for quotations for contracts and the directors expect the number of contracts and sales revenue to fall substantially next year. However, costs are expected to reduce by a similar proportion and the company should be able to carry on its business within its available overdraft limit. The directors are not aware of any reason why this overdraft facility might be withdrawn. Consequently they have adopted the going concern basis for preparing the financial statements.'

**A larger company**

'The company's business activities, and the factors that are likely to affect its future business performance, are set out in the Business Review in this document. The company's financial position, including its cash flows, liquidity position and borrowing facilities are described in the Finance Director's Review. In addition, notes to the financial statements include a description of the company's objectives and policies and processes for managing its capital; its financial risk management objectives; and its exposures to credit

---

> risk and liquidity risk. The company has considerable financial resources. As a consequence, the directors believe that the company is well placed to manage its business risks successfully in spite of the uncertain economic outlook.
>
> The directors therefore continue to adopt the going concern basis of accounting in preparing the annual financial statements.'

The directors may be personally liable if they make a statement that the company is a going concern without giving the matter full and careful consideration. Liability could arise if the company subsequently goes into liquidation within the next 12 months and shareholders claim that they relied on the going concern statement when making their investment decisions.

### Going concern assumption: factors to consider

The going concern assessment process should have two related elements:

- a review of the company's solvency and liquidity position and significant risks informed by the company's business planning processes, risk management framework and internal controls; and
- Based on that review, a decision by the board as to whether the financial statements should be prepared on a going concern basis and whether there are material uncertainties about the company's ability to continue as a going concern.

All directors, including NEDs, should be aware of factors that should be considered when deciding to support a statement that the company is a going concern. It is a subjective area where judgement is usually required to assess the uncertainties in the assumptions that are being made.

Factors that may cast doubt on the going concern status of a company include:

- recurring operating losses;
- a heavy dependence on short-term finance for long-term assets;
- working capital deficiencies (such as a large bank overdraft, or exceptionally low levels of inventory);
- high financial gearing (a high ratio of debt capital to equity);
- loan interest payments in arrears;
- excessive inventory or obsolete inventory;
- a deterioration in the entity's relationships with its banks (evidenced, perhaps, in written correspondence);

- the company uses out-of-date technology;
- there is a low level of current sales orders;
- there are legal proceedings that may jeopardise the company's ability to continue in business;
- there has been a loss of key management or staff; and
- there has been a loss of a key customer or supplier.

## Sharman Panel of Inquiry

The FRC established the Sharman Panel of Enquiry in 2011, in response to concerns about the limited information provided by companies about their going concern status.

The main concern was that going concern statements were restricted to informing shareholders about the possibility of financial catastrophe in the foreseeable future.

The Panel recommended that to improve the robustness and reporting of the going concern assessment, the boards of companies complying with the FRC's Corporate Governance Code should:

- over a period longer than 12 months, consider the threats to the company's business model and capital adequacy 'looking through the economic cycle and the company's own business cycle';
- have a high level of confidence that solvency and liquidity risks can be managed effectively for a period of at least 12 months from approval of the annual financial statements;
- as part of its discussion of principal risks in the business review, disclose the significant risks to the company's solvency and liquidity and how they are being managed; and
- confirm that it has undertaken a 'robust' going concern assessment.

The Panel also recommended that the company's auditors should consider the board's report on the robustness of its assessment and the disclosures about going concern status in the annual report, and confirm in the audit report that there is nothing they wish to add or draw attention to.

The FRC issued a consultation paper on the Sharman Panel recommendations in 2013. At the time of going to press, there had not been any further developments.

## 5 THE NEED FOR AN AUDIT COMMITTEE

The UK Corporate Governance Code (Principle C.3) requires that a board of directors should establish formal and transparent arrangements for:

- considering how they should apply the corporate reporting and risk management and internal control principles; and
- maintaining an appropriate relationship with the company's auditors.

For this purpose, the company should establish an audit committee as a committee of the board, which should be given certain responsibilities. A part of the role of the audit committee relates to risk management and internal control. This aspect of its work is described in Chapter 9. This chapter concentrates on the role of the audit committee with regard to financial reporting and the external auditors.

There is now also a statutory requirement for an audit committee in quoted companies, with the implementation of the EU Statutory Audit Directive in the UK from 2008. However, for listed companies the existing provisions of the UK Code (formerly the Combined Code) were sufficient to meet the requirements of the EU Directive.

# 6   THE ROLE AND RESPONSIBILITIES OF THE AUDIT COMMITTEE

## UK Corporate Governance Code provisions

The role and responsibilities of the audit committee are specified in the UK Corporate Governance Code, and supplementary guidance on audit committees is provided in the FRC's *Guidance on Audit Committees*, which adopted previous guidance known as the Smith Guidance.

The UK Code lists the role and responsibilities of an audit committee. Excluding those concerned with risk management, internal control and internal audit, they are to:

- monitor the integrity of the company's financial statements and any formal announcements relating to the company's financial performance. In doing so, it should review 'significant financial judgements' that these statements and announcements contain;
- make recommendations to the board for the appointment, reappointment or removal of the company's external auditors, for recommending to the shareholders for approval at a general meeting of the company (usually the AGM);
- approve the remuneration and terms of engagement of the external auditors (the initial negotiation is between executive management and the auditors);

- review and monitor the independence and objectivity of the external auditors, and also the effectiveness of the audit process;
- develop and implement the company's policy on using the external auditors to provide non-audit services. This should take into account any 'relevant ethical guidance', for example, from the audit profession. The audit committee should report to the board on any actions or improvements that it considers necessary and recommend the steps to be taken.

The terms of reference of the audit committee should be 'made available', and a separate section of the annual report should describe the work of the committee.

### Statutory Audit Directive and the audit committee's responsibilities

The EU Statutory Audit Directive requires that the responsibilities of an audit committee must, as a minimum, include the following:

- monitoring the financial reporting process;
- monitoring the statutory audit;
- monitoring the effectiveness of the company's internal control, risk management systems and (where applicable) internal audit; and
- reviewing and monitoring the independence of the company's external auditors, including the provision of non-audit work to the auditors.

The provisions of the UK Code and FRC *Guidance* are consistent with this.

### The audit committee and the board of directors

It is important to recognise that although these responsibilities are delegated by the board to the audit committee, the board as a whole, and each individual director, is responsible for providing financial statements that give a true and fair view of the company's position and performance. The FRC *Guidance* includes the following observations:

- 'While all directors have a duty to act in the interests of the company, the audit committee has a particular role, acting independently from the executive, to ensure that the interests of the shareholders are properly protected in relation to financial reporting and internal control.'
- However, audit committee arrangements need to be proportionate to the task, and will therefore vary with the size, complexity and risk profile of the company.
- The audit committee is just a committee of the board and all board directors are equally responsible for the company's affairs, as a matter of law. 'Any disagreement within the board, including disagreement between the

audit committee's members and the rest of the board, should be resolved at board level.'

- Management has an obligation to ensure that the audit committee is fully informed. In addition, the executive directors have a common law duty to provide all directors with the information they need to discharge their responsibilities: this includes a legal duty to keep the audit committee properly informed.

- The audit committee in turn has a responsibility to keep the board informed. Provision C.3.4 of the UK Code states that where requested by the board, the audit committee should provide advice on the annual report and accounts, and whether these are fair, balanced and understandable. The audit committee should therefore be expected to provide advice to the full board that will enable the board to fulfil its responsibilities for financial and business reporting.

The FRC Guidance states that the audit committee should report to the board on how it has discharged its responsibilities, including:

- the significant issues that it considers in relation to the financial statements, and how these were addressed;

- its assessment of the effectiveness of the external audit process and its recommendation on the appointment or reappointment of the external auditor; and

- issues where the board has asked for the audit committee's opinion.

Note: The Quoted Companies Alliance (QCA) has published an Audit Committee Guide for Smaller Quoted Companies, which can be found on the QCA website (see the Directory).

## 7 THE COMPOSITION OF THE AUDIT COMMITTEE AND THE SKILLS OF ITS MEMBERS

The UK Code states that an audit committee should consist of at least three members, who should all be independent NEDs (Code Provision C.3.1). The audit committee of smaller companies (companies outside the FTSE 350) should consist of at least two members, all independent NEDs.

At least one of the committee members should have 'recent and relevant financial experience'. Ideally this individual should have a professional accountancy qualification, and the financial knowledge required from the other committee members will vary according to the nature of the company and the complexity of its business.

In smaller companies the chairman of the company may be a member of the audit committee (but not the committee chairman), provided they were considered independent when first appointed to the board chairmanship.

As a matter of good governance practice, the company secretary should act as secretary to the audit committee. One of the functions of the company secretary should be to ensure that there are good communication flows between the audit committee and the main board.

The FRC *Guidance* also recommends that:

- appointments to the audit committee should be made by the board of directors, on the recommendation of the nomination committee in consultation with the audit committee chairman;
- appointments should initially be for a three-year period, and extendable by no more than two additional three-year periods, subject to the requirement that the director must remain independent.

### Skills, experience and training

The FRC *Guidance* suggests that the company should provide a suitable induction programme for new members of the committee, and there should be ongoing training for committee members. This should include training in an understanding of the principles of and developments in financial reporting and related company law.

Both the induction and the ongoing training may take the form of attendance at formal courses and conferences, internal company talks and seminars, and briefings by external advisers.

## 8 THE WORK OF THE AUDIT COMMITTEE

The FRC *Guidance* comments that many of the core duties of the audit committee are expressed in terms of 'oversight', 'assessment' and 'review'. The committee is not responsible for carrying out functions that properly belong with the company's executive management, such as the responsibility to prepare the financial statements.

Similarly, the audit committee should satisfy itself that there is a proper allocation of management responsibilities for the day-to-day monitoring of financial controls, but the committee should not do the monitoring itself.

However, the high-level oversight function of the committee may occasionally lead it into much more detailed work when something seems to be seriously wrong. For example, if the audit committee is not satisfied by the explanation from executive management and the auditors about the use of a particular accounting policy, the committee may be forced to look into the matter in some detail, and obtain independent professional advice if necessary.

## Frequency of meetings of the committee

The audit committee chairman, in consultation with the company secretary, should decide the frequency and timing of meetings. This will depend on the exact responsibilities of the committee.

The FRC *Guidance* suggests that there should be at least three meetings each year, to coincide with key points in the audit cycle. These might be when:

- the audit plans for the year are available;
- the interim financial statements are near completion;
- the preliminary announcement of the annual results, or the full annual report and accounts, are near completion.

Figure 8.1 provides a suggested annual cycle of audit committee activity based on three meetings a year.

The audit committee should also meet with the external auditors at least once each year, without any executive directors or management present, to discuss any matters relating to the work of the committee and matters arising from the audit.

Only the committee chairman and members are entitled to attend meetings of the committee. However, the committee can decide to invite other individuals to attend for an entire meeting or for a particular agenda item. The FRC *Guidance* comments that it should be expected that the committee will regularly invite the lead partner of the external auditors and the company's finance director.

The *Guidance* also comments that although formal meetings of the audit committee are 'at the heart of its work', it should be expected that the committee chairman (and to a lesser extent the other committee members) will want to keep in touch with various key people on a continuing basis – such as the board chairman, CEO, finance director, audit lead partner and head of internal audit.

## 9 THE AUDIT COMMITTEE AND FINANCIAL REPORTING

As a part of its responsibility for monitoring the integrity of the financial statements, the audit committee should review the significant financial issues and judgements that have been made by management in connection with the preparation of the statements.

- Management is responsible for preparing complete and accurate financial statements.

| PHASE | 1 INTERIM CLEARANCE MEETING | 2 RISK REVIEW AND YEAR-END PLANNING MEETING | 3 YEAR-END CLEARANCE MEETING |
|---|---|---|---|
| ACTIVITIES [Key areas of focus at certain points in the year] | 1.1 Review and approve the Interim Accounts 1.2 Meet the external auditors to review Interims and agree plans for the year-end 1.3 Comment on accounting policies/procedures 1.4 Consider reports from internal audit and / or other assurance providers 1.5 Review Audit Committee performance assessment and any training needs | 2.1 Undertake initial review of internal control and risk management 2.2 Approve draft external audit plans, fees and timetable 2.3 Consider any technical matters (i.e. pensions, related parties) 2.4 Approve internal audit / assurance plans or review the need for an internal audit function/capability 2.5 Consider 'whistleblowing' arrangements | 3.1 Agree internal control, corporate governance and Audit Committee reports 3.2 Consider and recommend Board approval of the Annual Report and Accounts 3.3 Meet the external auditors and review their report(s) 3.4 Undertake post-audit review and approve external audit fees 3.5 Consider internal audit / assurance reports and summary of year's activities |
| INTERACTION [If no Internal Audit, may be other internal / external functions] | – The Board – Finance Director and Finance – External Auditors – Internal Audit | – The Board – Senior Management and Business Units – Internal Audit | – The Board – Finance Director and Finance – External Auditors – Internal Audit |
| DOCUMENTS [Example documents to be reviewed / approved] | ➤ Interim Accounts ➤ External audit plans and fees ➤ Accounting policies and procedures ➤ Internal audit and other assurance reports | ➤ Formal objectives and terms of reference ➤ Risk and control register ➤ External audit planning memorandum / engagement letter ➤ Internal audit / assurance annual plan | ➤ Annual Report and Accounts ➤ Audit Committee report and internal control report ➤ External audit reports (management letter) ➤ Internal audit / assurance review of the year |

**Figure 8.1** Audit committee: annual audit cycle

- The audit committee is responsible for considering significant accounting policies and any significant estimates or judgements that have been made in preparing the financial statements.

The committee should also review the clarity and completeness of disclosure in the financial statements, particularly in the notes to the accounts.

It should also review related information that is published with the report and accounts, such as the business review or (from 1 October 2013) the strategic report and the corporate governance statements relating to the audit and risk management.

### Health checks

The audit committee, taking suitable advice if necessary, should assess the apparent 'health' of the financial statements. The finance director may be asked to answer questions from the audit committee.

Examples of 'health checks' that the audit committee might wish to make (at a level consistent with their financial literacy) include whether:

- the accounting policies used by the company are consistent with those used by other companies in the industry;
- the policy on accounting recognition is appropriate, so that revenue is not recognised too early in the income statement (profit and loss account);
- there have been substantial asset write-downs due to impairment;
- the policy on capitalisation of expenditure (such as development expenditure and expenditures incurred in relation to the acquisition of new assets) is appropriate and not too 'aggressive';
- there are unusual trends and features in the accounts, such as high profits and poor cash flows;
- there are large provisions in the accounts and, if so, whether these seem appropriate. (Provisions can be used to move profits from one year to another, possibly in order to 'smooth' profits between different years.)

When the audit committee is dissatisfied with any aspect of the company's financial reporting, it should report its concerns to the full board.

## 10 THE AUDIT COMMITTEE AND THE EXTERNAL AUDITORS

An important function of the audit committee is to support the relationship between the company's external auditors and the senior executive management.

The auditors must work closely with the executive management when they conduct the annual audit. However, when there is a close working relationship, especially a relationship that has existed for many years, there is a risk that the auditors and management will become too familiar with each other. This leads to a risk that the auditors might be too willing to accept the views and judgements of management when they should perhaps be submitting these to much more rigorous scrutiny.

There is also a risk that a firm of auditors may become over-reliant financially on the work that it does for a particular corporate client. This may be both audit and non-audit work.

When an audit firm relies heavily on a particular company for fee income, and when decisions about awarding the work to the audit firm are taken by executive management, there is a strong risk that the audit firm will lose its independence. It will be in the best financial interests of the audit firm to cause as few difficulties for the company as possible when performing the audit, in order to improve their chances of:

- being awarded the audit work next year; and also
- being awarded non-audit work.

### Maintaining a proper relationship with the external auditors
A proper relationship between a company and its auditors means making sure that the auditors perform their work in an objective, independent and professional way. It is therefore appropriate corporate governance practice for the audit committee to be given various responsibilities with regard to the auditors.

These include the responsibility for:

- monitoring the continuing independence of the external auditors;
- deciding policy about awarding non-audit work to the company's external auditors;
- reviewing the work of the auditors; and
- making recommendations about the appointment, reappointment or removal of the auditors.

### Auditor independence
The FRC *Guidance* recommends that the audit committee should have procedures for ensuring each year the independence and objectivity of the external auditors. This assessment should involve the following:

- A consideration of all the relationships between the company and the audit firm, including non-audit work. The relationship may become too close, for example, when the audit firm receives a large amount of non-audit work from the company, or when the same audit partner acts as lead audit partner for the same company's audit for a long time.

- Obtaining reassurance that the audit firm and its staff have no connections with the company – family, financial, employment, investment or business relationship – that could adversely affect the auditor's independence and objectivity. To this end the audit committee should obtain each year from the audit firm information about the policies and procedures used by the firm to ensure its own independence from the company, including its policy on the rotation of audit partners for the company audit.

The audit committee should also agree with the board the company's policy on employing former employees of the audit firm – for example, appointing a former audit manager to a senior accounting position in the company. The Institute of Chartered Accountants in England and Wales (ICAEW) has introduced a rule that public companies should not be allowed to appoint a former auditor of the company to the board for at least two years after the individual concerned has left the audit firm.

---

CASE EXAMPLE
................

## SCHRODERS

Schroders announced in 2013 that it would be replacing PriceWaterhouseCoopers (PwC) as its auditor with KPMG. PwC had been the company's auditor for 50 years. The audit work is valuable: in 2011 PwC earned £2.7 million for its annual audit work and £1.8 million for other services to the company during the year.

This development may reflect the increasing willingness of large companies to change their auditors, but in the case of Schroders, the change may not have come as a surprise. The company had announced that it would be replacing its departing CFO with someone who had previously been a partner of PwC who had acted as the company's auditor. The new CFO would be taking up his position in May 2013, just 26 months since he worked as the company's auditor.

---

The risk is that when a company employs a former employee of the audit firm, the relationship between the company and the audit firm may become closer and more familiar.

The audit committee should also ensure that the audit firm complies with professional ethical guidelines about the **rotation** of **audit partners**. Currently, for the audit of listed companies in the UK, audit firms are required to change the audit engagement partner for a company's audit at least every five years.

The independence of the audit firm may also be put at risk by the amount of non-audit work performed by the audit firm for the company – especially if the non-audit work will be subject to audit during the annual audit cycle.

### Provision of non-audit work by the audit firm

Non-audit work may include matters such as:

- advice or consultancy on tax matters, especially tax planning;
- advice and assistance with IT systems;
- investigating targets for a potential takeover bid;
- doing some book-keeping work;
- providing outsourced internal audit services.

A problem with the audit firm doing non-audit work is that when the firm audits transactions that have been recommended to the company by its own consultants, it will be difficult for the auditors to take an independent view of the transactions, by questioning or disagreeing with the advice of the firm's own experts.

There are three broad approaches to the regulation of non-audit work by audit firms:

- There may be no restrictions at all on the provision of non-audit work by the audit firm.
- There may be a total prohibition on the provision of non-audit work by the audit firm. The Institute of Chartered Accountants in England and Wales (ICAEW) has commented, however: 'A blanket prohibition on the provision of non-audit services to audit clients can be inefficient for the client and is neither necessary to ensure independence, nor helpful in contributing to the knowledge necessary to ensure the quality of the audit.'
- There may be a partial prohibition or restriction. This could take either of two forms. There could be a prohibition on the external audit firm from taking on certain types of consultancy work where the independence of the firm could be put at risk, but no restrictions on other types of work. Alternatively a limit may be set on the fees that the audit firm should be allowed to earn each year from non-audit work.

As a matter of good corporate governance, these explanations should be based on good and convincing reasons.

The FRC *Guidance* makes the following recommendations:

- The audit committee should develop and recommend to the board a policy on the provision of non-audit services by the auditor. The policy objective should be to ensure that giving non-audit work to the audit firm will not put at risk the independence and objectivity of the auditors. The audit committee, in formulating such a policy, should consider:
  - whether the skills and experience of the audit firm make it an appropriate choice of supplier of the non-audit service;
  - whether there are safeguards in place to ensure that the independence and objectivity of the auditors will not be threatened;
  - the nature of the non-audit work and the level of fees – and in particular the total amount of fees for all non-audit work by the audit firm;
  - the criteria that govern the compensation/pay of individuals who carry out the audit.
- The audit committee should set and apply a formal policy specifying the types of non-audit work:
  - from which the audit firm must be excluded;
  - for which the audit firm may be engaged without referral to the audit committee, and;
  - for which a case-by-case decision is necessary. (It may be appropriate to give approval in advance for non-audit work in this category, subject to a limit on the fee, without prior reference for approval. However, decisions to award this work to the audit firm should be ratified at the next meeting of the audit committee.)

As a general rule, non-audit work should not be given to an audit firm when:

- the audit firm will have audit work done by its own staff (for example, book-keeping work); or
- an employee of the audit firm could potentially make management decisions on behalf of the company; or
- the work creates a mutual interest between the audit firm and the company; or
- the audit firm is put in a position of advocating the company's position to any other organisation, for example, in a legal dispute.

Note: The Auditing Practices Board (APB) (see Directory) has issued a number of Ethical Standards for auditors. These include Standards on integrity, objectivity and independence, and on non-audit services provided to audit clients. These Standards establish principles and essential procedures for auditors in their audit work, and outline safeguards that could be put in place, but they do not contain specific rules or regulations.

### Reviewing the work of the auditors

The FRC *Guidance* recommends that the audit committee should review the work of the auditors, at the beginning, during and at the end of the annual audit cycle.

- At the beginning of the audit cycle, the audit committee should ensure that appropriate plans are in place for the audit. It should consider whether the audit work plan is consistent with the scope of the audit engagement and what the auditors are required to accomplish. It should also satisfy itself that the audit firm proposes to commit enough resources to the audit, having regard to the seniority, expertise and experience of the audit team members.
- During the progress of the audit, the audit committee should review the issues raised by the auditors. It should:
  - discuss with the external auditors any issues that they have raised with the management, and whether or not these issues have been resolved;
  - review the key estimates and judgements used by management in preparing the financial statements;
  - review any errors discovered by the auditors and where these are material obtain a satisfactory explanation from management.
- The audit committee should review the contents of any representation letters provided by management to the auditors, and consider whether the information provided by management is, as far as the committee is aware, both complete and appropriate.
- The committee should review the contents of the 'management letter' provided by the audit firm to management at the end of the audit, containing observations and recommendations for improvements in financial reporting systems and controls.

At the end of the audit cycle, the audit committee should assess the effectiveness of the audit process, and in particular it should consider:

- whether the auditors met the agreed audit plan;
- the 'robustness and perceptiveness' of the auditors in their handling of key accounting and audit judgements;
- the views from key people in the company (such as the finance director and the head of internal audit) about the conduct of the audit by the auditors;
- whether the auditors' management letter to the company's management is based on a good understanding of the company's business.

The committee should also report to the board on the effectiveness of the external audit process.

The ICAEW has issued a booklet providing guidance for audit committee members on the evaluation of the external auditors. This can be viewed on the ICAEW website (see Directory).

### The appointment, reappointment and removal of the external auditors

Company law requires companies to submit to the shareholders each year (at the AGM) a proposal for the election or re-election of the external auditors.

The audit committee should have the primary responsibility for making a recommendation on the appointment, reappointment and removal of the external auditors. The recommendations should be submitted to the full board for approval. If the board does not accept the committee's recommendation, the annual report should include:

- a statement from the audit committee explaining its recommendation; and
- an explanation of why the board did not accept the recommendation of the committee.

An audit committee's recommendation to remove the existing auditors may be based on its assessment of:

- the expertise and resources of the audit firm and whether these are adequate;
- its assessment of the effectiveness of the audit process;
- the independence and objectivity of the audit firm.

A requirement was introduced into the UK Corporate Governance Code in 2012 that FTSE 350 companies should **put the external audit out to tender at least every ten years**.

This requirement is also stated in the FRC's *Guidance on Audit Committees*, which adds the explanation that the purpose of the tendering process should be to enable the audit committee (acting on behalf of the board) to compare the quality and effectiveness of the services provided by the incumbent auditor with those of other firms.

There will be a transition period for the introduction of this change, so that 350 FTSE companies do not have to put their audit out to tender all in the same year, every ten years; consequently there will be about 35 companies in each year putting their audit out to tender.

## Terms and remuneration of the auditors

The audit committee should approve the terms of engagement of the external auditors and the fee to be paid for their audit services. It should satisfy itself that the fee is appropriate. The fee should be reasonable for the amount of services provided. It should not be too large, but neither should it be too low. With a low audit fee there may be some risk that the scope of the audit, or the quality of the audit, may be insufficient.

The committee should also review the scope of the audit with the auditor. If it considers the proposed scope to be insufficient, the committee should arrange for additional audit work to be undertaken (FRC *Guidance*).

## Competition Commission report: statutory audit services market investigation

In 2013, the Competition Commission published a report on its investigation into the statutory audit services market. The findings of the report were as follows:

- Competition in the market is restricted by factors that deter companies from switching audit firms and by a tendency for audit firms to focus on satisfying management rather than the needs of the shareholders of the companies they audit.
- Companies are reluctant to switch auditors, partly because it is difficult for them to compare the services of different auditors and partly because the costs of switching would be high. Companies therefore lack bargaining power with their auditors.
- Too often auditors focus on the needs of senior management, who are the key decision-takers on whether to retain their services.
- Companies and audit firms invest in a relationship of mutual trust and confidence 'from which neither will lightly walk away'.
- Mid-tier audit firms face 'experience and reputational barriers' to their selection as auditors for FTSE 350 companies.

The report concluded that the Competition Commission would be investigating the following possible combinations of remedies:

- mandatory tendering for audits (already a UK Code requirement);
- mandatory rotation of audit firms;
- prohibition of 'Big-4-only' clauses in loans to companies by banks;
- greater accountability of the auditors to the audit committee;
- enhanced engagement between the auditors and the shareholders; and
- extended reporting requirements.

In July 2013, the Commission announced its intention to propose mandatory tendering of audits by FTSE350 companies every five years, rather than every ten years. This proposal was criticised by the Financial Reporting Council, and at the time of writing it is not yet known whether the Commission's proposal will be implemented.


# 11 AUDIT COMMITTEE REPORT TO SHAREHOLDERS

There should be a separate section in the annual report describing the work of the audit committee (UK Code Provision C3.8). This requirement 'deliberately puts the spotlight on the audit committee and gives it an authority that it might otherwise lack' (the FRC *Guidance*).

This report should include:

- the significant issues that the committee considered in relation to the financial statements, and how these issues were addressed (having regard to matters communicated by the external auditors);
- an explanation of how it has assessed the effectiveness of the external audit process;
- an explanation of the approach it has taken to the appointment or reappointment of the external auditor, and information on the length of tenure of the current audit firm and when the tender process was last conducted (so that shareholders can understand why the committee reached its decision about a reappointment or change of auditors); and
- an explanation to shareholders, whenever the audit firm provides non-audit services, how the objectivity and independence of the auditors is safeguarded.


# 12 MODEL TERMS OF REFERENCE FOR AN AUDIT COMMITTEE

Model terms of reference for an audit committee have been produced by the ICSA in a guidance note, which can be downloaded from the ICSA website (see Directory). These model terms are consistent with the recommendations of the FRC's *Guidance on Audit Committees*. They include the following provisions:

- Members of the audit committee should be appointed by the board on the recommendation of the nomination committee and in consultation with the chairman of the audit committee.

- The chairman of the board may not be a member of the audit committee.
- Only members of the committee have a right to attend committee meetings, but the committee may invite other individuals to attend, such as the head of risk compliance, the head of internal audit, the board chairman, the CEO or the finance director, as and when this is considered appropriate.
- The external auditor will be invited to attend committee meetings on a regular basis.
- There should be at least four meetings of the committee each year, at appropriate times during the audit and reporting cycle.
- Meetings of the committee may be called by the committee secretary (who may be the company secretary) at the request of any member of the committee or the external or internal auditor if they consider a meeting necessary.

The model terms of reference set out the duties of the audit committee, which are consistent with those set out in the FRC *Guidance*. Some of these relate to internal control and internal audit, and these are described in Chapter 9. The duties relating to financial reporting and the external auditors are:

- to monitor the integrity of the company's financial statements and in particular:
    - the consistency of and any changes in accounting policies;
    - whether the company has complied with relevant accounting standards and has made appropriate estimates and judgements, taking into consideration the advice of the external auditors;
    - the clarity of the disclosures in the financial reports; and
    - all material information within the financial statements, including the business review and the corporate governance statement, insofar as this relates to the audit and risk management;
- to make recommendations to the board concerning the appointment, and reappointment or removal of the external auditors, and to oversee the selection process for any new audit firm;
- to oversee the relationship with the external auditors: make recommendations about their remuneration, approve their terms of engagement, assess their continuing independence (annually), monitor their compliance with current professional and ethical guidance and monitor the relationship as a whole, including the provision of non-audit services by the audit firm;
- to review and approve the annual audit plan and review the findings of the audit with the auditors;

- to meet regularly with the external auditors, including once at the audit planning stage and once after the audit (at the financial reporting stage of the cycle). The committee should meet with the external auditors at least once a year with no management present at the meeting;
- to review management's response to the recommendations of the auditors;
- to produce a report on the committee's work to go into the company's annual report; and
- to carry out a periodic review of its own performance and make recommendations for any changes/improvements to the board.

## 13 AUDITORS' LIABILITY: COMPANIES ACT 2006

The Companies Act 2006 (sections 534–538) includes a provision on the liability of the company's external auditors for negligence, breach of duty or breach of trust in connection with the conduct of the audit. The provision was introduced following lobbying by the audit profession, which was concerned about the likelihood that following the collapse of a company, a court might decide that it is reasonable for the audit firm to be held liable for all the losses suffered by the company or its investors (on the grounds that only the auditors, and not the company directors or anyone else, would have enough money to pay the amounts claimed in law suits).

The new provision in the Act allows a company to reach an annual agreement with its auditors for a liability limitation agreement. This is an agreement that will limit the potential liability of the external auditors for negligence etc. in the event of the company's financial collapse.

- A liability limitation agreement should be for one year only.
- It must be approved by the shareholders, either before or after the agreement is made.
- It must be disclosed in the annual report and accounts.
- An agreement cannot limit the potential liability of the auditors to an amount that is less than what is reasonable in the circumstances. The limit on the auditors' liability might be expressed as a sum of money, by a formula, or as a proportion of any loss suffered by the company.

The NAPF's *Corporate Governance Policy and Voting Guidelines* recommend that shareholders should vote against any form of auditor liability limitation agreement other than one that provides for proportional liability, unless there are compelling reasons why this would not be appropriate.

If companies decide to make liability limitation agreements with their auditors, it seems likely that the audit committee will be involved in the negotiations before the board recommends the agreement to the shareholders for their approval.

## 14 CHECKLIST FOR AN AUDIT COMMITTEE

The following checklist sets out some of the essential requirements for an effective audit committee.

### 1 General requirements

1.1 Do the members of the audit committee have sufficient financial skills and literacy to do their work effectively? ☐

1.2 Are the committee members able to give sufficient time to the work? ☐

1.3 Does the audit committee review all important financial announcements by the company before their public release? ☐

1.4 Does the audit committee report to the board on how it has discharged its responsibilities? ☐

1.5 Does the audit committee provide advice to the board on the fairness, balance and understandability of the annual report and accounts? ☐

1.6 Has the audit committee investigated to its satisfaction the going concern status of the company? ☐

1.7 Does the audit committee carry out regular and rigorous reviews of the internal control system and risk management in the company? Is the system of regular reviews working successfully? ☐

1.8 Does the audit committee regularly confirm to its own satisfaction that the internal audit function is monitoring risk management and internal control systems efficiently? ☐

1.9 Does the committee meet with the head of internal audit without other executives present? ☐

1.10 Does the audit committee take the lead in the company's relationship with the external auditors? Does it actively monitor the effectiveness and the independence of the external auditors, and the quality of the audit work? ☐

### 2 Relationship with the external auditors ☐

2.1 Does the audit committee have the lead role in the appointment of new auditors? ☐

2.2 Does the audit committee have plans for putting the audit out to tender at the appropriate time in the future? Is the company required to comply with the ten-year rule on putting the audit out to tender?

2.3   Does the audit committee have a point of contact with the external auditors, for ☐
      regular communication as needed? Is there a positive relationship between the
      audit committee and the external auditor?

2.4   Does the audit committee review objectively the independence of the external ☐
      auditors?

2.5   Does the audit committee review company policy on giving non-audit work ☐
      to the auditors, and is it satisfied that this policy remains appropriate? Can
      the committee justify to shareholders its opinion that the external auditors are
      independent?

2.6   Does the audit committee discuss the annual audit with the auditors at the ☐
      planning stage?

2.7   Does the audit committee review the findings of the external audit, and does it ☐
      have meetings with the auditors without executive managers present?

2.8   Does the audit committee review the quality of the audit? ☐
      For example, is it satisfied that sufficient resources have been put into the audit?

# CHAPTER NINE

# Internal control and risk management

......................

## OVERVIEW

The board of directors has a governance responsibility for risk management systems. This is recognised in the UK Corporate Governance Code.

Companies should have a structured framework for managing risk and the directors should satisfy themselves that this framework is suitable and adequate. Risks might be categorised broadly as external or internal business risks, and the latter may include areas such as financial, operational and compliance risks.

The UK Code requires the boards of listed companies to review the adequacy of the system of internal control and risk management systems. Guidance on this review of internal control is provided by the Turnbull Guidance. The UK Code also requires listed companies to publish a statement on internal control in their annual reports and accounts, and this is supplemented by disclosure requirements in the Disclosure and Transparency Rules.

A further requirement of the UK Code is that the audit committee should monitor the internal audit function and review its effectiveness. If the company does not have an internal audit function, the committee should (annually) review the need for one.

Listed companies are expected to have a whistle-blowing system in place, and the UK Code requires that the audit committee review the arrangements the company has in place for whistle-blowing by its employees.

UK requirements for the board to review internal control and risk are less stringent than the requirements of the Sarbanes-Oxley Act (SOX) in the US. UK companies reporting to the Securities and Exchange Commission in the US are required to comply with SOX.


## 1  RESPONSIBILITY FOR RISK MANAGEMENT AND INTERNAL CONTROL SYSTEMS

The Cadbury Report (1992) described risk management as 'the process by which executive management, under board supervision, identifies the risk arising from business ... and establishes the priorities for control and particular objectives.'

The UK Code (Principle C.2) states that 'The board is responsible for determining the nature and extent of the significant risks it is willing to take in achieving its strategic objectives', and that 'the board should maintain sound risk management and internal control systems'.

Provision C.2.1 of the UK Code states that 'the board should, at least annually, conduct a review of the effectiveness of the company's risk management and internal control systems and should report to shareholders that they have done so.' This review is likely to be carried out by the audit committee, which should then report its findings to the full board.

### ICGN Corporate Risk Oversight Guidelines

The International Corporate Governance Network (ICGN) has issued guidelines on responsibilities for the oversight and management of corporate risk (2010).

- The risk oversight process begins with the board. The board is responsible for deciding the company's risk strategy and business model, and it should understand and agree the level of risk that goes with this. It should then have oversight of the implementation by management of a strategic and operational risk management system.
- Management has the responsibility for developing and implementing the company's strategic and routine operational risk management system, within the strategy set by the board and subject to board oversight.
- Shareholders have responsibility for assessing the effectiveness of the board in overseeing risk. Investors are not themselves responsible for the oversight of risk in the company.

The ICGN Guidelines provide guidance on processes for the oversight of corporate risk by the board and within the company, for investor responsibility and for disclosures by a company on its risk management oversight processes.

## 2 BUSINESS RISK

The board of directors should consider business risk when it makes strategic decisions. It should choose strategies that are expected to be profitable, but that take the business risks to a level that it considers acceptable. Consequently, both risk and return should be assessed in strategic decision-making.

---

Business risk arises from the possibility that an event or action will, against expectation, affect an organisation's ability to maximise stakeholder value and to achieve its business objectives. Business risk events may be favourable, creating unexpected profit, or adverse, causing unexpected loss.

Adverse aspects of business risk arise as much from the possibility that opportunities will not be realised as they do from the possibility that threats will materialise or that errors will be made.

Business risks arise from conditions in the business environment generally or within the industry, and from unexpected actions by competitors.

---

Making decisions about business risk may be expressed in terms of 'risk appetite' or 'risk tolerance'.

- Risk appetite refers to the amount of risk that a board is willing to take on in order to achieve its strategic objectives.

- Risk tolerance is the amount of risk that a board is willing to accept in the pursuit of its objectives.

Risk tolerance might be expressed in numerical terms by companies with sophisticated risk management systems. For example, in banking, loss limits may be set by a bank for each of its trading activities in the financial markets, and risk measures such as Value at Risk (VaR) may be used to control exposures to risk. Alternatively risk tolerance could be expressed more simply in terms of a total ban on certain types of business activity or behaviour, or a limit to the capital investment in a project.

---

### CASE EXAMPLE
..............
## MARCONI

In the 1990s, GEC was a major UK company, specialising mainly as a defence contractor. It had a reputation as a risk-averse company with a large cash pile. In 1996 the company founder, Lord Weinstock, was succeeded as chief executive by Lord Simpson, who led the board into a major change in the company's strategy. GEC sold off its defence interests and switched its business into telecommunications, mainly in the USA, buying large quantities of telecommunications assets. The company also changed its name to Marconi.

A number of factors, including a huge over-capacity in network supply, led to a collapse in the market for telecommunications equipment in 2001. Many of Marconi's competitors saw the downturn coming, but Marconi did not. It assumed, incorrectly, the market downturn would be brief and there would soon be recovery and growth.

Within a year, loss of shareholder confidence resulted in a collapse in the Marconi share price, reducing the value of its equity from about £35 billion to just £800 million. In July 2001, the company asked for trading in its shares to be suspended in anticipation of a profits warning. Not long afterwards, Lord Simpson was forced to resign. In retrospect, investors realised that the Marconi board had not understood the business risks to which their strategy decisions had exposed the business.

In 2006 the Marconi name and most of the assets were bought by the Swedish firm Ericsson.

---

A lesson from the Marconi experience is that the board of the company took a strategic risk without being fully aware of the scale of the risk. The risk management systems within the company were also unable to alert management and the board to the increasing risks to the telecommunications industry in 2001. This was poor governance, and as a result the company lost both value for shareholders and its independence.

---

CASE EXAMPLE
................

## A FAILURE OF RISK OVERSIGHT

Failures of risk management were demonstrated by the global banking crisis in 2007–09. The UK government-initiated Walker Report in 2009 was a review of the failures in the banking industry. The report commented that although there had been failures by the regulators of the banking industry, much of the blame for the crisis was attributable to poor risk management: 'Serious deficiencies in prudential oversight and financial regulation in the period before the crisis were accompanied by major governance failures within banks. These contributed materially to excessive risk-taking and the breadth and depth of the crisis.'

The report recommended that the board of directors should give much more attention to risk appetite and risk tolerance: 'Board-level engagement in risk oversight should be materially increased, with particular attention to the monitoring of risk and discussion leading to decisions on the entity's risk appetite and tolerance.'

---

## 3 INTERNAL CONTROLS

Business risks can be grouped into a range of categories. The three headline categories often used are financial risks, operational risks and compliance risks.

- **Financial risks** are risks of errors (or fraud) in accounting systems and financial reporting. They include the risks of failing to record transactions in the accounting system, failing to protect cash or to collect money from customers, and making errors in financial statements.
- **Operational risks** have been defined as 'the risk of losses resulting from inadequate or failed internal processes, people and systems, or external

events' (Basel Committee on Banking Supervision). Operational risks include the risks of failure by staff to carry out procedures, the risks of system failure from machine breakdown or software errors, the risk of losing information from computer files, the risk of injury to staff from inadequate health and safety measures, and so on.

- **Compliance risks** are risks of losses (for example, the costs of fines or compensation payments) from failure to comply with laws and regulations.

---

CASE EXAMPLE
················

## HEALTH AND SAFETY RISKS

Health and safety risks are an example of operational risks. A well-publicised example has been safety risks (and failures in safety controls) that led to a fire and explosion at the Texas City refinery of oil company BP in 2005. Fifteen people were killed and about 170 injured in the incident. In addition to the direct losses suffered by BP, the incident also led to over 1,000 civil legal actions against the company, and charges of criminal violations of federal environmental laws. In 2009, the company was fined for safety violations by the Occupational Safety and Health Administration, and for failure to deal with the safety risks revealed by the 2005 explosion.

BP had an even bigger disaster in 2010, the Deepwater Horizon oil spill in the Gulf of Mexico, which is thought to be the biggest accidental marine oil spill in history. An explosion and sinking of the Deepwater Horizon oil rig claimed 11 lives and led to extensive environmental damage. A gushing wellhead on the sea floor was not capped for 87 days. The company faced civil and federal prosecutions, and a large number of private prosecutions. The company settled a federal case in November 2012 by pleading guilty to 11 charges of manslaughter and agreeing to pay a very large fine. The financial and reputational implications of the disaster led the company into a major strategic review of its businesses.

---

### Examples of internal controls

These risks are reduced or avoided by different types of internal controls which may be:

- preventive controls – limiting the possibility of an undesirable outcome (i.e. segregation of duties);

- corrective controls – correcting undesirable outcomes that have been realised (i.e. contingency planning);
- directive controls – designed to ensure a particular outcome is achieved (i.e. by staff training); or
- detective controls – designed to identify where undesirable outcomes have been realised (i.e. reconciliations).

Further practical examples of internal controls include:

- supervision and checking that employees have carried out their work properly;
- reports to management, who can check that errors or problems have not occurred;
- physical measures to protect assets and confidential information, such as putting cash in a safe, and security measures to prevent unauthorised access;
- establishing an organisation structure with clear responsibilities and working procedures, so that everyone knows what they are expected to do;
- employing and training competent people;
- arranging work processes so that the work done by one person is checked by someone else;
- arithmetical checks, such as control total checks in book-keeping systems; and
- procedures to ensure that proper authorisation is given before work is carried out or transactions are made.

Internal controls are devised by recognising risks, deciding what needs to be done to deal with them, implementing the controls and monitoring them to make sure they are working.

## 4   ENTERPRISE RISK MANAGEMENT (ERM)

The board should ensure that there is a robust framework for risk management. Many companies have established an enterprise-wide risk management framework, so that the approach to risk management is consistent throughout the company/group.

The Committee of Sponsoring Organisations of the Treadway Commission (COSO) has provided guidelines on internal control and Enterprise Risk Management. It defines ERM as:

'a process, effected by an entity's board of directors, management and other personnel, applied in strategy-setting and across the enterprise, designed to identify potential events that may affect the entity, and manage risk to be within its risk appetite, to provide reasonable assurance regarding the achievement of entity objectives.'

Essentially, ERM is an approach to risk management that embraces the entire organisation and its activities and is applied in a consistent and integrated way throughout the organisation.

## The ERM cube

COSO portrays the structure of ERM as a cube, but this simply means that there are three dimensions to an integrated risk management system.

One dimension represents the different levels of the organisation, from an entity-wide level down to smaller operating units. The COSO cube shows four levels:

(1)  entity-wide level;

(2)  divisional level;

(3)  business unit level; and

(4)  subsidiary level.

Levels differ between entities according to their organisational structure. The same approach to risk management is applied at all levels.

The second dimension relates to the objectives of the entity and the risks that might prevent achievement of those objectives. Internal control risks were classified earlier in this chapter as financial, operational and compliance risks. COSO's ERM model classifies objectives and risks into four types:

(1)  **Strategic risks**: these relate to the high-level goals of the entity.

(2)  **Operations risks**: these relate to the effective and efficient use of resources.

(3)  **Reporting risks**: these relate to the objective of reliable reporting, including financial reporting, and the risks that may prevent achievement of this objective.

(4)  **Compliance risks**: these relate to the objective of compliance with all relevant laws and regulations, and the risks that may prevent compliance.

All four types of risk should be managed at all levels within the entity.

The third dimension of the ERM cube consists of eight components of risk management that apply to all four categories of objective and risk and at all levels within the entity. These eight components are as follows:

(1)  **Internal environment**: This is the tone or culture towards risk that exists within the organisation and its units. It includes attitudes to risk and also ethical values. An entity should seek to establish a suitable internal environment at all levels of its organisation.

(2)  **Objective setting**: There must be a process in place for setting objectives that are consistent with the overall strategic objectives of the entity and its risk appetite.

(3) **Event identification**: There must be processes for identifying risks and opportunities that may affect the ability of the entity to achieve its objectives.

(4) **Risk assessment**: Risks should be analysed in terms of their probability (likelihood) and potential severity (impact). This assessment should provide a basis for deciding how (and if) the risk should be managed. Risks should be assessed both in terms of their maximum potential effect and the residual risk after risk management measures have been applied.

(5) **Risk response**: Management decides on a response to the management of the risk. Possible responses are taking measures to avoid the risk, to reduce the risk to an acceptable level, to share the risk or to transfer the risk (for example, by means of insurance).

(6) **Control activities**: Policies and procedures should be designed and implemented to control the risks in accordance with the chosen risk response. Appropriate specialist risk management and assurance functions should be established where appropriate, such as capabilities in internal audit, health and safety management, IT assurance, insurance management and environmental risk management functions.

(7) **Information and communication**: Information and communication should be identified, captured and communicated 'in a form and timeframe that enable people to carry out their responsibilities' (COSO). Communication should flow upwards, downwards and horizontally throughout the entity.

(8) **Monitoring**: The ERM system should be monitored through regular review, to check whether it is still fulfilling its intended purpose effectively.

The COSO cube therefore looks as follows:

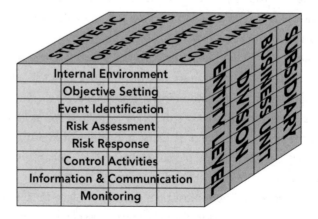

**Figure 9.1** The COSO ERM cube

In reviewing the effectiveness of internal control and risk management systems, the board (or audit committee or risk committee) should consider whether these eight components of risk management are applied sufficiently and consistently to all aspects of objectives and at all levels within the organisation.

## Establishing ERM

To establish a system of ERM, the initiative must come from the board and senior management. It requires a commitment and vision, the commitment of resources and the design and implementation of processes and procedures.

- Establishing the approach to risk management and creating a risk management 'vision'.
- Committing resources to risk management, and ensuring that an infrastructure for risk management is put in place and that the company/group has the capabilities and skills for managing risk.
- Implementing systems for risk assessment, the application of controls and other management systems for risk, and monitoring risks and the effectiveness of the risk management arrangements.

## Risk capabilities

The company should have the capabilities for managing risk, which might include:

- employees being given structured training in basic risk management procedures and internal control systems;
- individuals having personal objectives that make reference to their performance in areas of risk and control; or
- systems that are capable of providing early warning of any major control breakdowns or problems.

## Risk assessment

To implement risk management systems, there must first be processes or procedures for identifying risks and measuring them and assessing their potential significance. The measuring and assessment of risk is sometimes called 'risk profiling' or 'risk mapping'.

A simple example of risk mapping involves placing each identified risk in an appropriate position in a 2 × 2 matrix, according to:

- the frequency of adverse events or the probability that the risk will materialise and an adverse outcome will occur; and
- the expected loss or impact in the event of an adverse outcome.

A traditional approach to risk assessment is set out in Figure 9.2.

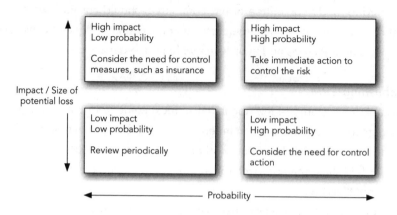

**Figure 9.2** Risk mapping

Companies in more complex business sectors may need a more sophisticated approach, using scenario analysis and arithmetic calculations.

All critical risks should be 'owned' by designated managers.

### The treatment of risk

Controls should be designed to mitigate the risk. There should also be some form of testing controls for both their design and their operating effectiveness.

- Controls for significant or 'critical' risks should be reviewed regularly to ensure that they are still an appropriate control to apply.
- The effectiveness of controls in reducing critical risks should be tested.
- 'Residual risk' is the risk that still remains after the controls have been put in place and implemented. Management should understand and monitor these residual risks, to ensure that they remain at acceptable levels.

### Monitoring risks

Risks should be monitored by managers who have responsibility for those risks. In addition, risks can be monitored at a more senior level through key performance indicators (KPIs) or key risk indicators (KRIs).

The board should be provided regularly by management with clear reports on risk management and internal control, such as reports on:

- the company's risk profile; and
- control testing, the results of those tests and action plans resulting from the test findings.

### ISO31000 on risk management

In 2009, the International Organization for Standardization issued a Standard on the Implementation of Risk Management Systems: ISO31000. ISO31000 may be used by any organisation in any industry or sector, and can be applied to any type of risk. Its purpose is to promote international standardisation in risk management systems.

In 2010, the Institute of Risk Management (IRM), in collaboration with the Association of Insurance and Risk Managers (Airmic) and the public risk management association Alarm, issued guidance on ISO31000. This guidance, 'A Structured Approach to Enterprise Risk Management (ERM) and the Requirements of ISO31000', is available on the IRM website at www.theirm.org/documents/SARM_FINAL.pdf.

ISO31000 uses the '7Rs and 4Ts' system of risk management as a framework for the implementation of a risk management system:

(1) Recognition/identification of risks.

(2) Ranking or evaluation of risk.

(3) Responding to significant risk where risk treatment covers one of four positions:

    (a) Tolerate: accept the exposure to risk.

    (b) Treat: take measures to control or eliminate the risk.

    (c) Transfer: transfer the risk to someone else.

    (d) Terminate: terminate the activity that gives rise to the risk.

(4) Resourcing controls.

(5) Reaction planning.

(6) Reporting and monitoring risk performance.

(7) Reviewing the risk management framework.

ISO31000 also puts forward a framework for risk management that has three main elements:

- **Risk architecture**: This consists of the roles and responsibilities for risk management within the organisation and the risk reporting structure. For example, it consists of the respective roles and responsibilities of the board, the audit committee, the group risk management committee, the risk disclosures committee, the CEO, business unit managers, individual employees, risk managers, specialist risk management functions and internal auditors.

- **Risk strategy**: The risk strategy of the organisation should be specified, including the risk appetite of the board. There should be a risk management action plan and resources to support risk management activities.

- **Risk protocols**: These are the rules and procedures for implementing risk management and the risk management methodologies that should be applied. For example, there should be rules, procedures and methodologies for risk assessments, risk responses, and incident reporting; a business continuity plan; and arrangements for auditing the efficiency and effectiveness of controls.

## 5 AN INTERNAL CONTROL SYSTEM

In the UK, corporate governance guidance has tended to focus mainly on internal control rather than risk management more generally. A useful definition of internal control was provided in 1992 in the US by the COSO Framework.

The COSO Framework defined internal control as 'a process, effected by an entity's board of directors, management and other personnel, designed to provide reasonable assurance regarding the achievement of objectives' in three particular areas: the effectiveness and efficiency of operations, the reliability of financial reporting, and compliance with applicable laws and regulations.

Note: The COSO Framework was updated in 2005 to give more focus to risk identification and risk assessment, and again in 2006 to cover the requirements of small companies.

---

### CASE EXAMPLE
......
## THE COLLAPSE OF BARINGS BANK

The collapse of Barings Bank in 1995 remains a major example of failures in internal control. The bank collapsed because of the activities of Nick Leeson, who was appointed as general manager of the bank's Singapore office in 1992. Leeson was qualified as a trader and he soon developed a position of considerable authority, becoming head trader and the effective head of 'back office operations' (including the recording and settlement of trading transactions) as well as the office general manager. There should have been controls to prevent traders from taking excessive risks, but because of his position of authority, Leeson was able to ignore them. He made speculative trading deals in the Singapore and Japanese markets, but made losses. Leeson was able to 'hide' the losses in an unused error account, and so was able to report profits on his activities when in fact the losses were mounting, from £2 million at the end of

---

1992 to £23 million at the end of 1993 and £208 million at the end of 1994. Leeson and his staff in the Singapore office were paid large bonuses on the basis of the reported profits. Leeson funded the losses by borrowing money from other parts of the bank and from client accounts (falsifying documentation and account records). His managers in London were not aware of what was happening.

Eventually, Leeson was unable to hide the losses any more, and in 1995 he fled from Singapore, leaving losses of over £800 million. Barings collapsed soon after and was taken over.

The collapse of Barings revealed enormous weaknesses in the bank's internal control system, which can be summarised briefly as:

- a poor control culture within the bank and lack of concern for risk;
- weaknesses in organisation structure;
- weaknesses in management and reporting processes;
- inadequate authorisation procedures;
- inadequate accounting controls; and
- failure by senior management in London and by the bank's board of directors to review the effectiveness of the internal control system.

## 6 THE UK CORPORATE GOVERNANCE CODE AND INTERNAL CONTROL

As stated earlier, a principle of the UK Code is that the board should maintain sound risk management and internal control systems. To this end it should conduct a review, at least annually, of the effectiveness of the company's risk management and internal control systems, and report to the shareholders that it has done so. The review 'should cover all material controls, including financial, operational and compliance controls'.

These principles and provisions are largely unchanged from similar requirements in the UK Combined Code that was issued 1998.

Although the board has overall responsibility for the internal control system, the UK Code (Provision C.3.2) states that **the audit committee should be given responsibility** within its terms of reference for:

- reviewing the company's internal financial controls;
- unless there is a separate risk committee of the board composed of independent NEDs, reviewing the company's entire internal control system and (business) risk management system.

A number of companies name the committee 'the Audit and Risk Committee', to emphasise the responsibility for review of the risk management system as well as internal control.

**A separate risk committee** of the board is unlikely to be established except in large companies (such as major banks), and the audit committee is responsible for reviewing the internal control and business risk management systems in most listed companies (and other non-listed companies that have audit committees).

The UK Code also gives the audit committee responsibilities for internal audit. These are described in more detail later.

## 7 TURNBULL GUIDANCE ON INTERNAL CONTROL

After the Combined Code was first published in 1998, there was some uncertainty about how the provisions relating to internal control should be applied. The Turnbull Committee was established to provide some guidance. The Turnbull Guidance, with small revisions, still applies and is the responsibility of the Financial Reporting Council.

The Turnbull Guidance reflects the principles-based approach in the UK Code to establishing a sound system of internal control and reviewing its effectiveness.

The Guidance recommends that a risk-based approach should be built into the company's normal management and governance processes. In particular, internal control should be embedded into the company's business processes, and the review of the effectiveness of internal control should not be treated as a separate exercise that is undertaken to meet regulatory requirements.

The Turnbull Guidance broadly follows the US COSO Framework for internal control, and considers the five essential elements of an internal control system. These essential elements for internal control are also components in COSO's model for an ERM system:

(1) **A control environment.** The board of directors must establish policies on risk management and internal control. It must also ensure that the company operates with integrity and in accordance with ethical values. There should be a culture of control throughout the organisation, from the board down to all employees, but the leadership must come from the board, which sets the 'tone at the top'.

(2) **Risk identification and assessment.** There should be a system for identifying and assessing internal control risks.

(3) **Control activities (internal controls).** Controls for mitigating or managing risks should be designed and implemented. Internal controls are a part of normal day-to-day operational activities and procedures. 'An effective internal control system requires that an appropriate control structure is set up, with controls defined at every business level. These should include: top-level reviews; appropriate activity controls for different departments or divisions; physical controls; checking for compliance ... and follow-up on non-compliance; a system of approvals and authorisations; and a system of verification and reconciliation.'

(4) **Information and communication.** An effective internal control system must have effective channels of communication, to ensure that all employees understand their responsibilities for control and that all relevant information reaches the individuals who need it.

(5) **Monitoring.** There should be regular monitoring and review of the effectiveness of the system of internal control. One way of monitoring internal control is to have an internal audit department, for carrying out reviews and reporting to senior management. However, the board of directors is ultimately responsible for maintaining a sound system of internal control, and this is recognised in the UK Corporate Governance Code.

In respect of the UK Code requirements the Turnbull Guidance focuses on:

- maintaining a sound system of internal control;
- reviewing the effectiveness of internal control; and
- the board's annual statement on internal control.

## Maintaining a sound system of internal control

The board of directors is responsible for the company's system of internal control:

- The board should set appropriate policies on internal control.
- It should regularly seek assurance that the system is working effectively.
- In deciding appropriate policies for internal control, the board will need to consider:
  - the nature and extent of the risks facing the company;
  - the extent of risks (and the types or categories of risk) that it regards as acceptable for the company to bear;
  - the likelihood that the risks will materialise;
  - the company's ability to reduce the effect of these risks on the business if they do materialise; and

> – the costs of applying controls to reduce the risk, relative to the benefits obtained from applying the controls.

The responsibility of management is to implement the board's policies on internal control and risk. To carry out these responsibilities, management should identify and evaluate risks faced by the company, for consideration by the board. Management should then design, operate and monitor a suitable system of internal control, applying the policies adopted by the board.

The system of internal controls should contain suitable operational controls, financial controls and compliance controls, which should be embedded into the operations of the company and form part of its culture. The system of controls should also be capable of responding quickly to risks as they change and evolve, due to internal factors within the company and also external factors in its business environment.

## Recognising the limits to internal control and its effectiveness

The Turnbull Guidance stresses that no system of internal control can eliminate risks:

> 'A sound system of internal control reduces, but cannot eliminate, the possibility of poor judgement in decision-making; human error; control processes being deliberately circumvented by employees and others; management overriding controls; and the occurrence of unforeseeable circumstances.
>
> 'A sound system of internal control therefore provides reasonable, but not absolute, assurance that a company will not be hindered in achieving its business objectives, or in the orderly and legitimate conduct of its business, by circumstances which may reasonably be foreseen. A system of internal control cannot, however, provide protection with certainty against a company failing to meet its business objectives or all material errors, losses, fraud or breaches of laws or regulations.'

## Reviewing the effectiveness of internal control

Reviewing the effectiveness of internal control is a key part of the board's responsibilities. The board should reach its own view about the effectiveness of the system, based on the information provided to them and the assurances given by management. The standard of care that directors should apply in carrying out this review is 'the standard of care generally applicable to directors in the exercise of their duties'.

In practice, this standard of care may not be very robust. The problem for directors is to find a way of carrying out this type of review in practice. Inevitably, they have to rely on reports and assurances from management, supported perhaps by reports from the internal auditors.

Management is accountable to the board for:

- monitoring the system of internal control; and
- providing assurances to the board that they have done so.

The board may delegate some responsibilities to the audit committee or other board committee, but the board as a whole is responsible for the disclosures in internal control in the annual report and accounts.

In order to review the effectiveness of the system, the board cannot simply rely on the embedded controls and procedures working as they should do. The board should receive regular reports on internal control, and it should also carry out an annual review.

When reviewing reports on internal control throughout the year, the board should:

- consider what the significant risks are, and how these have been identified, assessed and managed;
- assess the effectiveness of individual controls with regard to managing each of the significant risks, having regard to any weaknesses in internal control that were reported;
- consider whether appropriate actions were taken to deal promptly with any significant reported control weaknesses; and
- consider whether the findings of the reports indicate the need for more extensive monitoring of the system of internal control.

The annual review of the effectiveness of internal control should consider in particular:

- changes in the nature and significance of risks since the last annual review, and how well the company has responded to changes in its business and external environment;
- the scope and quality of the risk review;
- management's monitoring of significant risks, and the system of internal control;
- the extent and frequency of management reports to the board on internal control and risk monitoring, and the board's ability to build up a cumulative assessment of the system;

RESPONSIBILITIES

| MAINTAINING A SOUND SYSTEM OF INTERNAL CONTROL – THE TURNBULL GUIDANCE | **Factors to consider** | • The nature and extent of risks faced by the company.<br>• The extent and categories of risks that are acceptable for the company to bear.<br>• The likelihood of the risks materialising.<br>• The company's ability to reduce the incidence and impact of risks that do materialise (control activities in place).<br>• The costs of operating particular controls compared with the benefits they provide. |
|---|---|---|
| | **Internal control activities** | **The Board** should set policies on internal control and seek regular assurance that the system is functioning effectively. **Management** should implement board policies on risk and control; identify and evaluate risks for consideration by the board; design, operate and monitor the system of internal control.<br>**Employees** should consider internal control as part of their responsibility and accountability for achieving business objectives. They need the necessary knowledge, skills, authority and information relating to risk and control. |

**Figure 9.3** Turnbull Guidance summary

- any significant failing or weaknesses in control that have been identified at any time during the year, and the consequences that they have had; and
- the effectiveness of the company's public reporting processes.

In 2005 the Flint Committee was set up to review the Turnbull Guidance and to assess the need for a more rules-based approach, as adopted in the US with the Sarbanes-Oxley Act. After review and consultation, it was agreed that the Turnbull Guidance was the appropriate model for the UK and the only substantive change was for companies to disclose if any necessary action is taken to remedy any significant failings or weaknesses identified in their systems of internal control.

| KEY ELEMENTS | REVIEWING EFFECTIVENESS | THE BOARD STATEMENT |
|---|---|---|
| • Control environment.<br>• Risk assessment.<br>• Control activities.<br>• Information and communications.<br>• Monitoring procedures.<br>(A sound system of internal control reduces risk, but cannot eliminate it – due to the possibility of poor judgement, human error, management over-ride and unforeseeable circumstances.) | Reports from management to the board covering:<br>• A balanced assessment of the risks identified.<br>• An assessment of the critical control activities.<br>• Details of any significant weaknesses that have been identified. | The board should consider:<br>• Changes since the previous assessment.<br>• The scope and quality of management's reviews.<br>• The extent and frequency of communications. |
| **Internal control:** the policies, processes, tasks and behaviours that, taken together:<br>• **enable a response to** business, operational, financial and compliance **risks** (and other risks) to the achievement of business objectives;<br>• **safeguard assets** from inappropriate use, or from loss and fraud;<br>• help to ensure the **quality of internal and external reporting**;<br>• help to **ensure compliance** with applicable laws and regulations and internal policies, with regard to the conduct of business. | Effective monitoring on a **continuous basis** is essential for a sound system of internal control. The board should **receive and review reports on internal control regularly**. In addition, there should be an annual assessment. The board should define the process to be used. Management is accountable to the board for monitoring the control system. | The board should disclose that there is an **ongoing process** for identifying, evaluating and managing **significant risks**, and that this process is reviewed regularly by the board and **accords with the Turnbull guidance**. This process needs to have been in place for the entire year under review. |

At the time of writing, the FRC had announced its intention to publish proposals for a review of the Turnbull Guidance, which would be issued for consultation during 2013.

## 8  TURNBULL GUIDANCE SUMMARY

A high-level summary of the Turnbull Guidance in Figure 9.3 sets out some of the key aspects.

## 9 THE BOARD'S STATEMENT ON INTERNAL CONTROL AND THE CORPORATE GOVERNANCE STATEMENT

The UK Corporate Governance Code states that the board should conduct a review of the effectiveness of the system of internal controls, at least every year, and should report to the shareholders that they have done so (Provision C.2.1). This report, which is included in the annual report and accounts, should cover all material controls – operational controls, financial controls and compliance controls.

Following the implementation of the revisions to the EU Fourth Company Law Directive, the UK Disclosure and Transparency Rules include a requirement for listed companies to publish a separate corporate governance statement each year (possibly as part of the directors' report). The DTR requirements call for additional disclosures about financial controls in this statement. The statement must include a description of the main features of the company's internal control and risk management systems, in relation to the company's process for preparing its financial statements.

The Disclosure and Transparency Rules overlap with the UK Code requirements. The DTR rules call for more detailed disclosures than the UK Code, but are restricted to controls in relation to the financial reporting process.

## 10 THE INTERNAL AUDIT FUNCTION

The Institute of Internal Auditors (UK and Ireland) defines internal audit as:

> '...an independent, objective assurance and consulting activity designed to add value and improve an organisation's operations. It helps an organisation accomplish its objectives by bringing a systematic, disciplined approach to evaluate and improve the effectiveness of risk management, control, and governance processes.'

### The need for an internal audit function

Internal audit is a key monitoring tool used to check and review the control of critical risks across the organisation. The actual role of an internal audit function varies between organisations. Traditionally, internal auditors tested financial controls in various parts of an organisation's operations. However, internal auditors may also carry out such investigations with a view to testing the effectiveness of operational or compliance controls.

Internal audit is viewed as a monitoring activity, reviewing the effectiveness of the control systems. As such it is an independent review function, reviewing systems and processes across all areas of the business.

The FRC *Guidance on Audit Committees* comments that the need for an internal audit function will vary depending on factors specific to the organisation, such as:

- the scale and diversity of its activities;
- the number of its employees; and
- considerations of the costs of controls and the benefits they provide.

The board and senior management may want to receive independent and objective advice and assurance on risk and control. This will depend on the company's risk profile. Any such advice could be provided by an internal audit function. However, it may be provided instead by:

- an external firm of risk and control advisers; or
- specialists in specific areas of risk, such as health and safety, regulatory and legal compliance, and environmental issues.

In the absence of an internal audit function, management should use other monitoring processes to assure themselves that the internal control system and its internal controls are working effectively. The audit committee should then consider whether these alternative monitoring processes provide sufficient and objective assurance.

### Reviewing the work of the internal audit function

The UK Corporate Governance Code states that the responsibilities of the audit committee should include a requirement to monitor and review the effectiveness of the internal audit activities (Provision C.3.6).

If there is no internal audit function in the company, the audit committee should comply with the following requirements:

- It should consider each year whether there is a need for an internal audit function, and it should make a recommendation to the board about whether (yes or no) an internal audit function should be established.
- The reasons for not having an internal audit function should be explained in the relevant section of the annual report.

The FRC *Guidance* suggests that in reviewing the work of the internal audit function, the audit committee should:

- make sure that the internal auditor has direct access to the board chairman and the audit committee, and is accountable to the audit committee;

- meet with the head of internal audit at least once a year without executive managers being present at the meeting; and
- monitor and assess the effectiveness of the internal audit function within the overall context of the company's risk management systems.

When the internal auditor reports to executive management only, such as the finance director, there is a risk that internal audit reports will not be objective, and will be influenced by the views and attitudes of senior executives.

For similar reasons, the FRC *Guidance* suggests that the audit committee should approve the appointment or termination of appointment of the head of internal audit.

The audit committee should also review the work of internal audit, and the value provided by the internal audit function. It should do this by:

- reviewing and assessing the annual work plan for the internal audit section;
- receiving periodic reports on the results of the work done by internal audit;
- reviewing and monitoring the responsiveness of management to the findings and recommendations of the internal auditor; and
- monitoring and assessing the role and effectiveness of internal audit within the overall context of the company's internal control and risk management system.

## 11 WHISTLE-BLOWING PROCEDURES

'Whistleblowing is the popular term used when someone who works in or for an organisation ... raises a concern about a possible fraud, crime, danger or other serious risk that could threaten customers, colleagues, shareholders, the public or the organisation's own reputation.'

(BSI: Whistleblowing Procedures: Code of Practice).

Listed companies should be expected to have a formal system in place for whistle-blowing. A specific provision in the UK Corporate Governance Code (Provision C.3.5) is that the audit committee should review the arrangements that are in place to allow employees to 'blow the whistle' on possible wrongdoing (such as fraud) in relation to financial reporting. The committee should also make sure that arrangements exist for appropriate independent investigation of any such allegations by whistle-blowers.

The exact wording of the UK Code is as follows:

'The audit committee should review arrangements by which staff of the company may, in confidence, raise concerns about possible improprieties in matters of financial reporting or other matters. The audit committee's objective should be to ensure that arrangements are in place for the proportionate and independent investigation of such matters and for appropriate follow-up action.'

In the UK, the most authoritative guide on whistle-blowing procedures is now probably 'Whistleblowing Arrangements Code of Practice' issued by the British Standards Institute (BSI) in 2008. (This is also referred to as Publicly Available Specification 'PAS 1998:2008'.)

## The Bribery Act and whistle-blowing

The Bribery Act 2010 introduced a new criminal offence of 'failure of commercial organisations to prevent bribery' by an employee or any other associated person. A company would have a 'full defence' against such an accusation if it can show that despite a particular case of bribery it nevertheless had adequate procedures in place to prevent persons associated with it from bribing.

A company could claim in defence against such a charge that it has an effective and functioning whistle-blowing system. However, a successful defence would need to demonstrate that the whistle-blowing procedures operate in practice and work well.

*The Financial Times* (28 February 2013) reported the ninth annual survey of in-house legal counsel by US law firm Fulbright & Jaworski, which found that 37% of UK companies surveyed in 2012 reported that they had been the 'target' of a would-be whistle-blower. About three-quarters of the allegations led to an in-house investigation and about half to a regulatory investigation. The reported cases in 2012 were significantly higher than in previous years. This suggests a possibility that the increase in whistle-blowing in the UK may have been connected to the Bribery Act and measures by companies to provide an infrastructure for whistle-blowers to make their allegations without fear of persecution.

## 12 MODEL TERMS OF REFERENCE FOR AN AUDIT COMMITTEE: INTERNAL CONTROL, RISK MANAGEMENT AND INTERNAL AUDIT

The ICSA's *Guidance on Terms of Reference* for audit committees was described in Chapter 8. For a company that does not have a separate risk committee of the board, the terms of reference of the audit committee should include the following provisions with regard to internal control.

- The committee should keep under review internal financial controls and the internal control and risk management systems (and review the statements for inclusion in the annual report regarding internal control and risk management).
- It should review the adequacy of whistle-blowing arrangements, the procedures for detecting fraud and the systems in place for preventing bribery.
- It should review the effectiveness of the internal audit function.
- It should approve the remit of the internal audit function and ensure that it has enough resources to carry out its duties effectively.
- The committee should approve the appointment or removal of the head of internal audit.
- It should approve the annual internal audit work plan, review reports addressed to the audit committee by the internal auditors and review management's response to recommendations from the internal auditors.
- The committee should meet at least once a year with the head of internal audit to discuss the remit of the internal audit function and any issues arising from the work of the internal audit function.

## 13 RISK COMMITTEE

The UK Corporate Governance Code recognises that some companies may choose to have a separate risk committee of the board, in addition to an audit committee. The Code does not go into much detail about risk committees, and there is much more detail in the Walker Report (2009) on governance failures in financial services companies and in the ICSA *Guidance on Terms of Reference* for a risk committee (2010).

The functions of the audit committee and risk committee, if there is one, would overlap to some extent, but in broad terms:

- the audit committee would be responsible for matters relating to financial reporting, the external audit and external auditors; and
- the risk committee would be responsible for matters relating to the effectiveness of the internal control and risk management systems.

### Walker Report recommendations about risk committees

The Walker Report (2009) suggested that a risk committee would be particularly appropriate for banks and other financial institutions, because a failure to understand and manage risk was a major contributor to the financial crisis in banking in

2007–09. The report therefore recommended that banks and life assurance companies in the FTSE 100 should establish a risk committee of the board, separate from the audit committee. A risk committee should have responsibility for and oversight of:

- the current risk exposures of the company; and
- future risk strategy, including the strategy for capital adequacy and liquidity management.

The board should be served by a chief risk officer who would be a member of the executive management team, but alongside reporting responsibilities to the CEO or finance director, the chief risk officer should also report to the risk committee and have direct access to the chairman of the risk committee in case of need.

The Report suggested that the risk committee should consist of a majority of NEDs and should be chaired by a NED. The finance director should either be a member of the committee or should attend meetings of the committee. The chief risk officer should also attend committee meetings. Since the functions of the risk committee and the audit committee overlap, the chairman of the audit committee should participate in the work of the risk committee, possibly as a member of the committee.

The committee should meet about every quarter, and there should be no fewer than three meetings each year.

### ICSA guidance on terms of reference for a risk committee

The ICSA's guidance on terms of reference for a risk committee contains the following provisions.

- Members of the risk committee should be appointed by the board on the recommendation of the nomination committee and in consultation with the chairman of the risk committee. The board should appoint the committee chairman.
- The finance director (if not a committee member) and chief risk officer should attend committee meetings. In addition the committee may invite other individuals to attend, such as the chief internal auditor, external auditor or compliance officer, as and when appropriate.
- The duties of the risk committee should be to:
  - advise the board on the company's overall risk appetite, risk tolerance and risk strategy;
  - oversee and advise the board on current risk exposures and future risk strategy;

- keep under review the company's risk assessment procedures that inform decision-making by the board;
- review the capability of the company to identify and manage new types of risk;
- advise the board on the risk aspects of proposed strategic transactions, such as a proposed acquisition;
- review reports on material breaches of risk limits and consider the adequacy of the measures taken in response;
- review the adequacy of the company's internal financial controls and internal control and risk management systems;
- review the adequacy of the company's whistle-blowing arrangements, and the procedures for detecting fraud and preventing bribery;
- consider the remit of the company's risk management function and ensure that it has sufficient resources to carry out its functions effectively;
- review the response of management to findings and recommendations of the chief risk officer.

## 14 SARBANES-OXLEY (SECTION 404) AND INTERNAL CONTROL

Companies that have to register with the US Securities and Exchange Commission (SEC) (for example, because their shares are traded in the US) are subject to the requirements of the Sarbanes-Oxley Act 2002 (SOX).

Section 404 of SOX imposes strict requirements on companies with respect to internal control over financial reporting. It requires companies to include two reports on internal financial control in their annual report: one from management and the other from the company's auditors.

The report from management should state the responsibility of management for establishing and maintaining an adequate internal control system and procedures for financial reporting. The report should also contain an assessment by management of the effectiveness of the internal control structure and procedures of the company over financial reporting.

The SEC has applied the requirements of section 404 of SOX:

- The management of each company must evaluate the effectiveness of the company's internal control over financial reporting. The CEO and principal finance officer have personal responsibility for this process. The framework for this evaluation must be one that is acceptable to the SEC. (This is usually the COSO Framework, but the Turnbull Guidelines are also an acceptable framework.)

- The internal control over financial reporting includes policies and procedures that:
    - relate to the maintenance of accurate financial records for transactions and assets;
    - provide reasonable assurance that transactions are recorded and that receipts and expenditures are made only in accordance with authorisations of management and directors; and
    - provide reasonable assurance about the prevention or timely detection of fraud that could have a material effect on the financial statements.
- Companies must maintain evidence, principally source documentation, to support management's assessment of the effectiveness of internal control over financial reporting. The source documentation will be in the form of narrative notes, flowcharts, and test programmes and the results of tests.

Management must disclose any material weaknesses in the internal control system for financial reporting, and they cannot conclude that the internal control system is effective when a single material weakness exists. Auditors must provide an 'attestation report' that gives either a 'clean' opinion or an adverse opinion: there is no middle ground.

Although the requirements of section 404 apply only to financial controls (not operational controls or compliance controls), the Act places a considerable burden on companies, and potentially exposes the company's CEO and finance director to personal liability (both a prison sentence and a fine) for improper reporting.

During 2007 both the SEC and the US Audit Standards body, the Public Company Accounting Oversight Board (PCAOB), looked closely at the SOX rules and guidelines and:

(1) issued 'Auditing Standard No. 5', which provides more clarification on how auditors should integrate their section 404 work on internal controls with the annual financial statements audit;

(2) provided companies with guidance on their responsibilities and the work they need to do (previously only auditors had such guidance); and

(3) published guidance specifically for smaller public companies, recognising that this work needs to be scaled to the size and complexity of companies.

# 15 CHECKLIST FOR THE REVIEW OF INTERNAL CONTROL AND RISK MANAGEMENT SYSTEMS

The Turnbull Guidance focuses mainly on the internal control system and the FRC *Guidance on Audit Committees* provides suggestions for the review of internal control and risk management. The UK Corporate Governance Code states that the board is responsible for the review of risk management systems in general, and not just internal control. The review should be carried out by the audit committee, unless it is carried out by the board itself or by another committee of the board consisting entirely of independent NEDs.

Some guidance for the review of risk management systems is provided as a checklist questionnaire in the Turnbull Guidance.

---

### 1 On risk assessment

| | | |
|---|---|---|
| 1.1 | Does the company have clear objectives? Have these objectives been communicated so as to provide clear direction to employees on risk assessment and control? For example, do the objectives include measurable performance targets and indicators? | ☐ |
| 1.2 | Are significant operational, financial, compliance and other risks (both internal and external) identified and assessed on an ongoing basis? | ☐ |
| 1.3 | Do management understand clearly what risks are acceptable to the board? | ☐ |

### 2 Control environment and control activities

| | | |
|---|---|---|
| 2.1 | Does the board have clear strategies for dealing with risks that have been identified? Is there a policy on managing risks? | ☐ |
| 2.2 | Is there an appropriate control environment? For example, do codes of conduct, human resource policies and performance reward systems support the company's business objectives, including its risk management and internal control system? | ☐ |
| 2.3 | Are authority, responsibility and accountability clearly defined, so that decisions are made and actions are taken by the appropriate people? | ☐ |
| 2.4 | Does the company communicate to employees what is expected of them, and what is the scope of their freedom to act? This may apply to areas such as customer relations; service levels for activities; health, safety and environmental protection; the security of assets; business continuity issues; expenditure matters; and accounting. | ☐ |
| 2.5 | Do people in the company (and providers of outsourced services) have the knowledge, skills and resources to support the achievement of the company's objectives and to manage effectively the risks to their achievement? | ☐ |

## 3  Monitoring

3.1  Are there ongoing processes, embedded in the company's operating systems, for monitoring the effective application of processes, policies and activities related to internal control and risk management? ☐

3.2  Do these processes monitor the company's ability to re-assess risks and adjust controls as appropriate, in response to changes in objectives, the business and the company's external environment? ☐

3.3  Are there effective follow-up procedures for ensuring that appropriate changes are made or action is taken in response to changes in risk and control assessments? ☐

3.4  Is there appropriate communication to the board (or board committees) on the effectiveness of monitoring processes for risk and internal control? ☐

3.5  Are there specific arrangements in place for management to monitor and report to the board matters of particular importance with regard to risk, such as suspected fraud, other illegal acts or matters that could seriously affect the company's reputation or financial position? ☐

# CHAPTER TEN

# Director development and board performance evaluation

....................

## OVERVIEW

Directors should remain fully qualified and capable of performing their duties well. New directors should receive a formal induction on joining the company, tailored to their specific needs. Directors should subsequently keep their skills and knowledge refreshed and up to date, through regular training and development initiatives.

Listed companies should undertake an annual review and evaluation of the performance of the board, its committees and individual directors.

The performance review is the responsibility of the chairman (except for the performance review of the chairman), possibly with assistance from external consultants.

There is no specified standard approach to carrying out a performance review. Each company should decide its own methods and approach, but the process should have some substance and structure.

Feedback from the annual performance review process may be used to agree further training or development initiatives for individual directors, and may also be used by the nomination committee to re-assess the composition of the board.

# 1 INDUCTION FOR NEW DIRECTORS

All newly appointed directors should receive induction. This is a process of introducing the director to their new role, by providing information about the company, its products and operations, and also about the responsibilities of being a director. The need for induction applies to executive directors as well as NEDs. The induction programme should be tailored to the requirements of the individual director, to allow for what they know already and what they do not know.

The UK Corporate Governance Code states that 'all directors should receive induction on joining the board' (Principle B.4) and that it is the responsibility of the chairman to ensure that all new directors receive 'a full, formal and tailored induction on joining the board'. The Code does not specify what induction should consist of, except that as part of the induction process, directors 'should avail themselves of opportunities to meet major shareholders'.

The task of devising and implementing an induction programme may be delegated to the company secretary or another senior company administrator. The aim should be to assist the new director to become an effective contributor to the board as soon as possible. The *Guidance on Board Effectiveness* suggests that the chairman should take the lead in ensuring that new directors are appropriately inducted.

The induction programme may last for several months with further induction added in stages over time.

An induction programme should be tailored to the needs of the company and the individual directors. As a general rule the programme will consist of a combination of:

- documents, such as minutes of previous board meetings and committee meetings (of any committee the new director will be joining), published reports and accounts, company brochures, the current business plan, and so on;
- presentations, by senior executives or external consultants or advisers;
- meetings with senior executives and other key employees, and meetings with the company's professional advisers (for example, the head of the external audit team);
- meetings with shareholders and other important stakeholders;
- site visits to important business locations;
- attendance at conferences or formal training courses; and
- mentoring. (The Walker Report (2009) on corporate governance in UK banks commented that in some financial institutions, the induction process

included mentoring of a new NED by a senior member of the executive team over an initial induction period.)

The Higgs Report suggested that the aims of an induction process should be to:

- understand the company's business and its markets; and
- build a link with the company's people, and understand the company's main relationships – with its major customers, suppliers and shareholders.

Getting to understand the company's business involves not just learning about its products and markets and current business strategies, but also about significant contracts and major competitors, regulatory constraints on the market, key performance indicators and the group structure (and major subsidiaries and joint ventures). New directors also need to know about the current business plan, profit expectations and the board's dividend policy.

Building links with the company's people should involve meetings with senior management and site visits. The Higgs Report also commented on the value of board 'away days' for discussing strategy, which allow NEDs to build working relationships with colleagues away from the formal setting of the boardroom.

The FRC *Guidance on Audit Committees* comments specifically on the need for induction for new members of the audit committee. This programme should cover the role and the terms of reference of the audit committee, the time commitment expected from committee members and the main 'financial dynamics and risks' in the business.

Every director should also be made aware of the duties and responsibilities of all directors of the company. An induction programme may therefore include the provision of information about:

- the role of the board, including matters reserved for the board;
- the powers and duties of directors;
- the company's constitution (articles of association);
- the board committees and their terms of reference;
- board reviews of the risk management and internal control systems;
- how the board operates (for example, the frequency of board meetings, the role of the company secretary);
- the company's major shareholders;
- compliance with corporate governance requirements;
- the rules for directors about restrictions on dealing in the company's shares (the Model Code or an equivalent used by the company);
- company policy on corporate social responsibility (environmental issues, ethical issues, sustainable business); and

- arrangements for the annual performance review of board members.

The ICSA has published a guidance note on Induction of Directors. This can be obtained from the ICSA website (see Directory).

## New directors induction checklist

Have you been given the following essential information?

| THE DUTIES OF DIRECTORS | | THE COMPANY'S BUSINESS | | BOARD ISSUES | |
|---|---|---|---|---|---|
| The role and responsibilities of directors (legal, regulatory, best practice) | ☐ | Current strategic/ business plan | ☐ | Copy of the company's constitution (articles of association) and a summary of the most significant articles | ☐ |
| Copy of Model Code (or comparable code used by the company) | ☐ | Market analysis | ☐ | Minutes of recent board meetings | ☐ |
| Guidelines on matters reserved for the board and delegated authorities | ☐ | Budget and any revised forecasts | ☐ | Description of procedures for board meetings (e.g. when papers are sent out, normal location and duration of meetings, routine business transacted) | ☐ |
| Policy on directors obtaining independent professional advice | ☐ | Latest annual report and accounts | ☐ | Brief biographical details of all directors and key executives, contact details, responsibilities (executive role, board committees) | ☐ |
| Any other policies and procedures about which the director should be aware – check with the company secretary | ☐ | Explanation of key performance indicators | ☐ | Details of board committees including terms of reference | ☐ |
| 'Fire drill' procedures in situations such as a hostile takeover bid | ☐ | List of major subsidiaries, associated companies and joint ventures (and parent company) | ☐ | Minutes of previous committee meetings, for any committee the new director will be joining | ☐ |

| THE DUTIES OF DIRECTORS | THE COMPANY'S BUSINESS | | BOARD ISSUES |
|---|---|---|---|
| | Summary of major group insurance policies, including directors' and officers' liability insurance | ☐ | |
| | Details of any current or potential litigation by or against the company | ☐ | |
| | Treasury matters: funding arrangements, dividend policy | ☐ | |
| | Other published information: corporate brochure, mission statement, environmental report | ☐ | |
| | Summary of main events over the past three years | ☐ | |

## 2 PROFESSIONAL DEVELOPMENT OF DIRECTORS

The UK Corporate Governance Code calls for continuing professional development for directors, as well as an induction programme: 'All directors ... should regularly update and refresh their skills and knowledge' (Principle B.4).

- The chairman should make sure that the directors update their skills continually and refresh their knowledge and familiarity with the company. This is necessary to enable the directors to fulfil their roles as board members and committee members effectively.
- The company should bear the costs of professional development. The Code states: 'The company should provide the necessary resources for developing and updating its directors' knowledge and capabilities.'

As with induction, the chairman is responsible for ensuring that directors receive the training and development they need.

The UK Code gives more emphasis than in the past to the need for continuing development of all directors, including NEDs. The guiding assumption should be that every director needs ongoing training and development to remain effective. Failure to keep up with developments could be an indication that a director is losing effectiveness and so should not be re-elected at the end of their current term in office.

Provision B.4.2 of the Code states that the chairman 'should regularly review and agree with each director their training and development needs'. This review of the professional development needs of directors will probably be an element in their annual performance review. (Performance evaluation is dealt with later in this chapter.)

Although the chairman is responsible for this review, individual directors should think about the training or development that they need, and be ready to discuss this with the chairman at a suitable time. All directors, even very experienced ones, need to consider how effectively they are contributing to the board, and whether their skill levels require refreshment or improvement.

The Higgs Report (2003) made the point that personal development is not simply a matter of receiving formal 'classroom training', although formal training will be suitable in many cases.

The Report commented:

'On appointment, non-executive directors will already have relevant skills, knowledge, experience and abilities. Nevertheless, a non-executive director's credibility and effectiveness in the boardroom will depend not just on their existing capability but on their ability to extend and refresh their knowledge and skills ... The word "training" in this context is not altogether helpful as it carries rather limited connotations of formal instruction in a classroom setting ... By contrast, what I envisage is continued professional development tailored to the individual.'

The company secretary may be given responsibility for ensuring the effectiveness of the arrangements for training and development, and will need to be given the resources and budget for this task.

### FRC Guidance on professional development for audit committee members

The FRC *Guidance on Audit Committees* is more specific about the ongoing training requirements for members of the audit committee. It states that training should be provided on an 'ongoing and timely basis', and may include:

- an understanding of developments in financial reporting and related company law;
- training in the understanding of financial statements and applicable accounting standards;
- the regulatory framework for the company's business; and
- the role of internal and external auditors and risk management.

## 3 THE REQUIREMENT FOR PERFORMANCE EVALUATION

A principle of the UK Corporate Governance Code (Principle B.6) is that there should be an annual review and evaluation of the performance of:

- the board as a whole;
- each committee of the board; and
- each individual director.

This review should be both formal and rigorous.

### The purpose of performance evaluation

The purpose of the performance review is to ensure that:

- the board is fulfilling its purpose and carrying out its responsibilities;
- the board committees are fulfilling their roles effectively;
- individual directors are contributing effectively to the work of the board and its committees; and
- the collective skills and experience of the board members remain appropriate.

The evaluation of the performance of individual directors is particularly important for NEDs. Executive directors commit all (or most) of their time to the company, and should be fully familiar with the company's business and its operations. As senior executives, they are also able to bring the views of executive management to the discussions of the board.

It is more likely that NEDs, because they are 'part-time', do not contribute as much as their company would like – or needs. The UK Code specifically states that the performance evaluation of individual directors 'should aim to show whether each director continues to contribute effectively and to demonstrate commitment to the role (including commitment of time for board and committee meetings and any other duties)'.

# 4 THE PERFORMANCE EVALUATION PROCESS

### Who carries out the performance evaluation?
The UK Code states that the board has the responsibility for this annual review, without stating specifically who should carry it out.

The *Guidance on Board Effectiveness* offers more specific advice, describing evaluation as a 'powerful and valuable feedback mechanism for improving board effectiveness, maximising strengths and highlighting areas for further development'.

The *Guidance* states that evaluation should be objective and rigorous, and tailored to the board concerned. It suggests that the chairman should have overall responsibility for the process, with the SID leading the process to evaluate the chairman. Chairs of board committees should also lead the evaluation of their committees.

The UK Code also includes a provision that larger UK listed companies (FTSE 350 companies) should have 'external facilitation' of the board evaluation at least every three years. The use of external specialists to carry out or assist with the process should mean that the evaluation process continues to be rigorous and that feedback from the review is acted on. The *Guidance on Board Effectiveness* suggests that a decision to use external facilitators for a performance review may also be triggered by events such as:

- the appointment of a new board chairman;
- a known problem that will need tactful and impartial handling; or
- an external perception that the board is, or has been, ineffective.

Companies may combine performance evaluation by the chairman personally (or senior independent director) with the use of external consultants, for example, by alternating the use of external consultants in one year with internal review by the chairman the next year. However, the *Guidance on Board Effectiveness* is clear that external facilitation can 'add value by introducing a fresh perspective and new ways of thinking'.

### Guidance on performance evaluation
There are no rules or standard procedures for performance evaluation, and the details of the evaluation process will vary depending on the specific needs and circumstances of the company concerned.

However, the *Guidance on Board Effectiveness* comments that evaluation should look at how the board operates as a unit as well as looking at the contributions made by individual directors. It also suggests some areas that may be considered, including:

- the mix of skills, experience, knowledge and diversity on the board;
- clarity of, and leadership given to, the purpose, direction and values of the company;
- succession and development plans;
- how the board works together as a unit, and the tone set by the chairman and the CEO;
- key board relationships, particularly chairman/CEO, chairman/senior independent director, chairman/company secretary and executive/non-executive;
- effectiveness of individual non-executive and executive directors;
- clarity of the senior independent director's role;
- effectiveness of board committees, and how they are connected with the main board;
- quality of the general information provided on the company and its performance;
- quality of papers and presentations to the board;
- quality of discussions around individual proposals;
- the process the chairman uses to ensure sufficient debate for major decisions or contentious issues;
- the effectiveness of the secretariat;
- clarity of the decision processes and authorities;
- processes for identifying and reviewing risks; and
- how the board communicates with, and listens and responds to, shareholders and other stakeholders.

### A structured approach to performance evaluation

A suggested structure for performance evaluation is set out in Figure 10.1.

Performance evaluation can be carried out from three perspectives, or at three levels:

- Purpose. There should be an evaluation of how well the board is fulfilling its role and responsibilities, and enabling the company to achieve its objectives. Similarly, there should be an evaluation of how well each board committee is fulfilling its role and achieving its objectives.
- People. There should be an evaluation of the people who make up the board and its committees. The purpose of this evaluation should be to ensure that the board and its committees develop the management competencies and

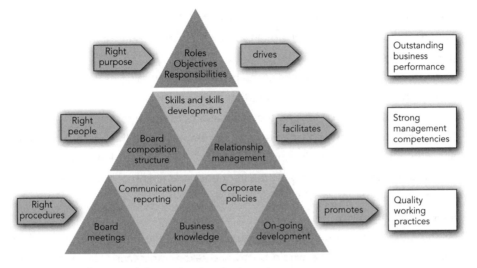

**Figure 10.1** A framework for evaluating the board

skills that the company needs from its leaders. This will involve an assessment of:

– the composition of the board and each committee;

– the skills and experience of the individual board members, and the combined skills and experience of the board (or committee) as a whole: whether these skills are appropriate and sufficient, and are being developed; and

– the success of the chairman in developing constructive relationships between the board (or committee) members.

- Procedures. There should also be an evaluation of the procedures of the board and its committees, to ensure that they use high-quality working practices and so function effectively. This will include an assessment of:

– the length and frequency of board meetings, and what the meetings have achieved;

– communication by the board to others and between board members;

– whether the knowledge of the individual board members is being used effectively (for example, in developing strategy);

– whether the board has developed suitable corporate policies (for example, for the use of the external auditors for non-audit work) and whether policies are continually reviewed; and

– whether the procedures of the board and its committees are subject to ongoing change and development.

## 5 USING PERFORMANCE EVALUATION

The UK Code states that the chairman should act on the results of the performance evaluation by:

- recognising the strengths of the board and addressing its weaknesses; and
- where appropriate, proposing that new members should be appointed to the board and/or seeking the resignation of some directors.

The chairman may also choose to review the composition of the board committees and whether a different chairman should be appointed to any of the committees. It may also be appropriate to review the frequency and timing of board meetings, so that arrangements for providing information to directors in advance of the meetings can be improved.

The *Guidance on Board Effectiveness* states that the outcome of evaluations should be shared with the whole board and taken into account, as appropriate, when considering issues such as board composition and the design of induction and director development programmes. The Guidance also suggests that it may be useful for boards to have 'a review loop' to consider the usefulness of the evaluation process.

One way of using performance evaluation constructively would be to identify training needs of individual directors. Any perceived weakness in the knowledge or skills of an individual director might be remedied by providing the director with an appropriate training or development programme.

The review of individual directors should also be used to consider whether the individual continues to contribute effectively, and whether a change in the composition of the board should be planned.

## 6 PERFORMANCE EVALUATION OF THE CHAIRMAN

The UK Corporate Governance Code (Provision B.6.3) states that the non-executive directors, led by the senior independent director, should be responsible for the performance evaluation of the chairman, but in doing this they should take account of the views expressed by the executive directors.

The issues for the review to consider should focus on the success of the chairman in providing effective leadership to the board and in performing the roles set out in the FRC's Guidance on Board Effectiveness.

Questions to consider may include the following:

- Has the chairman demonstrated ethical leadership for the board and the company?

- Does the agenda for board meetings focus mainly on strategy, performance, value creation and accountability, and does the board consider all matters reserved for its decision-making?
- Does the chairman ensure that board members receive a timely flow of high-quality supporting information?
- Does the chairman regularly consider succession planning and the composition of the board?
- Does the chairman provide effective management of board meetings and ensure that all members engage in discussions and that no person or small group dominates discussions?
- Does the chairman foster relationships based on mutual respect and open communication – both in and outside the boardroom – between the non-executive directors and the executive team?
- Does the chairman consult with the senior independent director on board matters?
- Does the chairman provide a strong lead on issues of director development, including through induction programmes for new directors and regular reviews with all directors?
- Does the chairman ensure effective communication with shareholders and other stakeholders and, in particular providers of debt capital?

## 7 REPORTING ON PERFORMANCE EVALUATION

The UK Corporate Governance Code (Provision B.6.1) states that the annual report of the company should state how the annual performance review of the board, its committees and individual directors has been conducted.

This requirement may also give weight to the view that external consultants should be used, because the company should be able to demonstrate that, by using consultants, the performance evaluation process has been:

- conducted in an objective manner;
- subjected to some degree of 'challenge'; and
- conducted with access to benchmarking against other, similar companies.

In the preface to the UK Code, the chairman of the FRC states that chairmen are encouraged in their statement in the annual report and accounts to explain personally how the principles relating to the role and effectiveness of the board have been applied.

## 8 CHECKLIST FOR EVALUATING BOARD PERFORMANCE

The following checklist sets out aspects of board performance within a structured framework for evaluation.

---

### 1 Roles, objectives and responsibilities

1.1 Each director has clearly-defined personal objectives linked to the overall strategy of the company. ☐

1.2 The objectives are communicated to the other directors and to senior management and key stakeholders, as appropriate. ☐

1.3 The board plays a significant role in defining long-term strategy. ☐

1.4 The board has approved an appropriate ethics policy and code of conduct. ☐

### 2 Board composition and structure

2.1 Selection. The process of making new appointments to the board has functioned well during the year. ☐

2.2 The board structure is clearly defined and has been subject to review. (UK Corporate Governance Code principle B.6, which deals with board evaluation, includes a specific reference to reviewing the composition of the board and its diversity, including gender.' Evaluation of the board should consider the balance of skills, experience, independence and knowledge of the company on the board, its diversity, **including gender**, how the board works together as a unit, and other factors relevant to its effectiveness.') ☐

2.3 The roles of the chairman and CEO are not combined. ☐

2.4 There are appropriate board committees with documented responsibilities. ☐

### 3 Skills and skills development

3.1 There is a unique and clear role description for each director. (Otherwise, why is that person on the board?) ☐

3.2 There are individual training plans for each director, including the non-executives. ☐

3.3 There is a formal but confidential system in place for the performance review of each individual director. ☐

### 4 Personal qualities and contribution

4.1 The individual directors have abilities in the areas of strategic perception, decision-making, analysis, communication, interpersonal interaction and the achievement of results. ☐

4.2 The individual director participates actively at board meetings, and asks probing and difficult questions at meetings and at other times. ☐

| | | |
|---|---|---|
| 4.3 | The individual works well with other people and communicates well. | ☐ |
| 4.4 | The individual makes valuable contributions to the board's deliberations and work including long-range/strategic planning decisions. | ☐ |
| 4.5 | The individual has a good attendance record at board and committee meetings. | ☐ |
| 4.6 | The individual comes to board meetings well-prepared. | ☐ |
| 4.7 | The individual NED is available when needed. | ☐ |
| 4.8 | The individual NED has suitable business knowledge and an awareness of the industry in which the company operates. | ☐ |

**5 Relationship management**

| | | |
|---|---|---|
| 5.1 | The board has a good working relationship with key stakeholders (management, other employees, external auditors, shareholders and other investors, analysts). | ☐ |
| 5.2 | There is a defined process for a continuous flow of information from management to the board and from the board to management. | ☐ |
| 5.3 | Directors are able to obtain independent professional advice on company matters. | ☐ |

**6 Board meetings**

| | | |
|---|---|---|
| 6.1 | There are regular board meetings – each quarter as a minimum. | ☐ |
| 6.2 | The attendance of directors at board meetings is recorded, and minutes of meetings are produced. | ☐ |
| 6.3 | Meetings have open discussions to ensure that the board comes to an informed and fully-considered decision. | ☐ |
| 6.4 | The NEDs meet on a regular basis, with management and other stakeholders, to keep up to date with the company's business. | ☐ |

**7 Communication and reporting**

| | | |
|---|---|---|
| 7.1 | The board regularly issues open communications across the company, to keep staff up to date with strategic developments. | ☐ |
| 7.2 | The board has open communication lines with investors and analysts. | ☐ |
| 7.3 | The board receives regular reports from teams across the business – operations, risk management and assurance functions. | ☐ |
| 7.4 | The board has complied with its disclosure guidelines for disclosures to various stakeholder groups. | ☐ |

**8 Business knowledge**

| | | |
|---|---|---|
| 8.1 | There is a formal orientation/induction programme for all directors. | ☐ |

8.2 Board members know, understand, apply and analyse strategic business direction. ☐

8.3 The board exhibits knowledge in all key areas (finance and accounting, risk management, marketing strategy, HR issues, improving business performance, change management). ☐

# 9 CHECKLIST FOR EVALUATING PERSONAL PERFORMANCE

Individual directors should be given an annual performance review. NEDs should self-review their own performance before the formal review takes place, and should be ready to discuss what they have achieved or failed to achieve since the previous review. The following checklist of questions is suggested as a guide to preparation. A score in the range 1 (poor) to 5 (very good) can be awarded as an answer to each question. Comments can be added to explain the rating in each case.

## 1 Contribution to board meetings and committee meetings

1.1 How well did I contribute to boardroom discussions?

Comment:

1 2 3 4 5
☐ ☐ ☐ ☐ ☐

1.2 How well did I contribute to decision-making?

Comment

1 2 3 4 5
☐ ☐ ☐ ☐ ☐

1.3 Do I consider myself to be independent in judgement, based on my boardroom contributions?

Comment

1 2 3 4 5
☐ ☐ ☐ ☐ ☐

## 2 Contribution of effort

2.1 Am I satisfied with the time I am contributing to the company?

Comment

1 2 3 4 5
☐ ☐ ☐ ☐ ☐

2.2 Have I attended all/most board meetings and committee meetings?

Comment

1 2 3 4 5
☐ ☐ ☐ ☐ ☐

2.2 Am I satisfied with my preparation for board meetings and committee meetings?

Comment

1 2 3 4 5
☐ ☐ ☐ ☐ ☐

## 3  Being informed

3.1  Am I satisfied with the information provided to me about the company's affairs, especially in advance of board and committee meetings?

1 2 3 4 5
☐☐☐☐☐

Comment

3.2  Do I have a sufficient knowledge of the company's business? Have I made site visits this year?

1 2 3 4 5
☐☐☐☐☐

Comment

3.3  Am I sufficiently aware of the company's risk management and Internal control systems, and the effectiveness of these?

1 2 3 4 5
☐☐☐☐☐

Comment

3.4  Am I sufficiently aware of developments in corporate governance and legislation relevant to the company?

1 2 3 4 5
☐☐☐☐☐

Comment

3.5  Am I satisfied with my training this year?

1 2 3 4 5
☐☐☐☐☐

Comment

## 4  Personal relationships

4.1  Do I have a good working relationship with the board chairman?

1 2 3 4 5
☐☐☐☐☐

Comment

4.2  Do I have a good working relationship with the other NEDs?

1 2 3 4 5
☐☐☐☐☐

Comment

4.3  Do I have a good working relationship with the executive directors?

1 2 3 4 5
☐☐☐☐☐

Comment

4.4  Do I make sufficient use of the services of the company secretary?

1 2 3 4 5
☐☐☐☐☐

Comment

## 5  Performance summary

5.1  What is the most pleasing aspect of my performance as NED this year?

5.2  What is the least satisfactory aspect of my performance as NED this year?

# CHAPTER ELEVEN

# Communication with stakeholders

1   *Relations with shareholders*

2   *UK Corporate Governance Code on relations with shareholders*

3   *Institutional investor guidelines: the UK Stewardship Code*

4   *Disclosures and transparency*

5   *Corporate social responsibility (CSR)*

.....................

## OVERVIEW

This chapter deals with several aspects of corporate governance that NEDs should be aware of, although they might not be closely involved with them. Companies should maintain good relations with their shareholders and should communicate with them. The responsibilities of the board for maintaining effective communications are set out in the UK Code on Corporate Governance. Institutional investors also have responsibilities, in the interests of their beneficiaries, for maintaining constructive relationships with the boards of companies in which they hold shares, and most UK institutional shareholders now subscribe to the principles of a UK Stewardship Code.

Another important aspect of good corporate governance is the need for adequate disclosures by companies to their shareholders and other stakeholders, and for transparency in those disclosures. Transparency is considered to be one of the fundamental principles of good corporate governance. In recent years, many stock market companies have expanded the quantity of information they provide, for example, in narrative reports, although this has not necessarily resulted in greater transparency.

There is also a view that companies have responsibilities to society as a whole and to the environment, and should not focus exclusively on making profits and creating value for shareholders. Corporate social responsibility is the concept that companies have responsibilities to act like a 'corporate citizen' in the societies in which they operate. A related issue is that companies, in accepting responsibilities to society and the environment, should report on these issues to a range of stakeholders and not just to their shareholders.

# 1  RELATIONS WITH SHAREHOLDERS

The directors of a company are responsible for running the company in the interests of its stakeholders, particularly its shareholders. In most large companies the major shareholders are not also directors, and it is therefore important that there should be good communications between the two groups. The shareholders need to be informed about how the company is performing, and the directors need to know the views of their shareholders.

Most communications between a company and its major shareholders are through the CEO, finance director and chairman. However, NEDs should be made aware of any issues that are of concern or interest to shareholders.

The UK Corporate Governance Code contains several principles and provisions concerned with relations with shareholders. There is also a UK Stewardship Code for institutional investors, and guidelines for members on a range of governance issues have been published by institutional investor organisations.

## Shareholder rights

The importance of relations between public companies and their shareholders arises partly from the fact that although equity shareholders are the legal owners of their company, shareholder rights are limited.

Shareholders of public companies are entitled to attend general meetings of the company, and at the AGM they vote on a number of items of routine business. They vote:

- on the re-election of directors proposed by the board;
- to appoint or reappoint the external auditors;
- to approve the recommended final dividend. They can vote in favour of the resolution or can vote for a lower dividend, but they cannot vote to increase the dividend above the recommended amount; and
- on the directors' remuneration report, but this is an advisory vote only and a vote against the report is not binding in any way on the board of directors.

Votes on ordinary business matters are passed by means of an ordinary resolution, requiring a simple majority. Other matters on which shareholders have a right to vote (such as votes on rights issues, the waiver of pre-emption rights, or a proposed amendment to the company's articles of association) may require a special resolution and a majority of at least 75%.

Resolutions are normally proposed at general meetings by the board of directors. However, shareholders are able to call an extraordinary general meeting if they hold at least 5% of the voting share capital, and they are also able to include a matter on the agenda for the AGM if they have at least 5% of the voting shares.

Shareholders have the right to remove a director before the end of their term of office. This requires an ordinary resolution in a general meeting (section 168, Companies Act 2006). In principle, 5% or more of shareholders could therefore call a general meeting to propose the removal of a director, but this would be an unusual event.

Taken together, shareholder voting rights are limited in scope. This creates the risk that shareholders will choose not to become involved in the affairs of their company, because there is relatively little they can do and they can sell their shares if they disapprove of the company's leadership, policies or performance.

To avoid the creation of a gap between the company and its shareholders, both boards of directors and institutional shareholders in listed companies are encouraged to 'engage' with each other.

## 2 UK CORPORATE GOVERNANCE CODE ON RELATIONS WITH SHAREHOLDERS

The UK Corporate Governance Code requires boards of directors to maintain relations with shareholders through dialogue and constructive use of the AGM.

### Dialogue with shareholders

A principle in the UK Code is that there should be a dialogue with institutional shareholders 'based on the mutual understanding of objectives' (Principle E.1).

The board as a whole has a responsibility to make sure that a satisfactory dialogue takes place.

- Although most shareholder contact is likely to be through the CEO and finance director, the chairman should ensure that all the directors are made aware of the issues that matter to the company's major shareholders, and their concerns.
- The board should keep in touch with shareholder opinion in whatever ways are most practical and efficient.

The Code also contains specific requirements (Provision E.1.1):

- The chairman of the board should ensure that the views of the shareholders are communicated to the board as a whole.
- The chairman should discuss governance and strategy with major shareholders.
- NEDs should be given the opportunity to attend scheduled meetings with major shareholders. They should also be expected to attend meetings where their attendance has been requested by major shareholders.
- The senior independent director should attend a sufficient number of meetings with a range of major shareholders, with the purpose of listening to their views and developing a balanced view of shareholder concerns.

Provision E.1.2 requires the board to state in the annual report the steps they have taken to ensure that the board members, **especially the NEDs**, develop an understanding of the views of the major shareholders about the company (for example, through face-to-face contact, analysts' briefings, or surveys of shareholder opinion).

This emphasis on maintaining contact with major shareholders, and taking opportunities to meet with major shareholders, is also part of the process of getting NEDs out of the boardroom, so that they gain much greater familiarity with the company and its affairs.

## Constructive use of the AGM

The UK Code also encourages boards to seek good relations with their shareholders through constructive use of the annual general meeting. 'The board should use the AGM to communicate with investors and to encourage their participation' (Principle E.2).

The board chairman should arrange for the chairmen of the nomination, remuneration and audit committees to attend the AGM and be available to answer questions. NEDs who are committee chairmen may therefore be expected to speak at the AGM during the shareholders' question time.

The Code also states that the board chairman should arrange for all directors to attend the AGM. Even if they do not speak at the meeting, directors will have the opportunity to hear shareholders' views.

Directors, including NEDs, often hold some shares in their company. As shareholders they are also entitled to vote.

Companies may provide in their articles of association for communications with shareholders to be by electronic means, typically via the company's website.

Information, such as the annual report and accounts and notices of general meetings) can be sent to shareholders in electronic form. Where electronic communications are used, shareholders are also able to appoint proxies electronically, to vote on their behalf on resolutions at a general meeting.

The UK Code includes some provisions relating to proxy voting at general meetings:

- The chairman should discuss governance and strategy with major shareholders.
- For each resolution voted on at any general meeting, proxy appointment forms should give shareholders the opportunity to vote for or against the resolution, or to record a 'vote withheld'. A vote withheld is not a vote in law: it records a positive decision 'not to vote' on the resolution. It therefore does not count when calculating the proportions of shares that have been voted for or against the resolution. However, votes withheld notify the board of shareholder concern about the resolution, which is strong enough to make them decide that they do not want to support it, but not strong enough to make them decide to oppose it.
- Where the vote on a resolution at a meeting is taken on a show of hands, rather than by poll, the company must make available at the meeting and also on its website certain information about the proxy voting (number of shares for which proxy appointments were made, number in favour of the resolution, the number against and the number of votes withheld).

Note: In UK law, private companies are not required to hold an AGM, but public companies must do so. Where a private company does not hold an AGM, the report and accounts must be sent to the shareholders, and there are special rules about the reappointment of the company's auditors.

## 3 INSTITUTIONAL INVESTOR GUIDELINES: THE UK STEWARDSHIP CODE

A counter-argument to the view that shareholders do not have many rights is that shareholders do have rights but do not use them effectively enough. Shareholders can exert influence over their company by engaging with them more. In addition there is an argument that institutional investors own their shares in the interests of other beneficiaries, such as members of pension funds, holders of life assurance policies and other investment clients. As 'stewards' for the investments of other beneficiaries, they should try to ensure that companies are governed in the interests of shareholders, by engaging constructively with them.

This view led to the issue of the UK Stewardship Code (2010, revised 2012) by the Financial Reporting Council. It is complementary to the UK Corporate Governance Code, and just as the Governance Code requires directors to seek good relations with shareholders, the Stewardship Code requires institutional investors to engage constructively with companies in which they hold shares. Engagement includes getting involved in constructive dialogue with companies on matters such as strategy, corporate performance and the management of risk and on other governance issues.

The Stewardship Code is aimed 'in the first instance' at UK fund managers ('asset managers'), who make investments on behalf of clients, and who are therefore the legal owners of the shares.

Clients of fund managers (asset owners) include pension funds and insurance companies. These are also encouraged by the FRC to apply the Stewardship Code on the same basis as asset managers.

The FRC has expressed its hope that the Code will also be applied by foreign investors in UK company shares.

The Institutional Shareholders Committee (ISC), a collective body for UK institutional investors, established the Institutional Investor Council in 2010, whose brief is to work with the FRC in promoting the UK Stewardship Code.

The Stewardship Code consists of seven principles, each with supporting guidance.

## The meaning of stewardship

The introduction to the 2012 revised version of the Stewardship Code comments that the aim of stewardship is to promote the long-term success of the company in such a way that the 'ultimate providers of capital' also prosper. The Code refers to 'investors' rather than 'shareholders', suggesting that long-term investors in debt capital have stewardship responsibilities as well as shareholders.

The Code goes on to state that responsibilities for stewardship are shared.

- The primary responsibility lies with the board of the company, which oversees the actions of management.
- Investors also have an important role, in holding the board to account for the fulfilment of its responsibilities.

For investors, stewardship involves voting at general meetings, and the way in which votes are used. However, stewardship for investors is more than just voting.

'Activities may include monitoring and engaging with companies on matters such as strategy, performance, risk, capital structure and corporate governance, including culture and remuneration. Engagement is purposeful dialogue with companies on these matters as well as on issues that are the immediate subject of votes at general meetings.'

The Code emphasises, however, that compliance with the Stewardship Code does not constitute an invitation to interfere in the management of companies; nor does it prevent investors from selling their shares, if this is thought to be in the best interests of their end-investors or beneficiaries.

### The seven principles of the UK Stewardship Code

The Code consists of seven principles, with some guidance for each principle.

**Table 11.1** The seven principles of the UK Stewardship Code

| PRINCIPLE | DETAILS |
| --- | --- |
| 1: Institutional investors should publicly disclose their policy on how they will discharge their stewardship responsibilities. | Discharging responsibilities means monitoring and engaging with companies. Public disclosure should be in a policy statement (or 'stewardship statement') by the institutional investor. The policy statement should reflect the institution's position within the 'investment chain', as asset owners or asset managers. |
| 2: Institutional investors should have a robust policy on managing conflicts of interest in relation to stewardship, which should be publicly disclosed. | Institutional investors should have a 'robust policy' on managing conflicts of interest in relationship to stewardship, and they should make public disclosure of this policy. Institutional investors should act in the interests of their clients or beneficiaries, but it is recognised conflicts of interest between beneficiaries or clients will inevitably arise from time to time. |
| 3: Institutional investors should monitor their investee companies. | Institutional investors should monitor the companies in which they invest, in order to decide when it is necessary to enter into an active dialogue with their board of directors. They should try to identify problems in a company at an early stage, to minimise the potential loss of shareholder value, and they should make their concerns known to appropriate members of the company's board. |

| PRINCIPLE | DETAILS |
|---|---|
| 4: Institutional investors should establish clear guidelines on when and how they will escalate their stewardship activities (escalating shareholder activism). | Institutional investors should set out the circumstances when they will intervene actively, for example, when they have concerns about the company's strategy, performance, corporate governance, remuneration or its approach to risks arising from environmental or social matters. Initial discussions with the company should be on a confidential basis, but if the company's board does not respond constructively, the institutional investor should consider whether to escalate their action. |
| 5: Institutional shareholders should be willing to act collectively with other investors where appropriate. | Institutional investors should be willing to act collectively with other investors where appropriate. 'At times collaboration with other investors may be the most effective manner in which to engage.' Collaborative engagement may be particularly appropriate at times when the company is under severe stress, or when risks threaten to 'destroy significant value'. |
| 6: Institutional investors should have a clear policy on voting and disclosure of voting activity. | Institutional investors should seek to vote all the shares that they hold. They should not automatically support the board of directors. Where they have been unable to reach a satisfactory outcome through dialogue, they should consider withholding their vote on resolutions at a general meeting, or voting against. It is good practice to notify the company of an intention to vote against a resolution or withhold their vote. |
| 7: Institutional investors should report periodically on their stewardship and voting activities. | Institutional investors should report periodically on stewardship and voting activities. Investment managers should report to their clients, and institutions that represent the interests of an end-investor or act as principals should report at least annually to those people to whom they are accountable. |

## 4 DISCLOSURES AND TRANSPARENCY

Disclosure and transparency are important principles in corporate governance.

- Disclosure refers to the requirement for companies to provide information to shareholders (and other investors and stakeholders) about their performance, situation, affairs and prospects.
- Transparency refers to the requirement that information provided by a company about itself should be clear and easy to understand. A company should not hide anything, or make its intentions or position unclear.

In the UK and the European Union more generally, in recent years there has been much greater recognition of the need for disclosures. Disclosures are a combination of statutory, regulatory and voluntary. Statutory disclosures are required, for example, by the Companies Act. Regulatory disclosures, including disclosures about corporate governance arrangements, are required for listed companies by the Disclosure and Transparency Rules. Disclosures on corporate governance are also required by the UK Corporate Governance Code. Companies may also choose to publish voluntary reports, notably on corporate social responsibility matters.

### Business review

The Companies Act 2006 (section 417) requires all companies other than small companies to include a business review in their annual report. This review is given other names in published accounts, such as operating and financial review (OFR). It may also be included within the directors' report.

A business review must contain a review of the company's business (including an analysis of the development and performance of the company during the year and its position at the end of the year) and a description of the principal risks and uncertainties facing the company.

Quoted companies are required to publish an enhanced business review, which should contain (to an extent necessary for an understanding of the company's business) information about:

- the main trends and factors likely to affect the company's business in the future;
- environmental matters (including the impact of the company's business on the environment), the company's employees and social and community issues; and
- (with exceptions) information about any person with whom the company has a contractual arrangement that is essential to its business.

In addition, the review should include (to the extent necessary for an understanding of its business) some quantitative information:

- analysis using key financial performance indicators (KPIs); and
- where appropriate, analysis using non-financial key performance indicators, such as KPIs relating to employee matters and environmental matters.

The Companies Act includes 'safe harbour provisions' for misleading statements in the business review (or omissions), as explained in Chapter 2.

*Strategic report: changes to narrative reporting from October 2013*

The UK government has announced its commitment to improved narrative reporting. In September 2011, the Department for Business, Innovation and Skills (BIS) issued a consultation paper, which stated as one of its aims the elimination of 'useless clutter' from narrative reports. Following this consultation the government introduced proposals for new regulations for narrative reporting, which come into effect from October 2013 as amendments to the Companies Act 2006.

Directors should prepare a strategic report to replace the business review. This should be placed at the front of the annual report and separate from the directors' report. For quoted companies, the report will have to include information about: the company's strategy and business model; numbers of women who are directors, senior managers and employees; greenhouse gas emissions; and other environmental and employee matters. (There is a small companies exemption from the requirement to produce a strategic report, and disclosure requirements in the report are not as extensive for non-quoted companies.)

The **strategic report** should contain essentially the same information as required previously for the business review, but with additional reporting requirements for quoted companies, relating to:

- requirements for quoted companies to report on their strategy and their business model (however, most UK listed companies already do this);
- human rights issues; and
- diversity on the board.

The strategic report must contain a fair review of the company's business and a description of the principal risks and uncertainties facing the company.

The report should provide a 'balanced and comprehensive analysis' of the development and performance of the business of the company during the financial year and the position of the company's business as at the end of the year. The review should be consistent with the size and complexity of the business.

In the case of an unquoted company, the report should include:

- a description of the company's strategy;
- a description of the company's business model;
- the main trends likely to affect the future of the company's business;
- information about environmental matters, including the company's effect on the environment;
- information about the company's employees;
- information about social, community and human rights issues, including any company policies on these matters and the effectiveness of those policies; and

- information about the number of persons of each sex who are directors of the company, managers of the company and employees of the company.

A strategic report will be mostly narrative in form, but for a quoted company it should also include:

- key financial performance indicators (KPIs); and
- where appropriate, key non-financial performance indicators, including information of environmental and employee matters.

It will be a criminal offence for a director to approve the strategic report knowing that it does not comply with the requirements of the Act.

There will be **safe harbour provisions** reducing the potential liability of the board for making forward-looking statements in the report that prove subsequently to have been incorrect. The purpose of these provisions is to give directors confidence to make forward-looking statements without fear of criminal prosecution or other legal action that would otherwise restrict their willingness to make predictions.

### Disclosures about corporate governance

Listed companies are required, by the UK Corporate Governance Code and the Disclosure and Transparency Rules (DTR), to make extensive disclosures about corporate governance issues in their annual report and accounts. Many of these disclosures have been mentioned in previous chapters. They are summarised briefly in Table 11.2.

The UK Code requires other disclosures, for example, a going concern statement by the directors and a report on the annual performance review of the board.

### CSR reports

In some aspects of reporting and disclosures, many companies provide additional voluntary information, and the majority of FTSE 100 companies now publish an annual corporate social responsibility report. This may be given a different name, such as a social and environmental report or a sustainability report, and is usually published as a separate document from the annual report and accounts, but at the same time (see below).

## 5 CORPORATE SOCIAL RESPONSIBILITY (CSR)

Corporate social responsibility (CSR) is not an issue of corporate governance. However, it is an issue that attracts the interest of various institutional investors, and NEDs ought to be aware of how CSR could affect their company.

CSR has been defined in various ways:

- It is 'a concept whereby companies integrate social and environmental concerns in their business operations and their interaction with their stakeholders on a voluntary basis'.

**Table 11.2** Corporate governance disclosure requirements

| UK CODE REQUIREMENT | DTR REQUIREMENT | COMPARISON |
|---|---|---|
| **The board and its committees.** The annual report should include a statement about how the board operates and its membership. The annual report should also include a description of the work of the nomination committee and audit committee. A description of the work of the remuneration committee should be made available. | Listed companies should produce a corporate governance statement that includes a description of the composition and work of the board and its committees. | Compliance with the requirements of the UK Code will result in compliance with the DTR, but only if the annual report also includes a report on the composition and work of the remuneration committee and any other board committees, in addition to the nomination and audit committees. |
| **Audit committee.** The Code makes provisions about the size and composition of the audit committee and the annual report should include disclosures in an audit committee report about the membership and functions of the committee. | Companies must have an audit committee and must comply with minimum rules for its composition. The annual report must include disclosures about the composition and functions of the committee. | Compliance with the UK Code means that the company will also comply with the DTR. |
| **Internal control and risk management.** The board must carry out a review of the effectiveness of the internal control and risk management systems and report that it has done so. | Within their corporate governance statement, companies must describe the main features of their internal control and risk management systems for the financial reporting process (only). | The requirements of the UK Code and DTR are different, but both can be met within the same report on internal control and risk management. |

- 'While there is no single, commonly-accepted definition of corporate social responsibility … it generally refers to business decision-making linked to ethical values, compliance with legal requirements, and respect for people, communities and the environment' (Business for Social Responsibility).

An important element of CSR is that it goes beyond compliance with legal and regulatory obligations, and involves voluntary initiatives and investment in people and the environment, and better relations with all stakeholders, not just shareholders and other investors.

### Sustainability and sustainable development

CSR is also associated with the concept of sustainable business development, which is the view that businesses should seek to develop in a way that can be sustained into the future, without depleting the earth's natural resources or causing irrecoverable environmental damage.

Companies that are seen to cause damage to the environment may suffer from a loss of reputation among customers, suppliers and government. This can have implications for fines and other penalties, civil legal action, lost contracts, clean-up costs and possibly falling sales. The impact on oil group BP of the explosion at a drilling rig in the Gulf of Mexico in 2010, and the subsequent environmental damage it caused, is a clear example of the potential risks and the need for companies to consider social and environmental issues, particularly in industries such as oil extraction, mining and energy production.

Interest in sustainable development has come from several sources:

- governments, concerned about the implications for society of environmental damage and loss of natural resources;
- investors, many of whom now consider the ethical, social and environmental implications of the investments they make ('socially responsible investment' or SRI); and
- companies themselves, who may identify business opportunities – developing new products or reducing costs – in environmentally-friendly initiatives. For example, in 2009, Mars announced a strategy for producing its entire cocoa supply in a sustainable manner by 2010 and pharmaceuticals group GlaxoSmithKline announced targets to cut waste in medicine production at its factories by two-thirds by 2015.

### CSR reports and sustainability reports

With the exception of the disclosures in the business review, described above, UK companies are under no obligation to report on the corporate social responsibility policies or initiatives. However, many listed companies now publish voluntary annual reports on CSR. They may be called social and environmental reports or CSR reports, and are usually published each year at the same time as the annual report and accounts but in a separate document or booklet. These reports set out their ethical values and commitment to CSR principles, and describe what they have done in this area during the financial year.

A CSR report might be largely descriptive, providing narrative descriptions of how the company has contributed to reductions in waste or pollution, promoting sustainable business or engaging in charitable activities and community development activities.

There is now growing recognition of the need to provide social and environmental information as quantified performance measurements, so that actual achievements can be assessed better against targets or benchmarks. Sustainability reports provide quantified measurements of performance in three areas of achievement: financial performance, social performance and environmental performance. Since these reports provide quantified performance measurements or results, sustainability reports are also described as triple bottom line reporting.

### The relevance of CSR to NEDs

NEDs need to be aware of the reporting requirements and voluntary reporting initiatives about CSR issues.

In addition, it may be important to understand how a company might suffer financially from a poor track record on CSR issues:

- Bad publicity about social and environmental issues could damage the public image of the company and its brands ('brand reputation risk').
- Companies may be affected by preferences of stakeholders, for companies with positive policy objectives on social and environmental issues. There are some investment organisations that focus on these issues. More significantly, perhaps, high-quality employees may prefer to work for 'ethical' companies.

NEDs also need to understand the growing significance of CSR for many institutional investors. For example, the UNEP Finance Initiative (UNEP is the United Nations Environment Programme) has over 200 members from the financial services sector, such as banks and investment institutions. The aim of this initiative is to promote a set of principles that define best practice for responsible investment by institutional investors that have the full support of the UN and also of leading institutional investors worldwide.

A view underlying the initiative is that institutional investors should make sustainable development an issue when making decisions on investment in companies. The UN Global Compact, which launched the UNEP Financial Initiative, has stated:

'Institutional investors with clear information on company behaviour can take action, via proxy voting and other means, to pressure companies not to focus on short-term gains at the expense of long-term performance particularly in developing and developed nations.'

In the UK, the Association of British Insurers updated its guidelines and issued 'Responsible Investment Disclosure Guidelines' (2007). These are directed at listed companies, and specify information about environmental, social and governance issues that they should be expected (as a minimum) to disclose.

# The UK Corporate Governance Code

## SEPTEMBER 2012

## CONTENTS

**The UK Corporate Governance Code**

## GOVERNANCE AND THE CODE

1. The purpose of corporate governance is to facilitate effective, entrepreneurial and prudent management that can deliver the long-term success of the company.

2. The first version of the UK Corporate Governance Code (the Code) was produced in 1992 by the Cadbury Committee. Its paragraph 2.5 is still the classic definition of the context of the Code:

   Corporate governance is the system by which companies are directed and controlled. Boards of directors are responsible for the governance of their companies. The shareholders' role in governance is to appoint the directors and the auditors and to satisfy themselves that an appropriate governance structure is in place. The responsibilities of the board include setting the company's strategic aims, providing the leadership to put them into effect, supervising the management of the business and reporting to shareholders on their stewardship. The board's actions are subject to laws, regulations and the shareholders in general meeting.

3. Corporate governance is therefore about what the board of a company does and how it sets the values of the company, and is to be distinguished from the day to day operational management of the company by full-time executives.

4. The Code is a guide to a number of key components of effective board practice. It is based on the underlying principles of all good governance: accountability, transparency, probity and focus on the sustainable success of an entity over the longer term.

5. The Code has been enduring, but it is not immutable. Its fitness for purpose in a permanently changing economic and social business environment requires its evaluation at appropriate intervals.

6. The new Code applies to accounting periods beginning on or after 1 October 2012 and applies to all companies with a Premium listing of equity shares regardless of whether they are incorporated in the UK or elsewhere.

## PREFACE

1. The FRC's review of the implementation of the Code in 2011 reinforced the two principal conclusions reported in the preface to the 2010 edition. First, that much more attention needed to be paid to following the spirit of

the Code as well as its letter. Secondly, that the impact of shareholders in monitoring the Code could and should be enhanced by better interaction between the boards of listed companies and their shareholders. The UK Stewardship Code, which provides guidance on good practice for investors, should be seen as a companion piece to this Code.

2. Nearly two decades of constructive usage have enhanced the prestige of the Code. Indeed, it seems that there is almost a belief that complying with the Code in itself constitutes good governance. The Code, however, is of necessity limited to being a guide only in general terms to principles, structure and processes. It cannot guarantee effective board behaviour because the range of situations in which it is applicable is much too great for it to attempt to mandate behaviour more specifically than it does. Boards therefore have a lot of room within the framework of the Code to decide for themselves how they should act.

3. To follow the spirit of the Code to good effect, boards must think deeply, thoroughly and on a continuing basis about their overall tasks and the implications of these for the roles of their individual members. Absolutely key in this endeavour are the leadership of the chairman of a board, the support given to and by the CEO, and the frankness and openness of mind with which issues are discussed and tackled by all directors.

4. The challenge should not be underrated. To run a corporate board successfully is extremely demanding. Constraints on time and knowledge combine with the need to maintain mutual respect and openness between a cast of strong, able and busy directors dealing with each other across the different demands of executive and non-executive roles. To achieve good governance requires continuing and high-quality effort.

5. The Code's function should be to help boards discharge their duties in the best interests of their companies. In recent reviews of the Code, the FRC has focused on changing the 'tone' of the Code by making limited but significant changes to signal the importance of the general principles which should guide board behaviours. It is to be hoped that these changes will promote greater clarity and understanding with regard to the tasks of a board and that communication with shareholders will be more effective as a result.

6. Chairmen are encouraged to report personally in their annual statements how the principles relating to the role and effectiveness of the board (in Sections A and B of the Code) have been applied. Not only will this give

investors a clearer picture of the steps taken by boards to operate effectively but also, by providing fuller context, it may make investors more willing to accept explanations when a company chooses to explain rather than to comply with one or more provisions. Above all, the personal reporting on governance by chairmen as the leaders of boards might be a turning point in attacking the fungus of 'boiler-plate' which is so often the preferred and easy option in sensitive areas but which is dead communication.

7. While in law the company is primarily accountable to its shareholders, and the relationship between the company and its shareholders is also the main focus of the Code, companies are encouraged to recognise the contribution made by other providers of capital and to confirm the board's interest in listening to the views of such providers insofar as these are relevant to the company's overall approach to governance.

Financial Reporting Council
September 2012

## COMPLY OR EXPLAIN

1. The 'comply or explain' approach is the trademark of corporate governance in the UK. It has been in operation since the Code's beginnings and is the foundation of the Code's flexibility. It is strongly supported by both companies and shareholders and has been widely admired and imitated internationally.

2. The Code is not a rigid set of rules. It consists of principles (main and supporting) and provisions. The Listing Rules require companies to apply the Main Principles and report to shareholders on how they have done so. The principles are the core of the Code and the way in which they are applied should be the central question for a board as it determines how it is to operate according to the Code.

3. It is recognised that an alternative to following a provision may be justified in particular circumstances if good governance can be achieved by other means. A condition of doing so is that the reasons for it should be explained clearly and carefully to shareholders[1], who may wish to discuss the position with the company and whose voting intentions may be influenced

---

1   References to shareholders in this section also apply to intermediaries and agents employed to assist shareholders in scrutinising governance arrangements.

as a result. In providing an explanation, the company should aim to illustrate how its actual practices are consistent with the principle to which the particular provision relates, contribute to good governance and promote delivery of business objectives. It should set out the background, provide a clear rationale for the action it is taking, and describe any mitigating actions taken to address any additional risk and maintain conformity with the relevant principle. Where deviation from a particular provision is intended to be limited in time, the explanation should indicate when the company expects to conform with the provision.

4. In their responses to explanations, shareholders should pay due regard to companies' individual circumstances and bear in mind in particular the size and complexity of the company and the nature of the risks and challenges it faces. Whilst shareholders have every right to challenge companies' explanations if they are unconvincing, they should not be evaluated in a mechanistic way and departures from the Code should not be automatically treated as breaches. Shareholders should be careful to respond to the statements from companies in a manner that supports the 'comply or explain' process and bearing in mind the purpose of good corporate governance. They should put their views to the company and both parties should be prepared to discuss the position.

5. Smaller listed companies, in particular those new to listing, may judge that some of the provisions are disproportionate or less relevant in their case. Some of the provisions do not apply to companies below the FTSE 350. Such companies may nonetheless consider that it would be appropriate to adopt the approach in the Code and they are encouraged to do so. Externally managed investment companies typically have a different board structure which may affect the relevance of particular provisions; the Association of Investment Companies' Corporate Governance Code and Guide can assist them in meeting their obligations under the Code.

6. Satisfactory engagement between company boards and investors is crucial to the health of the UK's corporate governance regime. Companies and shareholders both have responsibility for ensuring that 'comply or explain' remains an effective alternative to a rules-based system. There are practical and administrative obstacles to improved interaction between boards and shareholders. But certainly there is also scope for an increase in trust which could generate a virtuous upward spiral in attitudes to the Code and in its constructive use.

## THE MAIN PRINCIPLES OF THE CODE

### Section A: Leadership

Every company should be headed by an effective board which is collectively responsible for the long-term success of the company.

There should be a clear division of responsibilities at the head of the company between the running of the board and the executive responsibility for the running of the company's business. No one individual should have unfettered powers of decision.

The chairman is responsible for leadership of the board and ensuring its effectiveness on all aspects of its role.

As part of their role as members of a unitary board, non-executive directors should constructively challenge and help develop proposals on strategy.

### Section B: Effectiveness

The board and its committees should have the appropriate balance of skills, experience, independence and knowledge of the company to enable them to discharge their respective duties and responsibilities effectively.

There should be a formal, rigorous and transparent procedure for the appointment of new directors to the board.

All directors should be able to allocate sufficient time to the company to discharge their responsibilities effectively.

All directors should receive induction on joining the board and should regularly update and refresh their skills and knowledge.

The board should be supplied in a timely manner with information in a form and of a quality appropriate to enable it to discharge its duties.

The board should undertake a formal and rigorous annual evaluation of its own performance and that of its committees and individual directors.

All directors should be submitted for re-election at regular intervals, subject to continued satisfactory performance.

### Section C: Accountability

The board should present a fair, balanced and understandable assessment of the company's position and prospects.

The board is responsible for determining the nature and extent of the significant risks it is willing to take in achieving its strategic objectives. The board should maintain sound risk management and internal control systems.

The board should establish formal and transparent arrangements for considering how they should apply the corporate reporting, risk management and internal control principles and for maintaining an appropriate relationship with the company's auditors.

## Section D: Remuneration

Levels of remuneration should be sufficient to attract, retain and motivate directors of the quality required to run the company successfully, but a company should avoid paying more than is necessary for this purpose.

A significant proportion of executive directors' remuneration should be structured so as to link rewards to corporate and individual performance.

There should be a formal and transparent procedure for developing policy on executive remuneration and for fixing the remuneration packages of individual directors. No director should be involved in deciding his or her own remuneration.

## Section E: Relations With Shareholders

There should be a dialogue with shareholders based on the mutual understanding of objectives. The board as a whole has responsibility for ensuring that a satisfactory dialogue with shareholders takes place.

The board should use the AGM to communicate with investors and to encourage their participation.

## SECTION A: LEADERSHIP

### A.1 The Role of the Board

**Main Principle**

**Every company should be headed by an effective board which is collectively responsible for the long-term success of the company.**

**Supporting Principles**

The board's role is to provide entrepreneurial leadership of the company within a framework of prudent and effective controls which enables risk to be assessed and managed. The board should set the company's strategic aims, ensure that the necessary financial and human resources are in place for the company to meet its objectives and review management performance. The board should set the company's values and standards and ensure that its obligations to its shareholders and others are understood and met.

All directors must act in what they consider to be the best interests of the company, consistent with their statutory duties.[2]

**Code Provisions**

**A.1.1.** The board should meet sufficiently regularly to discharge its duties effectively. There should be a formal schedule of matters specifically reserved for its decision. The annual report should include a statement of how the board operates, including a high level statement of which types of decisions are to be taken by the board and which are to be delegated to management.

**A.1.2.** The annual report should identify the chairman, the deputy chairman (where there is one), the chief executive, the senior independent director and the chairmen and members of the board committees[3]. It should also set out the number of meetings of the board and those committees and individual attendance by directors.

**A.1.3.** The company should arrange appropriate insurance cover in respect of legal action against its directors.

## A.2 Division of Responsibilities

**Main Principle**

**There should be a clear division of responsibilities at the head of the company between the running of the board and the executive responsibility for the running of the company's business. No one individual should have unfettered powers of decision.**

**Code Provision**

**A.2.1** The roles of chairman and chief executive should not be exercised by the same individual. The division of responsibilities between the chairman and chief executive should be clearly established, set out in writing and agreed by the board.

---

2   For directors of UK incorporated companies, these duties are set out in the Sections 170 to 177 of the Companies Act 2006.
3   Provisions A.1.1 and A.1.2 overlap with FSA Rule DTR 7.2.7 R; Provision A.1.2 also overlaps with DTR 7.1.5 R (see Schedule B).

## A.3 The Chairman

**Main Principle**
**The chairman is responsible for leadership of the board and ensuring its effectiveness on all aspects of its role.**

**Supporting Principle**
The chairman is responsible for setting the board's agenda and ensuring that adequate time is available for discussion of all agenda items, in particular strategic issues. The chairman should also promote a culture of openness and debate by facilitating the effective contribution of non-executive directors in particular and ensuring constructive relations between executive and non-executive directors.

The chairman is responsible for ensuring that the directors receive accurate, timely and clear information. The chairman should ensure effective communication with shareholders.

**Code Provisions**
**A.3.1.** The chairman should on appointment meet the independence criteria set out in B.1.1 below. A chief executive should not go on to be chairman of the same company. If exceptionally a board decides that a chief executive should become chairman, the board should consult major shareholders in advance and should set out its reasons to shareholders at the time of the appointment and in the next annual report[4].

## A.4 Non-executive Directors

**Main Principle**
**As part of their role as members of a unitary board, non-executive directors should constructively challenge and help develop proposals on strategy.**

**Supporting Principles**
Non-executive directors should scrutinise the performance of management in meeting agreed goals and objectives and monitor the reporting of performance. They should satisfy themselves on the integrity of financial information and that

---

4   Compliance or otherwise with this provision need only be reported for the year in which the appointment is made.

financial controls and systems of risk management are robust and defensible. They are responsible for determining appropriate levels of remuneration of executive directors and have a prime role in appointing and, where necessary, removing executive directors, and in succession planning.

**Code Provisions**

A.4.1.  The board should appoint one of the independent non-executive directors to be the senior independent director to provide a sounding board for the chairman and to serve as an intermediary for the other directors when necessary. The senior independent director should be available to shareholders if they have concerns which contact through the normal channels of chairman, chief executive or other executive directors has failed to resolve or for which such contact is inappropriate.

A.4.2.  The chairman should hold meetings with the non-executive directors without the executives present. Led by the senior independent director, the non-executive directors should meet without the chairman present at least annually to appraise the chairman's performance and on such other occasions as are deemed appropriate.

A.4.3.  Where directors have concerns which cannot be resolved about the running of the company or a proposed action, they should ensure that their concerns are recorded in the board minutes. On resignation, a non-executive director should provide a written statement to the chairman, for circulation to the board, if they have any such concerns.

## SECTION B: EFFECTIVENESS

### B.1 The Composition of the Board

**Main Principle**

**The board and its committees should have the appropriate balance of skills, experience, independence and knowledge of the company to enable them to discharge their respective duties and responsibilities effectively.**

**Supporting Principles**

The board should be of sufficient size that the requirements of the business can be met and that changes to the board's composition and that of its committees can be managed without undue disruption, and should not be so large as to be unwieldy.

The board should include an appropriate combination of executive and non-executive directors (and, in particular, independent non-executive directors) such that no individual or small group of individuals can dominate the board's decision taking.

The value of ensuring that committee membership is refreshed and that undue reliance is not placed on particular individuals should be taken into account in deciding chairmanship and membership of committees.

No one other than the committee chairman and members is entitled to be present at a meeting of the nomination, audit or remuneration committee, but others may attend at the invitation of the committee.

**Code Provisions**

B.1.1.   The board should identify in the annual report each non-executive director it considers to be independent[5]. The board should determine whether the director is independent in character and judgement and whether there are relationships or circumstances which are likely to affect, or could appear to affect, the director's judgement. The board should state its reasons if it determines that a director is independent notwithstanding the existence of relationships or circumstances which may appear relevant to its determination, including if the director:

- has been an employee of the company or group within the last five years;
- has, or has had within the last three years, a material business relationship with the company either directly, or as a partner, shareholder, director or senior employee of a body that has such a relationship with the company;
- has received or receives additional remuneration from the company apart from a director's fee, participates in the company's share option or a performance-related pay scheme, or is a member of the company's pension scheme;
- has close family ties with any of the company's advisers, directors or senior employees;

---

5   A.3.1 states that the chairman should, on appointment, meet the independence criteria set out in this provision, but thereafter the test of independence is not appropriate in relation to the chairman.

- holds cross-directorships or has significant links with other directors through involvement in other companies or bodies;
- represents a significant shareholder; or
- has served on the board for more than nine years from the date of their first election.

**B.1.2.** Except for smaller companies[6], at least half the board, excluding the chairman, should comprise non-executive directors determined by the board to be independent. A smaller company should have at least two independent non-executive directors.

## B.2 Appointments to the Board

### Main Principle
**There should be a formal, rigorous and transparent procedure for the appointment of new directors to the board.**

### Supporting Principles
The search for board candidates should be conducted, and appointments made, on merit, against objective criteria and with due regard for the benefits of diversity on the board, including gender.

The board should satisfy itself that plans are in place for orderly succession for appointments to the board and to senior management, so as to maintain an appropriate balance of skills and experience within the company and on the board and to ensure progressive refreshing of the board.

### Code Provisions
**B.2.1.** There should be a nomination committee which should lead the process for board appointments and make recommendations to the board. A majority of members of the nomination committee should be independent non-executive directors. The chairman or an independent non-executive director should chair the committee, but the chairman should not chair the nomination committee when it is dealing with the appointment of a successor to the chairmanship. The nomination committee should make available its terms of reference, explaining its role and the authority delegated to it by the board[7].

---

6   A smaller company is one that is below the FTSE 350 throughout the year immediately prior to the reporting year.
7   The requirement to make the information available would be met by including the information on a website that is maintained by or on behalf of the company.

**B.2.2.** The nomination committee should evaluate the balance of skills, experience, independence and knowledge on the board and, in the light of this evaluation, prepare a description of the role and capabilities required for a particular appointment.

**B.2.3.** Non-executive directors should be appointed for specified terms subject to re-election and to statutory provisions relating to the removal of a director. Any term beyond six years for a non-executive director should be subject to particularly rigorous review, and should take into account the need for progressive refreshing of the board.

**B.2.4.** A separate section of the annual report should describe the work of the nomination committee[8], including the process it has used in relation to board appointments. This section should include a description of the board's policy on diversity, including gender, any measurable objectives that it has set for implementing the policy, and progress on achieving the objectives. An explanation should be given if neither an external search consultancy nor open advertising has been used in the appointment of a chairman or a non-executive director. Where an external search consultancy has been used, it should be identified in the annual report and a statement made as to whether it has any other connection with the company.

## B.3 Commitment

**Main Principle**
**All directors should be able to allocate sufficient time to the company to discharge their responsibilities effectively.**

**Code Provisions**

**B.3.1.** For the appointment of a chairman, the nomination committee should prepare a job specification, including an assessment of the time commitment expected, recognising the need for availability in the event of crises. A chairman's other significant commitments should be disclosed to the board before appointment and included in the annual report. Changes to such commitments should be reported to the board as they arise, and their impact explained in the next annual report.

8    This provision overlaps with FSA Rule DTR 7.2.7 R (see Schedule B).

**B.3.2.** The terms and conditions of appointment of non-executive directors should be made available for inspection[9]. The letter of appointment should set out the expected time commitment. Non-executive directors should undertake that they will have sufficient time to meet what is expected of them. Their other significant commitments should be disclosed to the board before appointment, with a broad indication of the time involved and the board should be informed of subsequent changes.

**B.3.3.** The board should not agree to a full time executive director taking on more than one non-executive directorship in a FTSE 100 company nor the chairmanship of such a company.

## B.4 Development

**Main Principle**
**All directors should receive induction on joining the board and should regularly update and refresh their skills and knowledge.**

**Supporting Principles**
The chairman should ensure that the directors continually update their skills and the knowledge and familiarity with the company required to fulfil their role both on the board and on board committees.

The company should provide the necessary resources for developing and updating its directors' knowledge and capabilities.

To function effectively all directors need appropriate knowledge of the company and access to its operations and staff.

**Code Provisions**
**B.4.1.** The chairman should ensure that new directors receive a full, formal and tailored induction on joining the board. As part of this, directors should avail themselves of opportunities to meet major shareholders.

**B.4.2.** The chairman should regularly review and agree with each director their training and development needs.

---

9 The terms and conditions of appointment of non-executive directors should be made available for inspection by any person at the company's registered office during normal business hours and at the AGM (for 15 minutes prior to the meeting and during the meeting).

## B.5 Information and Support

**Main Principle**
**The board should be supplied in a timely manner with information in a form and of a quality appropriate to enable it to discharge its duties.**

**Supporting Principles**
The chairman is responsible for ensuring that the directors receive accurate, timely and clear information. Management has an obligation to provide such information but directors should seek clarification or amplification where necessary.

Under the direction of the chairman, the company secretary's responsibilities include ensuring good information flows within the board and its committees and between senior management and non-executive directors, as well as facilitating induction and assisting with professional development as required.

The company secretary should be responsible for advising the board through the chairman on all governance matters.

**Code Provisions**
**B.5.1.** The board should ensure that directors, especially non-executive directors, have access to independent professional advice at the company's expense where they judge it necessary to discharge their responsibilities as directors. Committees should be provided with sufficient resources to undertake their duties.

**B.5.2.** All directors should have access to the advice and services of the company secretary, who is responsible to the board for ensuring that board procedures are complied with. Both the appointment and removal of the company secretary should be a matter for the board as a whole.

## B.6 Evaluation

**Main Principle**
**The board should undertake a formal and rigorous annual evaluation of its own performance and that of its committees and individual directors.**

**Supporting Principles**
Evaluation of the board should consider the balance of skills, experience, independence and knowledge of the company on the board, its diversity, including

gender, how the board works together as a unit, and other factors relevant to its effectiveness.

The chairman should act on the results of the performance evaluation by recognising the strengths and addressing the weaknesses of the board and, where appropriate, proposing new members be appointed to the board or seeking the resignation of directors.

Individual evaluation should aim to show whether each director continues to contribute effectively and to demonstrate commitment to the role (including commitment of time for board and committee meetings and any other duties).

## Code Provisions

**B.6.1.** The board should state in the annual report how performance evaluation of the board, its committees and its individual directors has been conducted.

**B.6.2.** Evaluation of the board of FTSE 350 companies should be externally facilitated at least every three years. The external facilitator should be identified in the annual report and a statement made as to whether they have any other connection with the company.

**B.6.3.** The non-executive directors, led by the senior independent director, should be responsible for performance evaluation of the chairman, taking into account the views of executive directors.

## B.7 Re-election

### Main Principle

**All directors should be submitted for re-election at regular intervals, subject to continued satisfactory performance.**

### Code Provisions

**B.7.1.** All directors of FTSE 350 companies should be subject to annual election by shareholders. All other directors should be subject to election by shareholders at the first annual general meeting after their appointment, and to re-election thereafter at intervals of no more than three years. Non-executive directors who have served longer than nine years should be subject to annual re-election. The names of directors submitted for election or re-election should be accompanied by sufficient biographical details and any other relevant information to enable shareholders to take an informed decision on their election.

**B.7.2.** The board should set out to shareholders in the papers accompanying a resolution to elect a non-executive director why they believe an individual should be elected. The chairman should confirm to shareholders when proposing re-election that, following formal performance evaluation, the individual's performance continues to be effective and to demonstrate commitment to the role.

## SECTION C: ACCOUNTABILITY

### C.1 Financial and Business Reporting

**Main Principle**
**The board should present a fair, balanced and understandable assessment of the company's position and prospects.**

**Supporting Principle**
The board's responsibility to present a fair, balanced and understandable assessment extends to interim and other price-sensitive public reports and reports to regulators as well as to information required to be presented by statutory requirements.

The board should establish arrangements that will enable it to ensure that the information presented is fair, balanced and understandable.

**Code Provisions**
**C.1.1.** The directors should explain in the annual report their responsibility for preparing the annual report and accounts, and state that they consider the annual report and accounts, taken as a whole, is fair, balanced and understandable and provides the information necessary for shareholders to assess the company's performance, business model and strategy. There should be a statement by the auditor about their reporting responsibilities[10].

---

10 This requirement may be met by the disclosures about the audit scope and responsibilities of the auditor included, or referred to, in the auditor's report pursuant to the requirements of ISA (UK and Ireland) 700, 'The Auditor's Report on Financial Statements'. Copies are available from the FRC website.

C.1.2.  The directors should include in the annual report an explanation of the basis on which the company generates or preserves value over the longer term (the business model) and the strategy for delivering the objectives of the company[11].

C.1.3.  The directors should report in annual and half-yearly financial statements that the business is a going concern, with supporting assumptions or qualifications as necessary[12].

## C.2 Risk Management and Internal Control[13]

### Main Principle

**The board is responsible for determining the nature and extent of the significant risks it is willing to take in achieving its strategic objectives. The board should maintain sound risk management and internal control systems.**

### Code Provision

C.2.1.  The board should, at least annually, conduct a review of the effectiveness of the company's risk management and internal control systems and should report to shareholders that they have done so[14]. The review should cover all material controls, including financial, operational and compliance controls.

## C.3 Audit Committee and Auditors[15]

### Main Principle

**The board should establish formal and transparent arrangements for considering how they should apply the corporate reporting and risk management and internal control principles and for maintaining an appropriate relationship with the company's auditors.**

11  It would be desirable if the explanation were located in the same part of the annual report as the Business Review required by Section 417 of the Companies Act 2006. Guidance as to the matters that should be considered in an explanation of a business model is provided in 'Reporting Statement: Operating And Financial Review'. Copies are available from the FRC website.

12  'Going Concern and Liquidity Risk: Guidance for Directors of UK Companies 2009' suggests means of applying this part of the Code. Copies are available from the FRC website.

13  'Internal Control: Guidance to Directors' suggests means of applying this part of the Code. Copies are available from the FRC website.

14  In addition FSA Rule DTR 7.2.5 R requires companies to describe the main features of the internal control and risk management systems in relation to the financial reporting process.

15  'Guidance on Audit Committees' suggests means of applying this part of the Code. Copies are available from the FRC website.

**Code Provisions**

C.3.1.  The board should establish an audit committee of at least three, or in the case of smaller companies[16] two, independent non-executive directors. In smaller companies the company chairman may be a member of, but not chair, the committee in addition to the independent non-executive directors, provided he or she was considered independent on appointment as chairman. The board should satisfy itself that at least one member of the audit committee has recent and relevant financial experience[17].

C.3.2.  The main role and responsibilities of the audit committee should be set out in written terms of reference[18] and should include:

- to monitor the integrity of the financial statements of the company and any formal announcements relating to the company's financial performance, reviewing significant financial reporting judgements contained in them;
- to review the company's internal financial controls and, unless expressly addressed by a separate board risk committee composed of independent directors, or by the board itself, to review the company's internal control and risk management systems;
- to monitor and review the effectiveness of the company's internal audit function;
- to make recommendations to the board, for it to put to the shareholders for their approval in general meeting, in relation to the appointment, re-appointment and removal of the external auditor and to approve the remuneration and terms of engagement of the external auditor;
- to review and monitor the external auditor's independence and objectivity and the effectiveness of the audit process, taking into consideration relevant UK professional and regulatory requirements;
- to develop and implement policy on the engagement of the external auditor to supply non-audit services, taking into account relevant ethical guidance regarding the provision of non-audit services by the external audit firm; and to report to the board, identifying any matters in respect of which it considers that action or improvement is needed and making recommendations as to the steps to be taken; and
- to report to the board on how it has discharged its responsibilities.

16  See footnote 6.
17  This provision overlaps with FSA Rule DTR 7.1.1 R (see Schedule B).
18  This provision overlaps with FSA Rules DTR 7.1.3 R (see Schedule B).

**C.3.3.** The terms of reference of the audit committee, including its role and the authority delegated to it by the board, should be made available.[19]

**C.3.4.** Where requested by the board, the audit committee should provide advice on whether the annual report and accounts, taken as a whole, is fair, balanced and understandable and provides the information necessary for shareholders to assess the company's performance, business model and strategy.

**C.3.5.** The audit committee should review arrangements by which staff of the company may, in confidence, raise concerns about possible improprieties in matters of financial reporting or other matters. The audit committee's objective should be to ensure that arrangements are in place for the proportionate and independent investigation of such matters and for appropriate follow-up action.

**C.3.6.** The audit committee should monitor and review the effectiveness of the internal audit activities. Where there is no internal audit function, the audit committee should consider annually whether there is a need for an internal audit function and make a recommendation to the board, and the reasons for the absence of such a function should be explained in the relevant section of the annual report.

**C.3.7.** The audit committee should have primary responsibility for making a recommendation on the appointment, reappointment and removal of the external auditors. FTSE 350 companies should put the external audit contract out to tender at least every ten years. If the board does not accept the audit committee's recommendation, it should include in the annual report, and in any papers recommending appointment or re-appointment, a statement from the audit committee explaining the recommendation and should set out reasons why the board has taken a different position.

**C.3.8.** A separate section of the annual report should describe the work of the committee in discharging its responsibilities.[20] The report should include:
- the significant issues that the committee considered in relation to the financial statements, and how these issues were addressed;
- an explanation of how it has assessed the effectiveness of the external audit process and the approach taken to the appointment or reappointment of the external auditor, and information on the length of tenure of the current audit firm and when a tender was last conducted; and

---

19  See footnote 7.
20  This provision overlaps with FSA Rules DTR 7.1.5 R and 7.2.7 R (see Schedule B).

- if the external auditor provides non-audit services, an explanation of how auditor objectivity and independence is safeguarded.

## SECTION D: REMUNERATION

### D.1 The Level and Components of Remuneration

**Main Principle**

**Levels of remuneration should be sufficient to attract, retain and motivate directors of the quality required to run the company successfully, but a company should avoid paying more than is necessary for this purpose. A significant proportion of executive directors' remuneration should be structured so as to link rewards to corporate and individual performance.**

**Supporting Principle**

The performance-related elements of executive directors' remuneration should be stretching and designed to promote the long-term success of the company.

The remuneration committee should judge where to position their company relative to other companies. But they should use such comparisons with caution, in view of the risk of an upward ratchet of remuneration levels with no corresponding improvement in performance.

They should also be sensitive to pay and employment conditions elsewhere in the group, especially when determining annual salary increases.

**Code Provisions**

D.1.1.    In designing schemes of performance-related remuneration for executive directors, the remuneration committee should follow the provisions in Schedule A to this Code.

D.1.2.    Where a company releases an executive director to serve as a non-executive director elsewhere, the remuneration report[21] should include a statement as to whether or not the director will retain such earnings and, if so, what the remuneration is.

---

21  As required for UK incorporated companies under the Large and Medium-Sized Companies and Groups (Accounts and Reports) Regulations 2008.

**D.1.3.** Levels of remuneration for non-executive directors should reflect the time commitment and responsibilities of the role. Remuneration for non-executive directors should not include share options or other performance-related elements. If, exceptionally, options are granted, shareholder approval should be sought in advance and any shares acquired by exercise of the options should be held until at least one year after the non-executive director leaves the board. Holding of share options could be relevant to the determination of a non-executive director's independence (as set out in provision B.1.1).

**D.1.4.** The remuneration committee should carefully consider what compensation commitments (including pension contributions and all other elements) their directors' terms of appointment would entail in the event of early termination. The aim should be to avoid rewarding poor performance. They should take a robust line on reducing compensation to reflect departing directors' obligations to mitigate loss.

**D.1.5.** Notice or contract periods should be set at one year or less. If it is necessary to offer longer notice or contract periods to new directors recruited from outside, such periods should reduce to one year or less after the initial period.

## D.2 Procedure

**Main Principle**
**There should be a formal and transparent procedure for developing policy on executive remuneration and for fixing the remuneration packages of individual directors. No director should be involved in deciding his or her own remuneration.**

**Supporting Principles**
The remuneration committee should consult the chairman and/or chief executive about their proposals relating to the remuneration of other executive directors. The remuneration committee should also be responsible for appointing any consultants in respect of executive director remuneration. Where executive directors or senior management are involved in advising or supporting the remuneration committee, care should be taken to recognise and avoid conflicts of interest.

The chairman of the board should ensure that the company maintains contact as required with its principal shareholders about remuneration.

**Code Provisions**

**D.2.1.** The board should establish a remuneration committee of at least three, or in the case of smaller companies[22] two, independent non-executive directors. In addition the company chairman may also be a member of, but not chair, the committee if he or she was considered independent on appointment as chairman. The remuneration committee should make available its terms of reference, explaining its role and the authority delegated to it by the board[23]. Where remuneration consultants are appointed, they should be identified in the annual report and a statement made as to whether they have any other connection with the company.

**D.2.2.** The remuneration committee should have delegated responsibility for setting remuneration for all executive directors and the chairman, including pension rights and any compensation payments. The committee should also recommend and monitor the level and structure of remuneration for senior management. The definition of 'senior management' for this purpose should be determined by the board but should normally include the first layer of management below board level.

**D.2.3.** The board itself or, where required by the Articles of Association, the shareholders should determine the remuneration of the non-executive directors within the limits set in the Articles of Association. Where permitted by the Articles, the board may however delegate this responsibility to a committee, which might include the chief executive.

**D.2.4.** Shareholders should be invited specifically to approve all new long-term incentive schemes (as defined in the Listing Rules[24]) and significant changes to existing schemes, save in the circumstances permitted by the Listing Rules.

## SECTION E: RELATIONS WITH SHAREHOLDERS

*E.1 Dialogue with Shareholders*

**Main Principle**

**There should be a dialogue with shareholders based on the mutual understanding of objectives. The board as a whole has responsibility for ensuring that a satisfactory dialogue with shareholders takes place[25].**

---

22  See footnote 6.
23  This provision overlaps with FSA Rule DTR 7.2.7 R (see Schedule B).
24  Listing Rules LR 9.4. Copies are available from the FSA website.
25  Nothing in these principles or provisions should be taken to override the general requirements of law to treat shareholders equally in access to information.

## Supporting Principles

Whilst recognising that most shareholder contact is with the chief executive and finance director, the chairman should ensure that all directors are made aware of their major shareholders' issues and concerns.

The board should keep in touch with shareholder opinion in whatever ways are most practical and efficient.

## Code Provisions

E.1.1.   The chairman should ensure that the views of shareholders are communicated to the board as a whole. The chairman should discuss governance and strategy with major shareholders. Non-executive directors should be offered the opportunity to attend scheduled meetings with major shareholders and should expect to attend meetings if requested by major shareholders. The senior independent director should attend sufficient meetings with a range of major shareholders to listen to their views in order to help develop a balanced understanding of the issues and concerns of major shareholders.

E.1.2.   The board should state in the annual report the steps they have taken to ensure that the members of the board, and in particular the non-executive directors, develop an understanding of the views of major shareholders about the company, for example through direct face-to-face contact, analysts' or brokers' briefings and surveys of shareholder opinion.

## E.2 Constructive Use of the AGM

## Main Principle

**The board should use the AGM to communicate with investors and to encourage their participation.**

## Code Provisions

E.2.1.   At any general meeting, the company should propose a separate resolution on each substantially separate issue, and should in particular propose a resolution at the AGM relating to the report and accounts. For each resolution, proxy appointment forms should provide shareholders with the option to direct their proxy to vote either for or against the resolution or to withhold their vote. The proxy form and any announcement of the results of a vote should make it clear that a 'vote withheld' is not a vote in law and will not be counted in the calculation of the proportion of the votes for and against the resolution.

E.2.2.  The company should ensure that all valid proxy appointments received for general meetings are properly recorded and counted. For each resolution, where a vote has been taken on a show of hands, the company should ensure that the following information is given at the meeting and made available as soon as reasonably practicable on a website which is maintained by or on behalf of the company:

- the number of shares in respect of which proxy appointments have been validly made;
- the number of votes for the resolution;
- the number of votes against the resolution; and
- the number of shares in respect of which the vote was directed to be withheld.

E.2.3.  The chairman should arrange for the chairmen of the audit, remuneration and nomination committees to be available to answer questions at the AGM and for all directors to attend.

E.2.4.  The company should arrange for the Notice of the AGM and related papers to be sent to shareholders at least 20 working days before the meeting.

## SCHEDULE A: THE DESIGN OF PERFORMANCE-RELATED REMUNERATION FOR EXECUTIVE DIRECTORS

The remuneration committee should consider whether the directors should be eligible for annual bonuses. If so, performance conditions should be relevant, stretching and designed to promote the long-term success of the company. Upper limits should be set and disclosed. There may be a case for part payment in shares to be held for a significant period.

The remuneration committee should consider whether the directors should be eligible for benefits under long-term incentive schemes. Traditional share option schemes should be weighed against other kinds of long-term incentive scheme. Executive share options should not be offered at a discount save as permitted by the relevant provisions of the Listing Rules.

In normal circumstances, shares granted or other forms of deferred remuneration should not vest, and options should not be exercisable, in less than three years. Directors should be encouraged to hold their shares for a further period after vesting or exercise, subject to the need to finance any costs of acquisition and associated tax liabilities.

Any new long-term incentive schemes which are proposed should be approved by shareholders and should preferably replace any existing schemes or, at least, form part of a well considered overall plan incorporating existing schemes. The total rewards potentially available should not be excessive.

Payouts or grants under all incentive schemes, including new grants under existing share option schemes, should be subject to challenging performance criteria reflecting the company's objectives, including nonfinancial performance metrics where appropriate. Remuneration incentives should be compatible with risk policies and systems.

Grants under executive share option and other long-term incentive schemes should normally be phased rather than awarded in one large block.

Consideration should be given to the use of provisions that permit the company to reclaim variable components in exceptional circumstances of misstatement or misconduct.

In general, only basic salary should be pensionable. The remuneration committee should consider the pension consequences and associated costs to the company of basic salary increases and any other changes in pensionable remuneration, especially for directors close to retirement.


## SCHEDULE B: DISCLOSURE OF CORPORATE GOVERNANCE ARRANGEMENTS

Corporate governance disclosure requirements are set out in three places:

- FSA Disclosure and Transparency Rules sub-chapters 7.1 and 7.2 (which set out certain mandatory disclosures);
- FSA Listing Rules 9.8.6 R, 9.8.7 R, and 9.8.7A R (which includes the 'comply or explain' requirement); and
- The UK Corporate Governance Code (in addition to providing an explanation where they choose not to comply with a provision, companies must disclose specified information in order to comply with certain provisions).

These requirements are summarised below. The full text of Disclosure and Transparency Rules 7.1 and 7.2 and Listing Rules 9.8.6 R, 9.8.7 R, 9.8.7A R are contained in the relevant chapters of the FSA Handbook.

The Disclosure and Transparency Rules sub-chapters 7.1 and 7.2 apply to issuers whose securities are admitted to trading on a regulated market (this includes all issuers with a Premium or Standard listing). The Listing Rules 9.8.6 R, 9.8.7 R and 9.8.7A R and UK Corporate Governance Code apply to issuers of Premium listed equity shares only.

There is some overlap between the mandatory disclosures required under the Disclosure and Transparency Rules and those expected under the UK Corporate Governance Code. Areas of overlap are summarised in the Appendix to this Schedule. In respect of disclosures relating to the audit committee and the composition and operation of the board and its committees, compliance with the relevant provisions of the Code will result in compliance with the relevant Rules.

## Disclosure and Transparency Rules

Sub-chapter 7.1 of the Disclosure and Transparency Rules concerns audit committees or bodies carrying out equivalent functions.

DTR 7.1.1 R and 7.1.3 R set out requirements relating to the composition and functions of the committee or equivalent body:

- DTR 7.1.1 R states than an issuer must have a body which is responsible for performing the functions set out in DTR 7.1.3 R, and that at least one member of that body must be independent and at least one member must have competence in accounting and/or auditing.
- DTR 7.1.2 G states that the requirements for independence and competence in accounting and/or auditing may be satisfied by the same member or by different members of the relevant body.
- DTR 7.1.3 R states that an issuer must ensure that, as a minimum, the relevant body must:
  (1) monitor the financial reporting process;
  (2) monitor the effectiveness of the issuer's internal control, internal audit where applicable, and risk management systems;
  (3) monitor the statutory audit of the annual and consolidated accounts;
  (4) review and monitor the independence of the statutory auditor, and in particular the provision of additional services to the issuer.

DTR 7.1.5 R sets out what disclosure is required. Specifically:

- DTR 7.1.5 R states that the issuer must make a statement available to the public disclosing which body carries out the functions required by DTR 7.1.3 R and how it is composed.
- DTR 7.1.6 G states that this can be included in the corporate governance statement required under sub-chapter DTR 7.2 (see below).

- DTR 7.1.7 G states that compliance with the relevant provisions of the UK Corporate Governance Code (as set out in the Appendix to this Schedule) will result in compliance with DTR 7.1.1 R to 7.1.5 R.

Sub-chapter 7.2 concerns corporate governance statements. Issuers are required to produce a corporate governance statement that must be either included in the directors' report (DTR 7.2.1 R); or in a separate report published together with the annual report; or on the issuer's website, in which case there must be a cross-reference in the directors' report (DTR 7.2.9 R).

DTR 7.2.2 R requires that the corporate governance statements must contain a reference to the corporate governance code to which the company is subject (for companies with a Premium listing this is the UK Corporate Governance Code). DTR 7.2.3 R requires that, to the extent that it departs from that code, the company must explain which parts of the code it departs from and the reasons for doing so. DTR 7.2.4 G states that compliance with LR 9.8.6 R (6) (the 'comply or explain' rule in relation to the UK Corporate Governance Code) will also satisfy these requirements.

DTR 7.2.5 R, DTR 7.2.7 R and DTR 7.2.10 R set out certain information that must be disclosed in the corporate governance statement:

- DTR 7.2.5 R states that the corporate governance statement must contain a description of the main features of the company's internal control and risk management systems in relation to the financial reporting process. DTR 7.2.10 R states that an issuer which is required to prepare a group directors' report within the meaning of Section 415(2) of the Companies Act 2006 must include in that report a description of the main features of the group's internal control and risk management systems in relation to the process for preparing consolidated accounts.
- DTR 7.2.6 R states that the corporate governance statement must contain the information required by paragraph 13(2)(c), (d), (f), (h) and (i) of Schedule 7 to the Large and Medium-sized Companies and Groups (Accounts and Reports) Regulations 2008 (SI 2008/410) where the issuer is subject to the requirements of that paragraph.
- DTR 7.2.7 R states that the corporate governance statement must contain a description of the composition and operation of the issuer's administrative, management and supervisory bodies and their committees. DTR 7.2.8 G states that compliance with the relevant provisions of the UK Corporate Governance Code (as set out in the Appendix to this Schedule) will satisfy these requirements.

## Listing Rules

Listing Rules 9.8.6 R (for UK incorporated companies) and 9.8.7 R (for overseas incorporated companies) state that in the case of a company that has a Premium listing of equity shares, the following items must be included in its annual report and accounts:

- a statement of how the listed company has applied the Main Principles set out in the UK Corporate Governance Code, in a manner that would enable shareholders to evaluate how the principles have been applied;
- a statement as to whether the listed company has:
  - complied throughout the accounting period with all relevant provisions set out in the UK Corporate Governance Code; or
  - not complied throughout the accounting period with all relevant provisions set out in the UK Corporate Governance Code, and if so, setting out:
    i.   those provisions, if any, it has not complied with;
    ii.  in the case of provisions whose requirements are of a continuing nature, the period within which, if any, it did not comply with some or all of those provisions; and
    iii. the company's reasons for non-compliance.

## The UK Corporate Governance Code

In addition to the 'comply or explain' requirement in the Listing Rules, the Code includes specific requirements for disclosure which must be provided in order to comply. These are summarised below.

The annual report should include:

- a statement of how the board operates, including a high level statement of which types of decisions are to be taken by the board and which are to be delegated to management (A.1.1);
- the names of the chairman, the deputy chairman (where there is one), the chief executive, the senior independent director and the chairmen and members of the board committees (A.1.2);
- the number of meetings of the board and those committees and individual attendance by directors (A.1.2);
- where a chief executive is appointed chairman, the reasons for their appointment (this only needs to be done in the annual report following the appointment) (A.3.1);
- the names of the non-executive directors whom the board determines to be independent, with reasons where necessary (B.1.1);

- a separate section describing the work of the nomination committee, including the process it has used in relation to board appointments; a description of the board's policy on diversity, including gender; any measurable objectives that it has set for implementing the policy, and progress on achieving the objectives. An explanation should be given if neither external search consultancy nor open advertising has been used in the appointment of a chairman or a non-executive director. Where an external search consultancy has been used it should be identified and a statement made as to whether it has any other connection with the company (B.2.4);

- any changes to the other significant commitments of the chairman during the year (B.3.1);

- a statement of how performance evaluation of the board, its committees and its directors has been conducted (B.6.1). Where an external facilitator has been used, they should be identified and a statement made as to whether they have any other connection to the company (B.6.2);

- an explanation from the directors of their responsibility for preparing the accounts and a statement that they consider that the annual report and accounts, taken as a whole, is fair, balanced and understandable and provides the information necessary for shareholders to assess and provide the company's performance, business model and strategy. There should also be a statement by the auditor about their reporting responsibilities (C.1.1);

- an explanation from the directors of the basis on which the company generates or preserves value over the longer term (the business model) and the strategy for delivering the objectives of the company (C.1.2);

- a statement from the directors that the business is a going concern, with supporting assumptions or qualifications as necessary (C.1.3);

- a report that the board has conducted a review of the effectiveness of the company's risk management and internal controls systems (C.2.1);

- where there is no internal audit function, the reasons for the absence of such a function (C.3.6);

- where the board does not accept the audit committee's recommendation on the appointment, reappointment or removal of an external auditor, a statement from the audit committee explaining the recommendation and the reasons why the board has taken a different position (C.3.7);

- a separate section describing the work of the audit committee in discharging its responsibilities, including: the significant issues that it considered in relation to the financial statements, and how these issues were addressed;

an explanation of how it has assessed the effectiveness of the external audit process and the approach taken to the appointment or reappointment of the external auditor, including the length of tenure of the current audit firm and when a tender was last conducted; and, if the external auditor provides non-audit services, an explanation of how auditor objectivity and independence is safeguarded (C.3.8);

- a description of the work of the remuneration committee as required under the Large and Medium-Sized Companies and Groups (Accounts and Reports) Regulations 2008, including, where an executive director serves as a non-executive director elsewhere, whether or not the director will retain such earnings and, if so, what the remuneration is (D.1.2);
- where remuneration consultants are appointed they should be identified and a statement made as to whether they have any other connection with the company (D.2.1); and
- the steps the board has taken to ensure that members of the board, and in particular the non-executive directors, develop an understanding of the views of major shareholders about their company (E.1.2).

The following information should be made available (which may be met by placing the information on a website that is maintained by or on behalf of the company):

- the terms of reference of the nomination, audit and remuneration committees, explaining their role and the authority delegated to them by the board (B.2.1, C.3.3 and D.2.1); and
- the terms and conditions of appointment of non-executive directors (B.3.2) (see footnote 9).

The board should set out to shareholders in the papers accompanying a resolution to elect or re-elect directors:

- sufficient biographical details to enable shareholders to take an informed decision on their election or re-election (B.7.1);
- why they believe an individual should be elected to a non-executive role (B.7.2); and
- on re-election of a non-executive director, confirmation from the chairman that, following formal performance evaluation, the individual's performance continues to be effective and to demonstrate commitment to the role (B.7.2).

The board should set out to shareholders in the papers recommending appointment or reappointment of an external auditor:

- if the board does not accept the audit committee's recommendation, a statement from the audit committee explaining the recommendation and from the board setting out reasons why they have taken a different position (C.3.6).

### Additional guidance

The FRC publishes guidance on going concern, risk management and internal control and audit committees, which contain further suggestions as to information that might usefully be disclosed in the statement that the business is a going concern (C.1.3), the statement on the board's review of the company's risk management and internal control systems (C.2.1) and the report of the audit committee (C.3.8) respectively. This guidance is available on the FRC website.

### APPENDIX

## Overlap between the Disclosure and Transparency Rules and the UK Corporate Governance Code

| DISCLOSURE AND TRANSPARENCY RULES | UK CORPORATE GOVERNANCE CODE |
| --- | --- |
| **D.T.R 7.1.1 R**<br>Sets out minimum requirements on composition of the audit committee or equivalent body. | **Provision C.3.1**<br>Sets out recommended composition of the audit committee. |
| **D.T.R 7.1.3 R**<br>Sets out minimum functions of the audit committee or equivalent body. | **Provision C.3.2**<br>Sets out the recommended minimum terms of reference for the audit committee. |
| **D.T.R 7.1.5 R**<br>The composition and function of the audit committee or equivalent body must be disclosed in the annual report<br>*DTR 7.1.7 R states that compliance with Code provisions A.1.2, C.3.1, C.3.2 and C.3.3 will result in compliance with DTR 7.1.1 R to DTR 7.1.5 R.* | **Provision A.1.2**<br>The annual report should identify members of the board committees.<br>**Provision C.3.8**<br>The annual report should describe the work of the audit committee. |
| **D.T.R 7.2.5 R**<br>The corporate governance statement must include a description of the main features of the company's internal control and risk management systems in relation to the financial reporting process.<br>*While this requirement differs from the requirement in the UK Corporate Governance Code, it is envisaged that both could be met by a single internal control statement.* | **Provision C.2.1**<br>The Board must report that a review of the effectiveness of the risk management and internal control systems has been carried out. |

| DISCLOSURE AND TRANSPARENCY RULES | UK CORPORATE GOVERNANCE CODE |
| --- | --- |
| **DTR 7.2.7 R**<br>The corporate governance statement must include a description of the composition and operation of the administrative, management and supervisory bodies and their committees. *DTR 7.2.8 R states that compliance with Code provisions A.1.1, A.1.2, A.4.6, B.2.1 and C.3.3 will result in compliance with DTR 7.2.7 R.* | This requirement overlaps with a number of different provisions of the Code:<br>**A.1.1:** the annual report should include a statement of how the board operates.<br>**A.1.2:** the annual report should identify members of the board and board committees.<br>**B.2.4:** the annual report should describe the work of the nomination committee.<br>**C.3.8:** the annual report should describe the work of the audit committee.<br>**D.2.1:** a description of the work of the remuneration committee should be made available. [Note: in order to comply with DTR 7.2.7 R this information will need to be included in the corporate governance statement.] |

The FRC is responsible for promoting high quality corporate governance and reporting to foster investment. We set the UK Corporate Governance and Stewardship Codes as well as UK standards for accounting, auditing and actuarial work. We represent UK interests in international standard-setting. We also monitor and take action to promote the quality of corporate reporting and auditing. We operate independent disciplinary arrangements for accountants and actuaries; and oversee the regulatory activities of the accountancy and actuarial professional bodies.

Financial Reporting Council
5th Floor, Aldwych House 71-91 Aldwych London WC2B 4HN
+44 (0)20 7492 2300
www.frc.org.uk
UP/FRC-BI12001
© The Financial Reporting Council Limited 2012
The Financial Reporting Council Limited is a company limited by guarantee. Registered in England number 2486368.
Registered Office: 5th Floor, Aldwych House, 71-91 Aldwych, London WC2B 4HN.

# FRC Guidance on Board Effectiveness

## 1. THE ROLE OF THE BOARD AND DIRECTORS

### An Effective Board

1.1. The board's role is to provide entrepreneurial leadership of the company within a framework of prudent and effective controls which enables risk to be assessed and managed.

1.2. An effective board develops and promotes its collective vision of the company's purpose, its culture, its values and the behaviours it wishes to promote in conducting its business. In particular it:

- provides direction for management;
- demonstrates ethical leadership, displaying – and promoting throughout the company – behaviours consistent with the culture and values it has defined for the organisation;
- creates a performance culture that drives value creation without exposing the company to excessive risk of value destruction;
- makes well-informed and high-quality decisions based on a clear line of sight into the business;
- creates the right framework for helping directors meet their statutory duties under the Companies Act 2006, and/or other relevant statutory and regulatory regimes;
- is accountable, particularly to those that provide the company's capital; and
- thinks carefully about its governance arrangements and embraces evaluation of their effectiveness.

1.3. An effective board should not necessarily be a comfortable place. Challenge, as well as teamwork, is an essential feature. Diversity in board composition is an important driver of a board's effectiveness – creating a breadth of perspective among directors, and breaking down a tendency towards 'group think'.

## The Role of the Chairman

1.4. Good boards are created by good chairmen. The chairman creates the conditions for overall board and individual director effectiveness.

1.5. The chairman should demonstrate the highest standards of integrity and probity, and set clear expectations concerning the company's culture, values and behaviours, and the style and tone of board discussions.

1.6. The chairman, with the help of the executive directors and the company secretary, sets the agenda for the board's deliberations.

1.7. The chairman's role includes:

- demonstrating ethical leadership;
- setting a board agenda which is primarily focused on strategy, performance, value creation and accountability, and ensuring that issues relevant to these areas are reserved for board decision;
- ensuring a timely flow of high-quality supporting information;
- making certain that the board determines the nature, and extent, of the significant risks the company is willing to embrace in the implementation of its strategy, and that there are no 'no go' areas which prevent directors from operating effective oversight in this area;
- regularly considering succession planning and the composition of the board;
- making certain that the board has effective decision-making processes and applies sufficient challenge to major proposals;
- ensuring the board's committees are properly structured with appropriate terms of reference;
- encouraging all board members to engage in board and committee meetings by drawing on their skills, experience, knowledge and, where appropriate, independence;
- fostering relationships founded on mutual respect and open communication – both in and outside the boardroom – between the non-executive directors and the executive team;
- developing productive working relationships with all executive directors, and the CEO in particular, providing support and advice while respecting executive responsibility;
- consulting the senior independent director on board matters in accordance with the Code;

- taking the lead on issues of director development, including through induction programmes for new directors and regular reviews with all directors;
- acting on the results of board evaluation;
- being aware of, and responding to, his or her own development needs, including people and other skills, especially when taking on the role for the first time; and
- ensuring effective communication with shareholders and other stakeholders and, in particular, that all directors are made aware of the views of those who provide the company's capital.

1.8. The chairman of each board committee fulfils an important leadership role similar to that of the chairman of the board, particularly in creating the conditions for overall committee and individual director effectiveness.

### The Role of the Senior Independent Director

1.9. In normal times the senior independent director should act as a sounding board for the chairman, providing support for the chairman in the delivery of his or her objectives, and leading the evaluation of the chairman on behalf of the other directors, as set out in the Code. The senior independent director might also take responsibility for an orderly succession process for the chairman.

1.10. When the board is undergoing a period of stress, however, the senior independent director's role becomes critically important. He or she is expected to work with the chairman and other directors, and/or shareholders, to resolve significant issues. Boards should ensure they have a clear understanding of when the senior independent director might intervene in order to maintain board and company stability. Examples might include where:
- there is a dispute between the chairman and CEO;
- shareholders or non-executive directors have expressed concerns that are not being addressed by the chairman or CEO;
- the strategy being followed by the chairman and CEO is not supported by the entire board;
- the relationship between the chairman and CEO is particularly close, and decisions are being made without the approval of the full board; or
- succession planning is being ignored.

1.11. These issues should be considered when defining the role of the senior independent director, which should be set out in writing.

## The Role of Executive Directors

1.12. Executive directors have the same duties as other members of a unitary board. These duties extend to the whole of the business, and not just that part of it covered by their individual executive roles. Nor should executive directors see themselves only as members of the CEO's executive team when engaged in board business. Taking the wider view can help achieve the advantage of a unitary system: greater knowledge, involvement and commitment at the point of decision. The chairman should make certain that executives are aware of their wider responsibilities when joining the board, and ensure they receive appropriate induction, and regular training, to enable them to fulfil the role. Executive directors are also likely to be able to broaden their understanding of their board responsibilities if they take up a non-executive director position on another board.

1.13. The CEO is the most senior executive director on the board with responsibility for proposing strategy to the board, and for delivering the strategy as agreed. The CEO's relationship with the chairman is a key relationship that can help the board be more effective. The Code states that the differing responsibilities of the chairman and the CEO should be set out in writing and agreed by the board. Particular attention should be paid to areas of potential overlap.

1.14. The CEO has, with the support of the executive team, primary responsibility for setting an example to the company's employees, and communicating to them the expectations of the board in relation to the company's culture, values and behaviours. The CEO is responsible for supporting the chairman to make certain that appropriate standards of governance permeate through all parts of the organisation. The CEO will make certain that the board is made aware, when appropriate, of the views of employees on issues of relevance to the business.

1.15. The CEO will ensure the board knows the executive directors' views on business issues in order to improve the standard of discussion in the boardroom and, prior to final decision on an issue, explain in a balanced way any divergence of view in the executive team.

1.16. The CFO has a particular responsibility to deliver high-quality information to the board on the financial position of the company.

1.17. Executive directors have the most intimate knowledge of the company and its capabilities when developing and presenting proposals, and when exercising judgement, particularly on matters of strategy. They should appreciate that constructive challenge from non-executive directors is an essential aspect of good governance, and should encourage their non-executive colleagues to test their proposals in the light of the non-executives' wider experience outside the company. The chairman and the CEO should ensure that this process is properly followed.

### The Role of Non-Executive Directors

1.18. A non-executive director should, on appointment, devote time to a comprehensive, formal and tailored induction which should extend beyond the boardroom. Initiatives such as partnering a non-executive director with an executive board member may speed up the process of him or her acquiring an understanding of the main areas of business activity, especially areas involving significant risk. The director should expect to visit, and talk with, senior and middle managers in these areas.

1.19. Non-executive directors should devote time to developing and refreshing their knowledge and skills, including those of communication, to ensure that they continue to make a positive contribution to the board. Being well-informed about the company, and having a strong command of the issues relevant to the business, will generate the respect of the other directors.

1.20. Non-executive directors need to make sufficient time available to discharge their responsibilities effectively. The letter of appointment should state the minimum time that the non-executive director will be required to spend on the company's business, and seek the individual's confirmation that he or she can devote that amount of time to the role, consistent with other commitments. The letter should also indicate the possibility of additional time commitment when the company is undergoing a period of particularly increased activity, such as an acquisition or takeover, or as a result of some major difficulty with one or more of its operations.

1.21. Non-executive directors have a responsibility to uphold high standards of integrity and probity. They should support the chairman and executive directors in instilling the appropriate culture, values and behaviours in the boardroom and beyond.

1.22. Non-executive directors should insist on receiving high-quality information sufficiently in advance so that there can be thorough consideration of the issues prior to, and informed debate and challenge at, board meetings. High-quality information is that which is appropriate for making decisions on the issue at hand – it should be accurate, clear, comprehensive, up-to-date and timely; contain a summary of the contents of any paper; and inform the director of what is expected of him or her on that issue.

1.23. Non-executive directors should take into account the views of shareholders and other stakeholders, because these views may provide different perspectives on the company and its performance.

## 2. BOARD SUPPORT AND THE ROLE OF THE COMPANY SECRETARY

2.1. The requirement for a company secretary of a public company is specified in section 271 of the Companies Act 2006. The obligations and responsibilities of the company secretary outlined in the Act, and also in the Code, necessitate him or her playing a leading role in the good governance of the company by supporting the chairman and helping the board and its committees to function efficiently.

2.2. The company secretary should report to the chairman on all board governance matters. This does not preclude the company secretary also reporting to the CEO in relation to his or her other executive management responsibilities. The appointment and removal of the company secretary should be a matter for the board as a whole, and the remuneration of the company secretary might be determined by the remuneration committee.

2.3. The company secretary should ensure the presentation of high-quality information to the board and its committees. The company secretary can also add value by fulfilling, or procuring the fulfilment of, other requirements of the Code on behalf of the chairman, in particular director induction and development. This should be in a manner that is appropriate to the particular director, and which has the objective of enhancing that director's effectiveness in the board or board committees, consistent with the results of the board's evaluation processes. The chairman and the company secretary should periodically review whether the board and the company's other governance processes, for example board and committee evaluation, are fit for purpose, and consider any improvements or initiatives that could strengthen the governance of the company.

2.4. The company secretary's effectiveness can be enhanced by his or her ability to build relationships of mutual trust with the chairman, the senior independent director and the non-executive directors, while maintaining the confidence of executive director colleagues.

## 3. DECISION MAKING

3.1. Well-informed and high-quality decision making is a critical requirement for a board to be effective and does not happen by accident. Flawed decisions can be made with the best of intentions, with competent individuals believing passionately that they are making a sound judgement, when they are not. Many of the factors which lead to poor decision making are predictable and preventable. Boards can minimise the risk of poor decisions by investing time in the design of their decision-making policies and processes, including the contribution of committees.

3.2. Good decision-making capability can be facilitated by:
- high-quality board documentation;
- obtaining expert opinions when necessary;
- allowing time for debate and challenge, especially for complex, contentious or business-critical issues;
- achieving timely closure; and
- providing clarity on the actions required, and timescales and responsibilities.

3.3. Boards should be aware of factors which can limit effective decision making, such as:
- a dominant personality or group of directors on the board, which can inhibit contribution from other directors;
- insufficient attention to risk, and treating risk as a compliance issue rather than as part of the decision-making process – especially cases where the level of risk involved in a project could endanger the stability and sustainability of the business itself;
- failure to recognise the value implications of running the business on the basis of self-interest and other poor ethical standards;
- a reluctance to involve non-executive directors, or of matters being brought to the board for sign-off rather than debate;
- complacent or intransigent attitudes;
- a weak organisational culture; or
- inadequate information or analysis.

3.4. Most complex decisions depend on judgement, but the judgement of even the most well intentioned and experienced leaders can, in certain circumstances, be distorted. Some factors known to distort judgement in decision making are conflicts of interest, emotional attachments, and inappropriate reliance on previous experience and previous decisions.

For significant decisions, therefore, a board may wish to consider extra steps, for example:

- describing in board papers the process that has been used to arrive at and challenge the proposal prior to presenting it to the board, thereby allowing directors not involved in the project to assess the appropriateness of the process as a precursor to assessing the merits of the project itself; or
- where appropriate, putting in place additional safeguards to reduce the risk of distorted judgements by, for example, commissioning an independent report, seeking advice from an expert, introducing a devil's advocate to provide challenge, establishing a sole purpose sub-committee, or convening additional meetings. Some chairmen favour separate discussions for important decisions; for example, concept, proposal for discussion, proposal for decision. This gives executive directors more opportunity to put the case at the earlier stages, and all directors the opportunity to share concerns or challenge assumptions well in advance of the point of decision.

3.5. Boards can benefit from reviewing past decisions, particularly ones with poor outcomes. A review should not focus just on the merits of the decision itself but also on the decision-making process.

## 4. BOARD COMPOSITION AND SUCCESSION PLANNING

4.1. Appointing directors who are able to make a positive contribution is one of the key elements of board effectiveness. Directors will be more likely to make good decisions and maximise the opportunities for the company's success in the longer term if the right skill-sets are present in the boardroom. This includes the appropriate range and balance of skills, experience, knowledge and independence. Non-executive directors should possess critical skills of value to the board and relevant to the challenges facing the company.

4.2. The nomination committee, usually led by the chairman, should be responsible for board recruitment. The process should be continuous and proactive, and should take into account the company's agreed strategic priorities. The aim should be to secure a boardroom which achieves the right balance between challenge and teamwork, and fresh input and thinking, while maintaining a cohesive board.

4.3.   It is important to consider a diversity of personal attributes among board candidates, including: intellect, critical assessment and judgement, courage, openness, honesty and tact; and the ability to listen, forge relationships and develop trust. Diversity of psychological type, background and gender is important to ensure that a board is not composed solely of like-minded individuals. A board requires directors who have the intellectual capability to suggest change to a proposed strategy, and to promulgate alternatives.

4.4.   Given the importance of committees in many companies' decision-making structures, it will be important to recruit non-executives with the necessary technical skills and knowledge relating to the committees' subject matter, as well as the potential to assume the role of committee chairman.

4.5.   The chairman's vision for achieving the optimal board composition will help the nomination committee review the skills required, identify the gaps, develop transparent appointment criteria and inform succession planning. The nomination committee should periodically assess whether the desired outcome has been achieved, and propose changes to the process as necessary.

4.6.   Executive directors may be recruited from external sources, but companies should also develop internal talent and capability. Initiatives might include middle management development programmes, facilitating engagement from time to time with non-executive directors, and partnering and mentoring schemes.

4.7.   Good board appointments do not depend only on the nomination committee. A prospective director should carry out sufficient due diligence to understand the company, appreciate the time commitment involved, and assess the likelihood that he or she will be able to make a positive contribution.

## 5. EVALUATING THE PERFORMANCE OF THE BOARD AND DIRECTORS

5.1.   Boards continually need to monitor and improve their performance. This can be achieved through board evaluation, which provides a powerful and valuable feedback mechanism for improving board effectiveness, maximising strengths and highlighting areas for further development. The evaluation process should aim to be objective and rigorous.

5.2. Like induction and board development, evaluation should be bespoke in its formulation and delivery. The chairman has overall responsibility for the process, and should select an appropriate approach and act on its outcome. The senior independent director should lead the process which evaluates the performance of the chairman. Chairs of board committees should also be responsible for the evaluation of their committees.

5.3. The outcome of a board evaluation should be shared with the whole board and fed back, as appropriate, into the board's work on composition, the design of induction and development programmes, and other relevant areas. It may be useful for a company to have a review loop to consider how effective the board evaluation process has been.

5.4. The Code recommends that FTSE 350 companies have externally-facilitated board evaluations at least every three years. External facilitation can add value by introducing a fresh perspective and new ways of thinking. It may also be useful in particular circumstances, such as when there has been a change of chairman, there is a known problem around the board table requiring tactful handling, or there is an external perception that the board is, or has been, ineffective.

5.5. Whether facilitated externally or internally, evaluations should explore how effective the board is as a unit, as well as the effectiveness of the contributions made by individual directors. Some areas which may be considered, although they are neither prescriptive nor exhaustive, include:

- the mix of skills, experience, knowledge and diversity on the board, in the context of the challenges facing the company;
- clarity of, and leadership given to, the purpose, direction and values of the company;
- succession and development plans;
- how the board works together as a unit, and the tone set by the chairman and the CEO;
- key board relationships, particularly chairman/CEO, chairman/senior independent director, chairman/company secretary and executive/non-executive;
- effectiveness of individual non-executive and executive directors;
- clarity of the senior independent director's role;
- effectiveness of board committees, and how they are connected with the main board;

- quality of the general information provided on the company and its performance;
- quality of papers and presentations to the board;
- quality of discussions around individual proposals;
- process the chairman uses to ensure sufficient debate for major decisions or contentious issues;
- effectiveness of the secretariat;
- clarity of the decision processes and authorities;
- processes for identifying and reviewing risks; and
- how the board communicates with, and listens and responds to, shareholders and other stakeholders.

## 6. AUDIT, RISK AND REMUNERATION

6.1. While the board may make use of committees to assist its consideration of audit, risk and remuneration, it retains responsibility for, and makes the final decisions on, all of these areas. The chairman should ensure that sufficient time is allowed at the board for discussion of these issues. All directors should familiarise themselves with the associated provisions of the UK Corporate Governance Code and its related guidance, and any relevant regulatory requirements.

6.2. Sufficient time should be allowed after committee meetings for them to report to the board on the nature and content of discussion, on recommendations, and on actions to be taken. The minutes of committee meetings should be circulated to all board members, unless it would be inappropriate to do so, and to the company secretary (if he or she is not secretary to the committee). The remit of each committee, and the processes of interaction between committees and between each committee and the board, should be reviewed regularly.

## 7. RELATIONS WITH SHAREHOLDERS

7.1. Communication of a company's governance presents an opportunity for the company to improve the quality of the dialogue with its shareholders and other stakeholders, generating greater levels of trust and confidence.

7.2. The Annual Report and Accounts is an important means of communicating with shareholders. It can also be used to provide well thought-out disclosures on the company's governance arrangements and the board evaluation exercise. Thinking about such disclosures can prompt the board to reflect on the quality of its governance, and what actions it might take to improve its structures, processes and systems.

7.3. The Code emphasises the importance of continual communication with major shareholders, and of the AGM, as two aspects of a company's wider communications strategy. The chairman has a key role to play in representing the company to its principal audiences, and is encouraged to report personally about board leadership and effectiveness in the corporate governance statement in the annual report.

# General Duties of Directors – Companies Act 2006 S170–177

*Introductory*

## 170 Scope and nature of general duties

(1) The general duties specified in sections 171 to 177 are owed by a director of a company to the company.

(2) A person who ceases to be a director continues to be subject –

    (a) to the duty in section 175 (duty to avoid conflicts of interest) as regards the exploitation of any property, information or opportunity of which he became aware at a time when he was a director, and (b) to the duty in section 176 (duty not to accept benefits from third parties) as regards things done or omitted by him before he ceased to be a director. To that extent those duties apply to a former director as to a director, subject to any necessary adaptations.

(3) The general duties are based on certain common law rules and equitable principles as they apply in relation to directors and have effect in place of those rules and principles as regards the duties owed to a company by a director.

(4) The general duties shall be interpreted and applied in the same way as common law rules or equitable principles, and regard shall be had to the corresponding common law rules and equitable principles in interpreting and applying the general duties.

(5) The general duties apply to shadow directors where, and to the extent that, the corresponding common law rules or equitable principles so apply.

*The general duties*

## 171 Duty to act within powers

A director of a company must –

    (a) act in accordance with the company's constitution, and

    (b) only exercise powers for the purposes for which they are conferred.

### 172 Duty to promote the success of the company

(1) A director of a company must act in the way he considers, in good faith, would be most likely to promote the success of the company for the benefit of its members as a whole, and in doing so have regard (amongst other matters) to –

(a) the likely consequences of any decision in the long term,

(b) the interests of the company's employees,

(c) the need to foster the company's business relationships with suppliers, customers and others,

(d) the impact of the company's operations on the community and the environment,

(e) the desirability of the company maintaining a reputation for high stand-ards of business conduct, and

(f) the need to act fairly as between members of the company.

(2) Where or to the extent that the purposes of the company consist of or include purposes other than the benefit of its members, subsection (1) has effect as if the reference to promoting the success of the company for the benefit of its members were to achieving those purposes.

(3) The duty imposed by this section has effect subject to any enactment or rule of law requiring directors, in certain circumstances, to consider or act in the interests of creditors of the company.

### 173 Duty to exercise independent judgement

(1) A director of a company must exercise independent judgement.

(2) This duty is not infringed by his acting –

(a) in accordance with an agreement duly entered into by the company that restricts the future exercise of discretion by its directors, or

(b) in a way authorised by the company's constitution.

### 174 Duty to exercise reasonable care, skill and diligence

(1) A director of a company must exercise reasonable care, skill and diligence.

(2) This means the care, skill and diligence that would be exercised by a rea-sonably diligent person with –

(a) the general knowledge, skill and experience that may reasonably be expected of a person carrying out the functions carried out by the director in relation to the company, and

(b) the general knowledge, skill and experience that the director has.

### 175 Duty to avoid conflicts of interest

(1) A director of a company must avoid a situation in which he has, or can have, a direct or indirect interest that conflicts, or possibly may conflict, with the interests of the company.

(2) This applies in particular to the exploitation of any property, information or opportunity (and it is immaterial whether the company could take advantage of the property, information or opportunity).

(3) This duty does not apply to a conflict of interest arising in relation to a transaction or arrangement with the company.

(4) This duty is not infringed –

   (a) if the situation cannot reasonably be regarded as likely to give rise to a conflict of interest; or

   (b) if the matter has been authorised by the directors.

(5) Authorisation may be given by the directors –

   (a) where the company is a private company and nothing in the company's constitution invalidates such authorisation, by the matter being proposed to and authorised by the directors; or

   (b) where the company is a public company and its constitution includes provision enabling the directors to authorise the matter, by the matter being proposed to and authorised by them in accordance with the constitution.

(6) The authorisation is effective only if –

   (a) any requirement as to the quorum at the meeting at which the matter is considered is met without counting the director in question or any other interested director, and

   (b) the matter was agreed to without their voting or would have been agreed to if their votes had not been counted.

(7) Any reference in this section to a conflict of interest includes a conflict of interest and duty and a conflict of duties.

### 176 Duty not to accept benefits from third parties

(1) A director of a company must not accept a benefit from a third party conferred by reason of –

   (a) his being a director, or

   (b) his doing (or not doing) anything as director.

(2) A "third party" means a person other than the company, an associated body corporate or a person acting on behalf of the company or an associated body corporate.

(3) Benefits received by a director from a person by whom his services (as a director or otherwise) are provided to the company are not regarded as conferred by a third party.

(4) This duty is not infringed if the acceptance of the benefit cannot reasonably be regarded as likely to give rise to a conflict of interest.

(5) Any reference in this section to a conflict of interest includes a conflict of interest and duty and a conflict of duties.

## 177 Duty to declare interest in proposed transaction or arrangement

(1) If a director of a company is in any way, directly or indirectly, interested in a proposed transaction or arrangement with the company, he must declare the nature and extent of that interest to the other directors.

(2) The declaration may (but need not) be made –

(a) at a meeting of the directors, or

(b) by notice to the directors in accordance with –

(i) section 184 (notice in writing), or

(ii) section 185 (general notice).

(3) If a declaration of interest under this section proves to be, or becomes, inaccurate or incomplete, a further declaration must be made.

(4) Any declaration required by this section must be made before the company enters into the transaction or arrangement.

(5) This section does not require a declaration of an interest of which the director is not aware or where the director is not aware of the transaction or arrangement in question.

For this purpose a director is treated as being aware of matters of which he ought reasonably to be aware.

(6) A director need not declare an interest –

(a) if it cannot reasonably be regarded as likely to give rise to a conflict of interest;

(b) if, or to the extent that, the other directors are already aware of it (and for this purpose the other directors are treated as aware of anything of which they ought reasonably to be aware); or

(c) if, or to the extent that, it concerns terms of his service contract that have been or are to be considered –

(i) by a meeting of the directors, or

(ii) by a committee of the directors appointed for the purpose under the company's constitution.

Note: The above statutory statement is a codification of directors' common law duties and does not cover all of the obligations that a director may owe to a company. Other duties may be found throughout the Companies Act 2006 and other legislation, for example, the Insolvency Act 1986.

# Directory

*Organisations and networking groups*

The Confederation of British Industry
www.cbi.org.uk

The Department for Business, Innovation and Skills
www.bis.gov.uk

The Institute of Chartered Accountants in England and Wales
www.icaew.com

The Institute of Chartered Secretaries and Administrators (ICSA)
www.icsa.org.uk

The Institute of Directors
www.iod.co.uk

The Institute of Risk Management
www.theirm.org

International Corporate Governance Network
www.icgn.org

Non-Executive Directors Association (NEDA)
www.nedaglobal.com

The Quoted Companies Alliance
www.theqca.com

*Resources*

Association of British Insurers (ABI) Responsible Investment Disclosure Guidelines
www.abi.org.uk

European Corporate Governance Institute – governance codes of practice from a range of European countries
www.ecgi.org/codes

Financial Reporting Council (FRC) – guardians of the UK Corporate Governance Code, the UK Stewardship Code and associated guidance, including:

- FRC Guidance on Audit Committees, Internal Control: Guidance for Directors and Improving Board Effectiveness
  www.frc.org.uk
- GC100 Companies Act (2006) – Directors' duties, GC100, GC100, Feb-07
  www.practicallaw.com/8-378-8813
- GC100 Guidance on Directors' Conflicts of Interest Authorisation Process, GC100, GC100, Aug-08
  http://uk.practicallaw.com/6-382-9094
  http://uk.practicallaw.com/3-382-9095

ICSA Reports and Guidance, including: Boardroom Behaviours Report and Guidance Notes
www.icsa.org.uk/policy-guidance

IoD Corporate Governance Guidance and Principles for Unlisted Companies
www.iod.com/MainWebsite/Resources

The Model Code (Annex 1 to Listing Rule 9, FSA Handbook)
http://fsahandbook.info/FSA/html/handbook/LR/9/Annex1

National Association of Pension Funds (NAPF) Corporate Governance Policy and Voting Guidelines
www.napf.co.uk/PolicyandResearch.aspx

QCA Corporate Governance Code for Small and Mid-sized Quoted Companies 2013
www.theqca.com

Review of the Role and Effectiveness of Non-Executive Directors (the Higgs Report), BIS, BIS, 2003
www.bis.gov.uk/files/file23021.pdf

# Index